BASIC SK

for

HOME-
SCHOOLING

Language Arts and Math for the
Middle School Years

Lee Wherry Brainerd, Jessika Sobanski, and Ricki Winegardner

LEARNINGEXPRESS

New York

Library of Congress Cataloging-in-Publication Data:
Brainerd, Lee Wherry.
   Basic skills for homeschooling : language arts and math for the middle school years / Lee Wherry Brainerd,
Jessika Sobanski, Ricki Winegardner.—1st ed.
       p. cm.
Includes bibliographical references.
     ISBN 1-57685-395-0 (pbk.)
   1. Home schooling—United States—Handbooks, manuals, etc. 2. Language arts (Middle school)—United
States—Handbooks, manuals, etc. 3. Mathematics—Study and teaching (Middle school)—United States—
Handbooks, manuals, etc. I. Sobanski, Jessika. II. Winegardner, Ricki. III. Title.
   LC40 .B75 2002
   371.04'2—dc21

                                                                                2002003296

Printed in the United States of America
9 8 7 6 5 4 3 2 1
First Edition

ISBN 1-57685-395-0

For more information or to place an order, contact LearningExpress at:
      900 Broadway
      Suite 604
      New York, NY 10003

Or visit us at:
      www.learnatest.com

CONTENTS

I

Overview

by
Ricki Winegardner

1

An Introduction to Homeschooling

*C*ongratulations! You are about to embark on the wondrous, exciting, and yes, sometimes-tedious journey of homeschooling your middle-school-aged child. Perhaps you are familiar with homeschooling, have homeschooled your child throughout elementary school, and are now continuing with the natural progression of teaching your child the more advanced skills of the middle school curriculum. Perhaps the homeschooling journey is new to you. Tentatively, you dip your toes into the water only to find out that it is really not so cold and soon you will be ready to dive headfirst into the world of educating your child, and yourself in the process.

Regardless of your child's educational history, it is your goal to make the middle school years as productive and successful as possible. It is our goal to provide you with some of the essential tools to make that happen.

This book is designed to give you information, suggestions, and actual supplementary lessons that will help you be a more effective parent-teacher to your "home-middle-schooler." The book aims to give you an overview of the issues surrounding homeschooling through these formative years, while also providing you with the practical resources necessary to challenge and supplement your child's learning. This first chapter presents an overview of what's to come. The next chapter concentrates on the nuts and bolts of homeschooling—from curriculum choices to coping with standardized testing and record keeping. The third chapter discusses learning and socialization and considers options best for you and your child as student and teacher. Advice on mainstreaming, should you decide to send your child to a traditional high school, is also included.

The next section of the book is devoted to teaching the basics of language arts. In five chapters, you will discover an overview of the academic goals for middle school, followed by a breakdown of reading, writing, listening, and speaking for socialization; information and understanding; critical analysis and evaluation; and literary response and expression. For mathematics, all the basics, including basic operations and number concepts; fractions and decimals; exponents and roots; ratios and proportions; percents, simple interest, and compound interest; and algebra are covered in six lessons. Finally, in the resources section you will find some of the best magazines, books, CD-ROMs and websites for you and your home learner. Also, a special section on resources for parents includes support groups, organizations, as well as vital education and legal references.

▶ A Brief History of Homeschooling

Is homeschooling a new fad? Are parents doing it just because it is the stylish thing to do? Well, if that were the case, we would have a hard time explaining how people such as Wilbur and Orville Wright came to be homeschooled.

Indeed, homeschooling, in some form or another, has been around for many centuries. While some children were given the opportunity to study with great philosophers, most learned life skills from their parents. Just as a parent teaches a child to walk and talk, the parent from centuries ago also taught the child to cipher, build, and create the tools necessary for day-to-day living. Children learned history from listening to stories being repeated by their older relatives. Today, we call that practice "oral history." Extended-family members may have taught the children specialized tasks, such as sewing or hunting, if that knowledge was not within the realm of one of the child's parents.

It is only in recent history that nuclear families have been isolated from their extended-family members, and this dynamic, in part, has changed the face of American education. While public schooling existed for many years, Massachusetts became the first state to enact a compulsory attendance law in 1852. Other states followed, and it wasn't long until most children were educated in public schools. During the Industrial Age of the United States, public schooling became the norm as more parents began to work in factories and service industries. By 1918, all of the states had laws similar to the compulsory attendance law in Massachusetts as mothers went to work outside of the home when fathers were sent to fight in the wars involving our country during the first half of the twentieth century. Children attended public schools during the day hours while their parents worked. This arrangement seemingly worked for everyone. Adults could work knowing that their young children were supervised and cared for by trained individuals while learning.

The modern homeschool movement, which began in the 1960s, is widely attributed to John Holt. A veteran of World War II who went on to become an educator, John Holt envisioned ways to reform what he saw as a crumbling educational system within the United States. Disillusioned with the conditions within public schools, Mr. Holt recommended that parents once again take control of their children's education. Initially, John Holt suggested a new concept—unschooling. To further his claims that children's minds are eager, unspoiled, and fertile grounds of learning, he suggested schools where children were not taught, but facilitated. Within these institutions, children would find all the tools they needed to learn without tests, quizzes, or report cards. There would be no rules, no mandatory attendance, and no structure—just uninhibited learning. While some followers of Holt's philosophy did set up these types of unschools, they were not widely successful—running out of resources and subsequently closing their doors.

> ### *Parents have become so convinced that educators know what is best for children that they forget that they themselves are really the experts.*
>
> **— MARIAN WRIGHT EDELMAN, FOUNDER AND PRESIDENT, CHILDREN'S DEFENSE FUND**

Realizing that the community unschool was not an easily accepted or viable solution to the worsening conditions within public schools, Mr. Holt encouraged his followers to unschool at home. Parents could serve as facilitators within their home unschools. This idea intrigued his followers, and a growing number of parents began to embark on educating their children at home. Eventually the words "homeschool" and "unschool" became used within newsletters and publications interchangeably, although it is important to note that within this book they mean two different things. Homeschooling means to educate your child at home, whereas unschooling refers to a specific, child-led methodology of learning. In a 1980 interview with *The Mother Earth News,* John Holt estimated that there were already 10,000 families within the United States who were homeschooling their children using a variety of methodologies. Mr. Holt died in 1985. During the same time period, Dr. Raymond Moore and Dorothy Moore, sometimes dubbed the "grandparents of the homeschooling movement," began to collect, analyze, and distribute information about the effects of conventional schooling methods. According to the Moore Method, a child's education should be customized or tailored to his or her particular needs and interests. Many homeschooling parents adhere to this principle, as parents are uniquely able to incorporate their child's interest and learning style into his education where the traditional school system, for practical reasons, is not.

While John Holt's opinions about how a child should learn are directly opposite of the conventional schooling that most government-sponsored public schools promote, many other leaders, such as the Moores, have emerged in the homeschooling society who have far less radical ideas about how to educate a child. Today, children are educated at home using a variety of approaches; some resemble miniature schools, with small in-home classrooms and schedules, while others follow the Holt unschooling approach, allowing a child to become excited about his surroundings and to learn through exploration and discovery. Most seem to fall somewhere in between, allowing children the flexibility to follow their interests while providing structure where necessary to ensure that the child is learning the basics.

It's a Fact!

Home-based learning or *home education* **means using your home as a base for learning, with community, travel, and nature as equally important "schools."** *School-at-home* **means using a structured curriculum with the same methodology as an institutional school, but in a family setting.** *Unschooling* **describes structure-free and student-led learning, with the parents serving as guides.** *Eclectic homeschooling* **is a mixture of methods. That said, there are probably as many individual styles of homeschooling as there are homeschoolers!**

Throughout the four-decade span of the modern homeschooling movement, attitudes and opinions about homeschooling have changed drastically. Once considered an option for hippies, radicals, and those who were on various political, religious, and social "fringes," homeschooling has consistently gained respect, popularity, and momentum as a viable and desirable family education choice.

▶ WHY HOMESCHOOL?

Parents should choose the form of education they want for their children.

—WILLIAM BENNETT, FORMER SECRETARY OF EDUCATION

Most parents spend at least a portion of their time educating their children at home—even those who enroll their children in conventional or public schools. Common is the snapshot of a preschooler perched upon a loved one's lap for story time. Happy is the child skipping along a nature trail stopping to gaze into a cricket's eye. Usually these vignettes evoke warm feelings, but how often do we think about the learning that is being done in these scenes? Your middle school child has outgrown your lap, and may be more interested in exploring a crater on Mars than exploring a single nature trail on planet Earth, but you remain your child's first teacher. Now that your child is entering middle school, you have decided to continue with the homeschooling tradition that you started during the elementary years. If this is your first year homeschooling, you are anxious to find your footing, get your sea legs about you, and embark on educating your middle school child.

Why Do Families Decide to Homeschool?

According to the U.S. Department of Education's National Center for Education Statistics (NCES), more than 850,000 children in the United States were homeschooled in 1999. Several other resources have estimated that these numbers are rising annually at rates ranging from 7 to 15 percent. Many families pursue the homeschooling path during a portion of their child's education—often the elementary years—whereas a smaller percentage chooses to homeschool exclusively, beginning in the elementary years and continuing through high school. Others have found that the middle years are where their children can benefit most from the personalized environment that homeschooling can provide. Of the 850,000 homeschooled children in the United States, over 186,000 of those students were in the middle school grades. Why are these families choosing homeschooling rather than the conventional classroom? Some of the most common reasons cited for homeschooling include:

♦ **Lack of Confidence in The Educational System**

According to a report released on August 1, 2001 by the NCES, the most prevalent reason for a parent to decide to homeschool is because they believed that they could give their child a better education at home than by sending their child to any of the other educational options available, public or private. Parents expressed that they did not feel that their children were kept suitably challenged in public school, nor were the standards as high as they would like. As well as believing that they could better educate their children at home, parents cited that they were unimpressed with the learning environment, or lack thereof, within local school systems.

♦ **Religious or Spiritual Beliefs**

Once the most common reason for homeschooling, religion has fallen to a distant second place. Still a rather prevalent reason for homeschooling, spiritual or religious beliefs accounted for over 300,000 of America's homeschooled children. Some religions dictate rules or beliefs that are best adhered to or met in a homeschool setting. Enrollment of a child in public school is perceived to be detrimental to the spiritual teachings of this family or church. While the decision on how to educate a child is a usually a family decision, there are cases where few, if any, children within a religious order or belief are educated in public schools. Those who choose to homeschool because of religious or spiritual beliefs can be found across all religions and all over the United States.

♦ **Special Needs**

A child with special needs—whether those needs are specific to learning style, development level, or overall physical health—may thrive in the homeschool atmosphere. Often these children, who may require more or specialized attention, instruction, and interaction from a teacher within a conventional classroom, will find that a tailored homeschooling curriculum is the key to educational success. Parents who are already aware of and in tune with these special needs will have a head start in finding the precise learning style of their child with special needs.

♦ **Parenting Philosophy/Morals and Values**

While there are many tangible reasons that people homeschool, such as studies showing higher test scores—homeschooled children averaged a score 80 points higher than the general population on the 2000 SAT test—and advanced logical thinking skills, there are also philosophical arguments. Many parents believe that they can better foster desirable character traits and morals in their child than might be encouraged in conventional schools. These parents find themselves opting to homeschool because they feel that the philosophies of the schools and staff do not complement their own family and parenting philosophies. These parents may also feel alienated by a failing school system or by a difficult environment on the school's campus.

◆ **Private Schooling Options Were Unattainable**

Some of the respondents to the NCES survey would have chosen to send their children to private schools, had they been more easily accessible to their children. The inability to afford private or parochial school tuitions prompted some families to choose to homeschool. Other parents chose homeschooling because their children were not accepted at private schools.

◆ **Other Reasons**

There were a variety of other reasons mentioned for homeschooling children. These reasons ranged from a parent's career to transportation and convenience, as well as children's behavior problems at school. Also, growing concern over school safety has led some parents to homeschooling. These reasons made up a much smaller percentage of the reasons cited; however, the numbers were significant enough to be included in the NCES report.

Resources Around You

 There are many individual decisions and choices to be made in home education, based on the needs of your family. Your community can help! A great place for ideas and resources is a local homeschooling *support group*. These range from sharing experiences at Park Days and Parents' Night Out, to youth clubs and cooperative classes (for example, Connor's mom teaches physics and Erin's dad teaches French). Support groups may organize field trips, teen events, study halls, drama clubs, sports teams, bands, and choirs. See Appendix G for how to find a local support group.

The Advantages and Challenges of Homeschooling

While there are many benefits to homeschooling, including a strengthened relationship between parent and child as well as a tailored educational process, there are certainly some negatives that should be discussed. You have probably heard many of the arguments for and against homeschooling while you were researching the topic, and again when you told family and friends that you had chosen the homeschooling path for your child's educational journey.

As with any major decision in your life, you have weighed the pros and cons very carefully before coming to a final decision—and *final* does not have to mean that you homeschool your child through graduation. The choice can be evaluated each year or when situations change. One homeschooling parent reports that she likes to consider homeschooling as an annual decision, not as a lifetime decision. Every year she gets out her scales and weighs the plusses and minuses of homeschooling. She knows that circumstances, such as family finances and schedules, change and that what works this year may not work next year. This annual evaluation allows her to become refocused, revitalized, and reaffirmed to her commitment. Also, she feels that the challenge of homeschooling a middle schooler sounds far less daunting if you break it down to a year-by-year commitment rather than a long-term decision.

Many people do not completely understand homeschooling or the flexibility it allows. This lack of understanding becomes evident when you hear a group of people having a homeschooling discussion. Since you have decided to homeschool, you may already be familiar with these issues. After each argument against homeschooling, we have supplied the unique advantages and challenges that you should be aware of as you embark on the homeschooling path. Knowing the objection points will not only help you reassure those people in your life who question your choice, but more important, it will help you to focus on developing well-rounded adolescent scholars.

◆ **Argument: Your children will not be properly socialized. Homeschooled children spend too much time interacting with (usually) one adult and do not learn the nuances of socializing with their peers that conventional schooling teaches them.**

Advantage: Because children who are homeschooled do have a fair amount of nonschool time, they also have time to go to the library, enjoy the park, e-mail their pen pals, or to talk on the telephone. There are plenty of opportunities for them to socialize with their peers. This can be done at youth organizations such as scouting programs or 4-H clubs, at church or synagogue youth activities, through sports programs in the community, and at libraries, as well as within a homeschooling organization in your community. Through these activities, homeschooled children learn to socialize constructively with people of varying ages.

Also, consider the structured socialization that is forced upon children in the school setting. Often children become accustomed to only socializing with those children with whom it is convenient to socialize, not those to whom they would gravitate naturally if given the opportunity.

Challenges: Because homeschooled children do not spend large amounts of time with children of similar maturity and age levels, there can be a tendency for a homeschooled child to become uncomfortable when faced with peer pressure situations. You, the parent, need to make the extra effort to ensure that your child does get the opportunity to experience some of the pleasures of childhood with friends. In addition to being exposed to children who share interests, children need to be allowed the opportunity to mingle in unstructured activities with children their own age. Also, socialization is as much a part of education as learning. Being able to function in social situations and to clearly express and debate ideas prepares children for life.

And, do not overlook the extra effort required on your part as you shuttle your child to organized activities around your area. Scheduling and planning learning segments with other homeschooling parents takes time and is well worth the energy required!

◆ **Argument: How are you going to teach a subject such as algebra if you never mastered it in school (or you have forgotten key principles)?**

Advantages: Being a prepared homeschooler allows you to make decisions about how to teach a specialized or advanced subject in which you may not be proficient. There are several options available to the homeschooling family. The teaching parent can study the subject prior to teaching it, thereby not only teaching the child but learning a new skill along the way. Remember that you can also enlist the help of a tutor, friend, or fellow homeschooling parent who is proficient in that subject. (Homeschooling parents often "swap skills"—your child goes to their house for math; their child comes over to your place for Spanish.) If none of these options work, then you may have the option to enroll your child part time in the local public school or community college so that she can learn that one subject. If the subject is music, art, or physical education, you can enroll your student in local classes given at the YMCA or another community center.

Fortunately, in today's information age, there are a myriad of resources available such as online courses or video instruction. Other options to look into are found at your local library. Many libraries have resources available to support home learning as well as umbrella programs that can work well with the homeschooling curriculum. And, even though you may not be actively teaching the lesson, you are still the one making the choices about your child's education.

Challenges: Again, you will need to have a plan for these situations. Because most states have a list of required courses for homeschooling, there are bound to be instances where you will need to call on the help of a friend or colleague or else teach yourself a new skill. If you suddenly need to enroll your child in classes, enlist the help of a tutor, or buy an online course or software package, this could become an unanticipated expense. Enrollment in public school ensures that your child will be offered instruction in all areas required for graduation, but if your issues are with the quality of the education in your local school, you may have to look further.

◆ **Argument: Your child has special needs that should be left to professional educators.**

Advantages: Who better to cater to a child's special needs than the person who has the closest interaction with him? Unfortunately, and through no fault of their own, most public school teachers do not have the luxury of forging a one-on-one relationship with a student in a classroom with up to twenty students. Often, by the time a teacher finds the methods that really click with a student with special needs, it is time for that student to move on to the next grade level. In the homeschooling environment, a parent can tailor a child's educational experience to fit the child's needs. Whether it is unschooling or curriculum-based learning, the child learns in the fashion that best fits his needs.

Challenges: Here's that term again—preparation. If you decide to homeschool your child with special needs, you will need to spend time researching and exploring learning methods that have proven successful with other children who share your child's special learning needs. Also, educating the child with special needs can be a daunting experience. While you may have moments of triumph, there is also the possibility for frustration and exhaustion along the way. Children with special needs who are sent to public school are assigned to a teacher or teachers who are specially trained to educate these students, and it may be difficult to undertake this specialized education, especially while educating other children at home. Check with your state to see what kind of special assistance your child is guaranteed by law, no matter where the child learns. For example, a deaf child is guaranteed an interpreter for public or private school. You may need an interpreter for the math tutor your family enlists to help in this area, and you should expect the same state-mandated assistance in your homeschool environment. Investigating policy takes time and patience. Do not expect the state to volunteer these and similar services to you, but they are there for you, so keep digging!

◆ **Argument: You will have to quit your job because teaching is a full-time job.**

Advantages: Actually, you don't have to quit your job. There are many families that have chosen to homeschool, and not by a long shot are all of them stay-at-home moms. Within the homeschooling population, you will find working parents, single parents, fathers, grandparents, and of course, stay-at-home moms. Because homeschooling is so flexible, you can keep your job, if you choose, while teaching your children during your hours at home. In some dual-parent households, both parents work half time or three-quarters time. In some cases, the logistics are addressed by telecommuting to work. And, in the age of self-employment in so many careers, many moms and dads work from a home-based office. They can write reports while their child writes a research paper, call clients while their child takes a spelling quiz, or conduct meetings while their child is at Cub Scouts.

And, bear in mind that many parents who send their kids to traditional school often return home from their jobs at night to an evening of homework with their preteen. Your family can enjoy a family meal and a Wednesday night movie because your schoolwork is finished.

Challenges: The decision to homeschool a child should not take the backseat to your career. Take an honest look at your situation to assess where you see homeschooling fitting into your daily routine. Find out if flextime is allowed at your job. Enlist relatives to help you and budget your time wisely.

Carschooling® Tricks

Many folks who drive a good deal see their vehicles as classrooms on wheels, complete with their collection of narrated books recorded on cassette or CD. And from a teaching point of view, discussing the story you have just heard with your child comes naturally (and you're already "trapped" in the car!). Books on tape, including family listening and unabridged books, are carried by most libraries and bookstores. Two other sources to explore are Books on Tape at www.booksontape.com or 800-88-BOOKS, and Audio Bookshelf at www.audiobookshelf.com or 800-234-1713. Jim Weiss, storyteller extraordinaire, produces a terrific library of fairy tales, folk tales, myths, short stories, and mysteries, related in his deep, satisfying voice. Get a free catalog from www.greathall.com or 800-477-6234.

Frequently Asked Questions

There are many reasons why homeschooling has gained popularity, but popularity should not be a parent's prime reason for considering homeschooling. Do your best to make your homeschooling decisions without influence from peers, extended family members, or the neighbors on either side of you.

As you embark on your homeschooling program, take some time out to review the following frequently asked questions, review our answers, and reflect on your own situation.

1. Am I qualified to homeschool my child?

Absolutely! Your love of learning and building relationships with your child makes you a perfect candidate to school your child. What your child will gain from your encouragement, love, and support cannot be taught in a conventional classroom. There are many who, in fact, believe that it sometimes helps if you don't have a teaching credential. And remember, identify areas where you think you will need outside help and secure it.

2. What if my child does not want to learn from me?

All children love to learn. Some children, however, have specialized learning styles and needs. Your job is to find the key to your child's interests. How can you correlate your child's interests to a writing assignment? In the process of becoming interested, learning, then becoming interested in something else, your child will gain valuable life skills and you will learn even more about what piques your child's intellectual curiosity.

3. Is homeschooling legal where I live?

Yes. Although homeschooling laws vary from state to state, homeschooling has been legal in all 50 states since the late 1980s. Please see Chapter 2 for specifics and where to find out about the regulations in your state.

4. Will I have the time to homeschool?

Contrary to what we may have been taught, educating a child does not take a full day. In the public school atmosphere, children spend a large amount of time waiting or preparing to learn. At home, your child is able to spend that waiting and preparing time doing the actual learning. And, remember, the schedule is flexible to your family's needs. You plan it, you do it, and you revise it. Only you know what schedule will work for your family, but remember that there are homeschooling families in which both parents work outside the home.

5. How will I socialize my child?

How do public school children remain socially active over the long summer vacation? Typically they engage in activities with their family members, neighborhood children, and by being a part of organized activity such as swim classes or dance instruction. Your homeschooled child will gain socialization skills in the same manner—by being active in local organizations, being family-aware, and spending time building relationships within their community.

6. **How will I teach my child a subject with which I am unfamiliar?**

Remember, you do not have to teach advanced subjects to your homeschooled child unless your child shows an interest in that topic or your local laws mandate it as a required course of study. You will not be performing advanced chemistry labs unless your middle schooler is pursuing that interest—and even then, there are options to pursue. If your child develops an interest in a topic with which you are unfamiliar, you can find alternative means of learning, such as by tutoring, through textbooks, or even in classes offered at community college or distance learning programs. Also, when a child wants to learn, she will learn. This is especially true in the homeschooled child because they are accustomed to using a wide variety of resources to find answers to their questions.

7. **How will I know that this is the right path for my family?**

You may know right away or you may spend a fair amount of time wrestling with your decision. It is important that you have a support network. There are many homeschool support groups and organizations both in geographical communities and in virtual communities on the Internet. Become an involved member and eventually you may find yourself as the veteran giving support to the novice.

8. **Can we afford homeschooling?**

Homeschooling can be as expensive or as inexpensive as you desire. In some families, one of the parents works while the other is a stay-at-home parent. In other homeschooling families, both parents work. There are homeschooling single-parent families. The point is that you can find a way to homeschool—sometimes it just means that you juggle your schedule a bit, change a few priorities, or find new avenues of making money and implement new practices for spending it.

9. **How do I prove what my child has learned?**

There are many opportunities for proving what your child has learned under your tutelage. This topic will be addressed more thoroughly in Chapter 2 as record keeping, standardized testing, and portfolios are discussed. Also, others will see for themselves how well you have done as a teacher when they meet your bright, inquisitive, and intellectually curious child.

10. **Will it work?**

This is where you need to trust yourself and your child. Consider all of the things that your child has taught himself since birth. Consider the learning environment that you are going to promote. How will he do anything else than to learn even more?

As you read through the next chapters, consider this—what do writer C. S. Lewis, country singer LeAnn Rimes, Supreme Court Justice Sandra Day O'Connor, General Douglas MacArthur, anthropologist Margaret Mead, artist Andrew Wyeth, Miami Dolphin Jason Taylor, and Nobel Prize–winning writer Pearl Buck have in common? You guessed it! All were homeschooled. Or consider Thomas Edison. Edison was called "unteachable" and "addled" by his teachers. His parents brought him home for schooling, and he went on to invent the electric light, the telephone transmitter, the electric generator, and many other great wonders!

Dive Into the Web

The Internet is a great place to find information and connect with other homeschooling parents who are just getting started. Here are two examples of the variety of resources available:

- Eclectic Homeschool Online maintains a collection of Beginning Homeschooling links (www.eho.org/beginning.htm), including FAQs, articles, curricular support, and legal information.
- Veteran homeschoolers offer their advice for new homeschooling parents—from "Learning at home means not only having time to enjoy learning but to enjoy life and enjoy being a family," to "Buy an electric pencil sharpener"—at www.nhen.org/nhen/pov/newhser/words_advice.html.

You can find a multitude of other sites by doing a Web search on "beginning homeschooling." Many of the organizations listed in Appendix A also provide information for new homeschoolers.

2

Curricular and Other Educational Decisions

*A**fter*** making the initial decision to teach your middle school child at home, you will need to make some other major decisions. Probably the first that will come to mind is, "What type of curriculum will I use?" This was a difficult question to answer during the early years of the modern homeschool movement because there were not many readily available resources from which homeschooling parents could choose. During those early years of the modern homeschooling movement, homeschooling families created their own curricula. They were unable to depend on support groups and plentiful resources because, quite frankly, this support was almost nonexistent. As the popularity of homeschooling increased, so did the number of curriculum resources available to parents. Further aiding the homeschooling community has been the growth of the Internet. Resources that were costly or unavailable a decade ago are now available at little or no cost to the Internet-connected family.

As a novice homeschooling parent, you may believe, as many do, that you must use a formal curriculum similar to those that public schools use to teach their students. Fortunately, this is not the case! Your own homeschool can resemble the public school environment as closely or as distantly as you desire. In fact, one of the greatest aspects of homeschooling is the freedom it allows you as you pick your tools of choice. For information on curricula, try *The Homeschooler's Cur-*

riculum Swap (www.theswap.com), the oldest used curriculum site on the Web, where homeschoolers buy and sell books and other resources for all subjects and skill levels.

If you are a veteran homeschooler, then you know a thing or two about picking out curricula and materials. And, you already may know that you have many choices available to you, and before you invest in a lot of materials that you may or may not use, you will want to weigh each of your options carefully.

► PLANES, TRAINS . . . AND BICYCLES?

A curriculum is a learning plan that you will use to map out your child's educational path. Choosing a curriculum is similar to choosing an itinerary for a trip. First you have to decide what mode of transportation you are going to use, then how that mode is going to get you to your destination. Before you embark on your homeschooling adventure, you will want to have an idea of where you are planning to go.

When planning your homeschooling itinerary, you will begin by choosing the mode of educational transportation from which you and your child will receive the most benefit. When considering your vehicle for learning, consider your child's learning style as well as your teaching style. The trip will not be very enjoyable if your child prefers a bicycle while you are traveling by airplane. Also, remember that you do not have to settle on one mode of transportation. The ability to choose one or several educational vehicles is just one of the many demonstrations of flexibility in homeschooling.

Consider your child—is he a rigid learner who likes routine and planning? He may prefer it if you settle on one and only one form of educational transportation. Perhaps your child is an explorer, sometimes very ambitious and exuberant, other times cerebral and thoughtful. You may want to consider several transportation options—essentially the planes, trains, and bicycles of learning—so that he can choose what best works for him. Still another group of children learn best when they get to choose the mode of transportation while on the trip. You may get partway through the year to find that you and/or your child need a change, either to go fast-forward, or to take things a bit more leisurely.

LEARNING STYLES

Among your middle schooler's friends, you have probably noticed a variety of personalities. There are some children who naturally take the lead and make decisions. Other children are more likely to follow or not make waves within the group. Some children are very active performers who entertain and amuse. Just as all of these children have very different personalities, so do they have very different learning styles.

A learning style is a method of perceiving and processing information. Think back to when your child was learning basic math facts. Which method of learning fit best? Did she write and rewrite the facts until they were committed to memory, or did she say them aloud over and over in an almost singsong fashion? Did your use of manipulatives and real life examples help etch the math facts indelibly into her brain? All are examples of how your child's learning style affected the way she studied and mastered tasks.

Having a keen understanding of your child's learning style(s) allows you to facilitate a learning environment tailored to her needs. Your child may have more than one learning style; in fact, it is most likely that your learner will possess at least two distinct learning styles. There are at least seven commonly recognized styles of learning. Find your child's learning style(s) from the following list:

Physical

The physical, or kinesthetic, learner is easily identified. You will notice them in a room—fidgeting, twisting their hair, and playing with their school supplies. Sitting still is a concept lost on these active people. It is best explained that these learners think well while moving. Usually, they enjoy sports, activities, and just plain "doing." They will enjoy acting out, interacting with manipulatives or teaching tools, and any sort of dance or movement. Examples of adult physical learners are professional athletes, craftspeople, surgeons, actors, and dancers.

Intrapersonal

It is possible that unless you are an intrapersonal learner, you may have trouble remembering one that you went to school with. Often times the intrapersonal learner is described as shy or introverted. Intrapersonal learners are not antisocial; they simply think better when they are allowed to focus completely and independently. Sometimes they are described as reserved, which is not truly accurate. Although they do sometimes march to the beat of their own drum, they usually are just busy thinking and processing information. They prefer to do things alone rather than as part of a large group. The intrapersonal learner excels when learning new information via self-paced activities or independent projects. Psychologists, philosophers, and computer programmers are all examples of careers where intrapersonal learners succeed.

Interpersonal

Now that we know what intrapersonal learners are, it is not difficult to surmise what an interpersonal learner is. These children are often described as social butterflies. You may have noticed them while volunteer chaperoning at a community-based field trip. The interpersonal learner is anxious to help others, volunteering for almost anything that will allow him the opportunity to interact with others. This type of learner enjoys group activities and relishes the time spent sharing ideas. The interpersonal learner cooperates with others and enjoys researching and performing tasks with small groups of people, rather than independently. Teachers, politicians, entertainers, and business executives often fall under this learning style.

Linguistic

The linguistic learner usually has a wonderful vocabulary and will use it in both written and spoken language. It is rare to see this child without a book. Linguistic learners enjoy giving speeches and oral reports almost as much as they enjoy reading and creative writing. Linguistic learners gain a lot of knowledge simply by listening to lectures, reading textbooks, and trading anecdotes. Linguistic learners often grow up to become authors, journalists, or lecturers.

Mathematical

Mathematical learners thrive in logic. These children understand and follow rules, often to the letter. They have a keen understanding of mathematics, numbers, and patterns. The mathematical learner enjoys brainteasers and math puzzles. This type of learner benefits most by experimenting and using statistics and calculations. Mathematical learners succeed in careers such as science, mathematics, accounting, and law.

Musical

Although this label tends to hint that a child with this learning style excels in music, that is not necessarily true. Simply, musical learners sing, hum, and feel musically. They hear and understand melodies in the world around them. Children who are musical learners often make up songs and rhymes to help them remember and recall facts. They thrive in environments where learning is accomplished with a variety of multimedia resources. Singers, musicians, and Web designers are often musical learners.

Visual

Visual learners are doodlers and artists and everything in between. They have a keen understanding of color and lines. Pictures, images, and art appeal to these learners. The visual learner enjoys painting, graphing, and creating maps. Drawing charts, creating diagrams, using colors and spatial relationships give understanding to the lessons they are learning. Visual learners often grow up to be architects, painters, and pilots.

By identifying the learning style(s) that best suit your child, you will possess the information that allows you to proactively find the methodologies to best help him on the path to educational success. If your child is struggling, refer to the learning style list to find some of the activity types that may work well with your child's individual style or combination of styles. After identifying those activity types, consult the following list to find activities that will give your child the best chance to perceive and process information. For more information on learning styles and a free assessment, visit Walter McKenzie's Surfaquarium site at www.surfaquarium.com/im.htm.

Consider Yourself—what teaching methodologies appeal to you? There are so many options available that you may become overwhelmed, but you can narrow down your field of curriculum choices if you carefully chart your goals. Are you familiar with the state and local laws that govern your community? Do you want complete control over the curriculum, or would you prefer guidance and supervision? Do you have access to a homeschooling support group that can assist you as you make your decisions (and perhaps share resources)? Do you want your child to participate in religious-based learning or does secular learning appeal to you? After assessing how you and your child interact along with what mix of teaching/learning styles you share, you will undoubtedly find a curriculum option that will prove successful as you school at home.

▶ RESEARCH

Research is the key to finding the correct curriculum for you and your children. A successful curriculum can consist of a commercial curriculum, correspondence school, some lessons that you put together yourself, or most likely a little bit of each. Bear in mind that many parents find that their first curriculum choice is not always their favorite or best choice. It is very likely that you will feel the same way. It is likely that you will choose one curriculum to get you started, and as you settle in to the routine it may become apparent that both you and your child need to tweak the curriculum a bit, making some changes here and there as you work toward a perfect fit.

Curriculum choice is one of the areas where parents and children are able to use the flexibility that homeschooling allows to their best advantage. The next section describes some common curriculum choices.

Commercial Curricula

There are many pre-packaged and marketed curricula for you to choose from. The companies who package these materials will provide you with the tools—workbooks, textbooks, and other materials—necessary to teach your child. It is up to you to do the teaching as well as the record-keeping associated with these curricula. Commercial curricula are available across a wide range of spiritual beliefs, as well as with no spiritual or philosophical tone built in. Some websites that sell commercial curricula include Curriculum Services (www.curriculumservices.com) and Core Curriculum of America (www.core-curriculum.com).

Correspondence or Umbrella Schools

While you and your child will be responsible for completing lessons, the materials and grading of assignments are provided for and are supervised by a larger school or organization. The materials will be made available to you as you are ready for them and you send them back to the supervisory institution upon completion. You may or may not work with a supervising teacher who will help you with any stumbling blocks you may find. Also, your child may be provided a report card of their progress on a regular basis. Again, you can find these types of schools or organizations to fit your religious needs if you so desire. Well-known umbrella schools include the American School (www.americanschoolofcorr.com) and Calvert School (home.calvertschool.org). Your local homeschooling parents association will likely offer ideas, support, and advice about umbrella schools in your area.

Custom-created Curricula

As you become more comfortable with the idea of homeschooling your child, or if you've been homeschooling for a few years now, you may decide to depend less on commercial materials and to create more of your own curriculum materials and guidelines. Your custom-created curriculum may be child-based, where your child chooses the path of learning by expressing her interests. In this type of learning you merely provide the tools to expand on natural curiosities. Other custom-created curricula may be made up of a collection of lessons and materials that you have gathered and created from a variety of resources. In this type of curriculum, you and your child are completely in control of the learning path and you have the freedom to stray off the beaten trail and into the wilderness as you create new paths.

Resources Around You

Everybody loves a fair! *Curriculum Fairs* **and** *Homeschool Conferences* **give homeschooling families a boost. They are usually sponsored by local homeschooling groups to bring together families for workshops, mutual support, and networking. You may find a used-curriculum swap and a vendor hall with new books, curricula, freebies, and catalogs. But beware of vendors pushing expensive programs—it** *is* **possible to homeschool successfully on a shoestring! Also, if you want the whole family to attend, be sure the conference or fair is kid-friendly—with workshops and activities for all ages.**

Multitask and Learn: Creating a Curriculum Around Choosing a Curriculum

If you are new to homeschooling, you will be very tempted to gather the latest curriculum catalogs, all the samples from your homeschooling friends, and any other curriculum materials you can get your hands on. Before you succumb to the temptation to use everything you have laid eyes upon, you may want to choose an interim curriculum. You can ease your children into life-based learning by creating a complete curriculum around choosing a curriculum. Imagine solving math problems by performing cost analysis on a variety of curriculum options. Research skills can be honed as your children find curriculum resources, compare those resources with state and local laws governing homeschooling, and report on them. Writing and grammar skills can be incorporated in the written reports that your children prepare explaining the pros and cons of the various curricula they research. Meanwhile, you are gaining insight on how your children learn and how you guide and teach, as well as all of the pertinent information about the various curriculum products available to you.

This interim methodology also provides a great transition from the public school system for the novice homeschooling family. Children will get a break from textbooks while parents will gain the much needed information and confidence necessary to succeed.

▶ BEFORE YOU DECIDE

Before you rush out and spend exorbitant amounts of money on flashily packaged curricula, attractive correspondence schools, or enough materials to educate your entire neighborhood, there are some basic questions that you will need to ask yourself, and have answers to, in order to successfully choose a curriculum that will work for you and your child.

1. Am I familiar with the state and local laws and guidelines governing homeschooling in my area? If you are not, stop here and continue after gaining more information.

2. Does my child have special needs—remedial or advanced—that I need to pay special attention to?

3. How structured do I want my child's learning to be? Do I prefer a school-at-home environment or a child-paced and interest-based environment?

4. Do I want to be completely responsible for my child's curriculum, or would I prefer an overseeing teacher?

5. Do I want to structure my teachings and therefore my child's learning around my beliefs?

▶ BASIC CURRICULUM GUIDE

Knowing what to teach and at what level can be daunting to a parent who is trying to create a curriculum, so we have put together a basic curriculum guide to outline some of the core topics taught in the major subject areas during the middle school years. Because "middle school" means different grades and ages to different people, remember that in this case, middle school covers grades six through eight. Depending upon your child's abilities, interest levels, and opportunities, he may cover some of these topics as early as the fifth grade or perhaps later in the ninth grade. Remember, these are meant to be *guidelines*, not absolutes in your child's education.

Mathematics

In the early middle school years, your child will be expected to master the basics of mathematics—addition, subtraction, multiplication, and division. Typically, the advanced middle school child will also have a basic knowledge of geometry and an understanding of charts and graphs. Depending on your child's interest level and ability, you may delve into some of the advanced math concepts, such as algebra and statistics. Please go to the mathematics section of this book to find out more about learning at home; lessons, practice questions and answer key, and activities to do in and around the home are included.

Language Arts

Language arts represents a complete set of skills necessary to speak, communicate, and understand the English language. The middle school child is expected to gain a greater vocabulary and understanding of the English language through the exploration of the written and spoken word. Expression through the written word will be explored more deeply than in earlier years. The middle school child also spends time becoming familiar with many genres of literature. This familiarity will enable your child to add literary terms to her growing vocabulary. After this basic exposure to literature, composition may be stressed, so that your child not only learns how to experience poetry and short stories, but how to compose these basic literary forms. Finally, life-skill writing is introduced as your child gains the ability to compose business letters, effectively outline, revise, and edit.

As you will see in the language arts section of this book, reading, writing, listening, and speaking skills are covered in depth in this book as they apply to:

◆ Social Interaction
◆ Information and Understanding
◆ Critical Analysis and Evaluation
◆ Literary Response and Expression

Most important, language arts are stressed across the entire curriculum through the reading, writing, listening, and speaking accomplished in all subjects. This book specializes in the mathematics and language arts areas. However, a brief overview of the often necessary components to a well-rounded, at-home education is mentioned in the following section.

Science

Science continues to be an area of high interest in pre-adolescents and adolescents alike, especially when you add plenty of hands-on activities and labs that your middle school child is both mentally and physically prepared to enjoy. In so many cases, the world around you can be your science textbook. Middle school science encourages exploration and the middle school child is often an eager explorer.

In biology, your child will study subjects such as the classification of living things, ecosystems, and the human body. Your child will spend these years learning about everything from microbes to plants to the human body. Also, expect that she will spend time studying Earth sciences, learning about topics such as climate, geology, meteorology, and conservation. Physical sciences will also be covered during the middle school years. Topics of interest often include electricity, energy, inventions and discoveries, and machines. Students are often introduced to chemistry, at least on a very basic level.

Imagine all of the opportunities to learn about these various topics right inside your own home! Touching on all of these topics, at least on the surface, will allow your child to discover new interests as well as gain some basic scientific knowledge.

Social Studies

Social studies, or the study of cultures and societies of our world, encourages your child to further learn about the global community in which he lives. Be prepared to discover not only today's world, but the societies of centuries gone by as well as the relationships and politics that have shaped the world around us.

Carschooling® Tricks

Playing audiotapes and CDs in the car enhances listening and speaking skills across subjects. Your library and bookstore carry audiotapes and CDs of fine books, learning songs, and seminars. Carschooling® guru Diane Flynn Keith recommends:

Lives of the Presidents is one answer to the question "How do you make American history interesting to kids?" . . . Each U.S. president from Washington to Clinton is profiled in brief biographical vignettes that describe his personality, temperament, quirks, and habits; his likes and dislikes in food, dress, and people; his interaction with White House staff, family members and pets; his education and life experience; and those matters that were of premiere importance during his presidency. The chatty format makes for easy listening—and having factual information peppered with gossipy tidbits is a stroke of narrative genius . . . Kathleen Krull's acclaimed series includes *Lives of the Musicians, Lives of the Writers,* and *Lives of the Artists.* Available at Audio Bookshelf, 174 Prescott Hill Road, Northport, ME 04849; 1-800-234-1713; www.audiobookshelf.com.

In social studies, as in science, your child will touch the surface of many topics, to gain a basic all-around knowledge of the world around him. Some common areas of study include global and regional studies; becoming familiar with the countries, customs, and cultures of Africa, Latin America, Asia, Australia, the Far East, and Europe. After learning about each of these geographical and cultural regions, your advanced middle school child may spend time learning about the relationships and politics between the people of these regions.

While learning about each of the major regions of our planet, your child will also spend time gaining geography skills such as map preparation and interpretation. Learning about the people who have shaped our world is also an important area of study for the pre-teen student. To round out the vast amounts of information that your child will have gained about the world around him, focus on advanced American studies, such as American history, politics, economics, and government.

Health

The mental, physical, and hormonal changes of a middle school child make these years the prime years to focus on health and safety issues. Information on puberty, hygiene, and general health is eagerly absorbed by the middle school mind. Understanding how their bodies work, how they are changing, and behaviors that could affect their minds, bodies, and futures will all be covered across the middle school years. You will probably reiterate some of the same topics over several years to help reinforce their importance.

Basic and obvious topics covered within the health and safety curriculum include diet and exercise. Your child may learn how a fundamentally healthy lifestyle complete with a healthy diet, plenty of rest, and sufficient exercise can positively affect their day-to-day performance as well as their overall mental and physical health. The intermediate middle school child may also become aware of some of the major diseases and health issues of our society, including diabetes, cancer, heart disease, and genetic disorders.

Often included in this course of study, at the basic, intermediate, and advanced levels, are general hygiene issues. Reinforcing the fact that hand washing can significantly reduce the chance of catching the common cold, further discussion of proper dental health, and the positive effects—both physically and mentally—of proper grooming are all common topics of discussion.

The middle school health and safety curriculum will optimally cover some of the temptations of the world around us. These are the prime years to discuss, in depth, the effects of drug and alcohol use and abuse. The middle school student may learn about the positive effects of prescription drugs as well as the darker side of chemical and drug abuse.

Human sexuality and reproduction become increasingly important during the advanced middle school years, which are marked by the hormonal changes of puberty. In addition to discussing the mechanics and physiological changes occurring within their bodies, the intermediate and advanced middle school years are the prime time to discuss healthy and unhealthy behavior. The difficult topics of sexually transmitted diseases, HIV, pregnancy, and contraception are at least introduced and then further discussed throughout the child's advanced middle and high school career.

Important first aid and accident prevention lessons will provide your middle school child with life skills that he will carry with him for a lifetime.

▶ TEACHING ACROSS THE CURRICULUM

No one expects you to be the only source of information for your child and that is why you can rest a bit easier when your child is ready for an advanced study and you are not. These situations do not only arise when a child's abilities surpass those of her parents, but also when a child's interests are not in line with her parents' interests. Children of the middle school age are beginning to find their own interests and paths in life, and unfortunately their interests may not always match with your proficiencies. It seems an inevitable joke of nature that the child of a math fanatic will grow to love the languages, or that an author will give birth to a chemist. When your child's abilities surpass yours, or when they have a special interest you don't share or are not expert in, there are many options available to you.

Teach Yourself

If you have the aptitude and the fortitude, you could try to teach yourself more about the subject that your child is interested in. This can be especially helpful if your child's interest is in one of the languages. Both you and your child can learn to speak French, for instance, and practice together. Consider that if you are going to be your child's primary educator, your mind will always be open to learning new skills.

Go Mining

When learning the material yourself is out of the question, then go looking for help. Whether you are looking for workbooks or videotapes, you can find a wide variety of materials at teacher supply stores, through homeschooling catalogs, and of course on the World Wide Web. There are many websites devoted to providing information to students. Be diligent in your searches to find great information. Try www.about.com and www.yahooligans.com, and turn to the resources in the back of this book for guidance.

Distance Learning

This tool is being used in public and private schools and could be a valuable tool for you in the homeschool setting. Many schools have found that when a student shows a high level of proficiency in a given subject that they do not offer onsite, they can turn to distance learning to provide that student with enrichment and instruction. Children who learn through distance learning have a teacher, a set curriculum, assignments, and even classmates. They can participate in discussion with their classmates via e-mail or discussion boards, and can interact with their teacher through e-mail. A few examples of distance learning institutions are Willoway CyberSchool (www.willoway.com), Apex Learning (apexlearning.com), and Northstar Academy (www.northstar-academy.org). Another good place to search for more information is the Jason Project (www.jasonproject.org).

Hire a Tutor

You can hire a tutor to help your child with a given topic. Do not be afraid to think creatively about a tutor. If your child wants to learn Spanish, why hire a special tutor when you have a homeschooling friend who speaks Spanish fluently? Perhaps she can teach your child Spanish, while you teach one of her children a subject in which you excel.

Investigate the Possibilities

Do not allow yourself to believe that you cannot teach your child a given subject. Where there is a will, there is a way, and it is up to you to find the way to educate your child. Today's Information Age provides so many options to homeschooling parents, whether through video courses, audio tools, or special curriculum materials. Also, remember that in some areas, the local public schools are amenable to your child attending public school or local colleges on a part time basis just to attend the one or two desired classes.

▶ STANDARDIZED TESTS

A highly controversial topic in both public school and homeschool circles, standardized testing is something that all parents need to be aware of, even if they are planning to homeschool. Some localities require that your child, whether public schooled or homeschooled, submit to certain standardized tests during milestone years in their educational career. Other localities do not require standardized testing. Even if your family does not reside in an area requiring standardized testing of homeschooled children, you still may want your child to be tested, or you may want, at the very least, to prepare your child for these tests. Your reasons for preparing for these tests could include one or many of those outlined in the following sections.

To Mainstream into Traditional Schools

Because so many public and private schools require standardized testing, having these test scores in your child's portfolio can provide objective information to the administration of the school in which you plan to mainstream your child.

To Prep for Taking the SAT, ACT, ASVAB, or AP Tests

There are some standardized tests that your homeschooled child may be required to take in her future to enter the military or apply to college. It is highly probable that your child will benefit when taking those tests by taking some other standardized tests, or at least practicing for them, now. Recent studies have shown that homeschooled children average a score on the SAT test that is 80 points higher than their conventionally-schooled peers.

If you are planning to enroll your child in college early, you will want to have a fair amount of information available for the desired college at the time of application. Standardized test results can help bolster an already-strong portfolio.

To Prep for Distance Learning, College Classes, or Correspondence Classes

When your middle school child is taking classes under someone else's tutelage, he will undoubtedly be subjected to testing. Because these classes are sometimes taken at a college or through a distance learning program, the testing format closely resembles standardized tests in that the answer sheet is filled in separately from the question sheet.

To Follow a Career Path that Requires Testing for Certification or Board Testing

Many careers, from cosmetology to criminology to those in the medical field, require the passing of professional standardized tests. These tests lead to certification or licensing. There are other career paths that do not require certification or licensure, but holding a level of certification can be desired. To provide your child with the highest level of preparedness possible, you may want your child to take some of the standardized tests available now, or at the very least, you may incorporate some level of standardized test preparation work into your child's curriculum.

To Practice Testing for Real-Life Experiences

There are very few of us who have not been evaluated at some time in our lives by some sort of standardized test. Your child will also experience some of those evaluations as an adult. While you are expanding his mind and encouraging his independence, also teach your child to be flexible enough to accept that this type of evaluation is something that he may experience.

To Possibly Gauge Where Student or Program Weaknesses are and to Help Families Adjust Future Curriculum

Some standardized tests can provide parents with very helpful information to assist them with curriculum preparation for the following years. If you are unsure about where your child's strengths are, where her weaknesses are, and where your child places overall when compared to others of the same age/grade level, you may consider standardized testing.

To Add to a Homeschooler's Portfolio or File

While you are homeschooling your child, your roles will include being both an educator and record keeper. The portfolio that you and your child assemble will often be used to help "prove" your child's level of aptitude and performance. Parents may want to consider adding standardized test results to this portfolio. Check with your state—they may require that you do so.

To Meet State Requirements

Remember, some states and localities require that your homeschooled child be subjected to routine standardized testing. Please check your state and local guidelines to be certain that you are aware of all tests that your child must submit to.

To Satisfy Doubtful Relatives or Friends That Your Homeschooling Program is "Successful"

Possibly one of the most personal and most satisfying reasons that you might want your child to take a standardized test is to keep your homeschool-reluctant friends and family members at bay. Although you may be telling them about your child's intellectual and psychological growth, it is not until they see the results of a recognized standardized test that they believe that the educational path that you and your child have chosen is indeed successful.

It's a Fact!

There are more than 800 colleges and universities—including Harvard and Stanford—that welcome and even recruit homeschoolers. Admissions officers appreciate that homeschoolers tend to be highly motivated, resourceful, and independent learners.

Colleges may base entrance on one or more of the following:

- interviews
- standardized test scores
- portfolios of work
- homemade transcripts
- letters of recommendation
- onsite testing

Find out more in Cafi Cohen's book *And What About College?: How Homeschooling Leads to Admissions to the Best Colleges and Universities* (New York: Holt, 2000).

▶ TEST PREPARATION

Because standardized tests, by nature, are much different than the type of learning and evaluation that your homeschooled child is accustomed to, you may want to spend some time preparing your child for standardized tests. Preparation for these tests should include learning how to do work within a set period of time, since most standardized tests have time limits associated with them. Also, remember that if he is not already accustomed to filling out answer sheets, your child may find the question book/answer key format clumsy.

It is up to you to prepare your child for the possibility of standardized tests. This preparation will help your child's performance on these tests, no matter what the reason is that they are taking them. You can work this test preparedness into your regular curriculum studies or you can specifically do test-prep exercises in addition to your regularly planned curriculum. One of the ways to work test-prep into your regular curriculum is to have your child perform timed tasks in one particular subject; for instance, see how many math facts your child can correctly complete within a given time limit. You can also require that your child complete some assignments using an answer sheet. Although it seems as though filling in an answer key is an easy task, you would be surprised how many children, when initially faced with an answer sheet, end up making simple, non-academic errors on them, such as accidentally marking answers in the wrong spot on the sheet.

Another way to prepare your child for standardized tests is to make a concerted effort to work at test prep outside of your regular curriculum. For those who desire test-prep tools, there are a wide variety available to parents and students. Depending on your child's learning style, you can choose software solutions, workbooks, or a combination of both.

Dive into the Web

If your child is preparing for a standardized test or just needs to brush up on her basic skills, LearnATest.com has a variety of practice tests and skill-building activities. The online courses and practice tests feature

- ▶ instant scoring
- ▶ personalized analysis of results
- ▶ individualized recommendations
- ▶ detailed answer explanations, so your child can understand why certain answers are right and others wrong

Online tests, courses, and books are available at multiple levels to sharpen your child's skills and help her pass the test and move on to the next level of her education.

► SUMMING IT UP

After reading all of the many topics within each of the subjects that you should or could cover while homeschooling your middle-school-aged child, your head may be swimming. Remember, in most cases, those are suggested guidelines. No matter what curriculum you decide on, a child's natural curiosity and eagerness to learn are going to propel him in the right direction. You only need to provide the right amount of mentoring, tutoring, and guidance to get your child there successfully.

As mentioned, the information above should mostly be considered a guideline to the types of subjects your middle school child may study. There are, however, some hard and fast rules, and they follow.

The Laws

Whether you agree with them or disagree with them, the fact of the matter is that there are laws that govern a child's education—more specifically, homeschooling. Children are expected to demonstrate a certain level of proficiency in a variety of subjects in order to be promoted through the grade levels. You may be asked to keep a portfolio of your child's work to serve as proof that you are educating your child. You may be required to have a certified teacher oversee your child's education. In some states, your child may be forced to undergo standardized testing—especially when he or she is in the eighth grade.

Keeping up with all of the federal, state, and local laws that govern homeschooling can become a task in itself. To find the best and most current information on requirements in your state, go to the website of the Home School Legal Defense Association (www.hslda.org) and enter your state. Information and options are included. Here are a few examples from the states of California, Minnesota, and Washington.

California Legal Home Schooling Options:

	Option: 1	Option: 2
Legal Option:	Qualify as a private school	Use a private tutor
Attendance:	None	175 days per year, 3 hours per day
Subjects:	Same as the public schools and in the English language	Same as the public schools and in the English language
Qualifications:	Must be "capable of teaching"	Teacher certification
Notice:	File an annual affidavit with the county superintendent between October 1 and 15	None
Recordkeeping:	Maintain an attendance register	None
Testing:	None	None

California Legal Home Schooling Options:

	Option: 3	Option: 4
Legal Option:	Enroll in an independent study program through the public school	Enroll in a private school satellite program, taking "independent study"
Attendance:	As prescribed by the program	As prescribed by the program
Subjects:	As prescribed by the program	As prescribed by the program
Qualifications:	None	Must be "capable of teaching"
Notice:	A de facto part of the enrollment process	None
Recordkeeping:	As prescribed by the program	As prescribed by the program
Testing:	As prescribed by the program	As prescribed by the program

Minnesota Legal Home Schooling Options:

	Option: 1
Legal Option:	Establish and operate a qualified home school
Attendance:	None
Subjects:	Reading, writing, literature, fine arts, math, science, history, geography, government, health, and physical education
Qualifications:	None
Notice:	File with the local superintendent by October 1 of each school year the name, age, and address of each child taught
Recordkeeping:	If teaching parent is not at least a college graduate, submit a quarterly report to the local superintendent showing the achievement of each child in the required subjects
Testing:	Administer an annual standardized test as agreed to by the local superintendent

Washington Legal Home Schooling Options:

	Option: 1	Option 2
Legal Option:	Establish and operate a home school	Operate under an extension program of an approved private school designed for parents to teach their children at home

Attendance:	Equivalent to: 2,700 total hours in grades 1–3; 2,970 total hours in grades 4–6; 1,980 total hours in grades 7–8; 4,320 total hours in grades 9–12	180 days per year or equivalent to: 2,700 total hours in grades 1–3; 2,970 total hours in grades 4–6; 1,980 total hours in grades 7–8; 4,320 total hours in grades 9–12
Subjects:	Occupational education, science, math, language, social studies, history, health, reading, writing, spelling, music and art appreciation, U.S. and Washington constitutions	Occupational education, science, math, language, social studies, history, health, reading, writing, spelling, music and art appreciation, U.S. and Washington constitutions
Qualifications:	Either: 1) be supervised by a certified teacher, or 2) have 45 college quarter credit hours or have completed a course in home education, or 3) be deemed qualified by the local superintendent	Must be under the supervision of a certified teacher employed by the approved private school
Notice:	File an annual notice of intent with the local (or applicable nonresident) superintendent by September 15 or within two weeks of the start of any public school quarter	None
Recordkeeping:	Maintain standardized test scores, academic progress assessments, and immunization records	None
Testing:	Annually administer and retain a state approved standardized test by a qualified person or have the child evaluated by a certified teacher currently working in the field of education	Progress must be evaluated by a certified teacher employed by the approved private school

▶ STANDARDIZED TESTS BY STATE

Standardized testing is always changing. At the time of publication, the information listed below was current and accurate. It is important to contact your child's school early in the year to confirm what tests are going to be given, what topics will be covered, and when the tests will be given.

States that require standardized testing in eighth grade include:

State:	Alaska
Name of Test:	Alaska Benchmark Examinations
Subjects Tested:	Reading, Writing, Mathematics
Month Given:	March

State:	Arizona
Name of Test:	Stanford 9
Subjects Tested:	Reading, Mathematics, Language
Month Given:	March, April

State:	California
Name of Test:	Stanford Achievement Test, 9th Edition (SAT 9)
Subjects Tested:	Reading, Writing, Spelling, Mathematics
Month Given:	March, April

State:	Colorado
Name of Test:	Colorado Student Assessment Program (CSAP)
Subjects Tested:	Reading, Mathematics, Science
Month Given:	March, April

State:	Connecticut
Name of Test:	Connecticut Mastery Test
Subjects Tested:	Reading, Writing, Mathematics
Month Given:	March, April

State:	Delaware
Name of Test:	Delaware Student Testing Program (DSTP)
Subjects Tested:	Reading, Writing, Mathematics, Science, Social Studies
Month Given:	April, May

State:	Florida
Name of Test:	Florida Comprehensive Assessment Test (FCAT)
Subjects Tested:	Reading, Mathematics
Month Given:	February, March

State:	Georgia
Name of Test:	Norm-referenced Tests (NRT), Criterion-referenced Competency Tests (CRCT)
Subjects Tested:	Reading, Writing, Mathematics, Science, Social Studies
Month Given:	March, April, May

State:	Illinois
Name of Test:	Illinois Standards Achievement Test (ISAT)
Subjects Tested:	Reading, Writing, Mathematics
Month Given:	April

State:	Indiana
Name of Test:	Indiana Statewide Testing for Educational Progress (ISTEP +)
Subjects Tested:	Mathematics, Reading, Language Arts
Month Given:	September, October

State:	Iowa
Name of Test:	Iowa Test of Basic Skills (ITBS)
Subjects Tested:	Reading, Writing, Mathematics
Month Given:	N/A

State:	Kansas
Name of Test:	Kansas Assessment Program (KAP)
Subjects Tested:	Reading, Writing, Mathematics, Social Studies
Month Given:	March, April

State:	Kentucky
Name of Test:	Kentucky Core Content Tests
Subjects Tested:	Mathematics, Social Studies, Arts, Humanities, Practical Living/Vocational Studies
Month Given:	April, May

State:	Louisiana
Name of Test:	Louisiana Educational Assessment Program for the 21st Century (LEAP 21)
Subjects Tested:	English Language Arts, Mathematics, Science, Social Studies
Month Given:	February, March

State:	Maine
Name of Test:	Maine Educational Assessment (MEA)
Subjects Tested:	Reading, Writing, Health, Mathematics, Social Studies, Science, Fine Arts
Month Given:	March, November, December

State:	Maryland
Name of Test:	Maryland School Performance Assessment Program (MSPAP)
Subjects Tested:	Reading, Writing, Language Arts, Mathematics, Science, Social Studies
Month Given:	April, May

State: Massachusetts
Name of Test: Massachusetts Comprehensive Assessment System (MCAS)
Subjects Tested: English Language Arts, Mathematics, Science and Technology, History and Social Science
Month Given: March, April

State: Michigan
Name of Test: Michigan Educational Assessment Program
Subjects Tested: Science, Writing, Social Studies
Month Given: N/A

State: Minnesota
Name of Test: Basic Standards Test (BST)
Subjects Tested: Reading, Mathematics
Month Given: February

State: Missouri
Name of Test: Missouri Assessment Program (MAP)
Subjects Tested: Mathematics, Language Arts, Fine Arts, Social Studies, Science, Health
Month Given: March, April

State: Montana
Name of Test: N/A
Subjects Tested: Reading, Communication Arts, Mathematics, Science, Social Studies
Month Given: April, May

State: Nevada
Name of Test: Nevada Writing Assessment Program/Terra Nova
Subjects Tested: Writing/Reading, Language Arts, Mathematics, Science
Month Given: N/A

State: New Jersey
Name of Test: Grade Eight Proficiency Exam (GEPA)
Subjects Tested: Reading, Writing, Mathematics, Science, Social Studies, Fine Arts (Health and World Languages will be added in 2002–2003 and 2003–2004, respectively)
Month Given: March

State: New York
Name of Test: New York 8th Grade Assessments
Subjects Tested: English Language Arts, Mathematics/Science, Social Studies
Month Given: January, February, May, June

State:	North Carolina
Name of Test:	8th Grade End-of-Grade Tests
Subjects Tested:	Reading, Writing, Mathematics
Month Given:	May, June

State:	North Dakota
Name of Test:	Test of Cognitive Skills, 2nd Edition (TCS/2), Terra Nova
Subjects Tested:	Reading, Language Arts, Mathematics, Spelling, Science, Social Studies
Month Given:	N/A

State:	Oklahoma
Name of Test:	Oklahoma Core Curriculum Tests (OCCT)
Subjects Tested:	Reading, Writing, Mathematics, Science, History, Geography, The Arts
Month Given:	March, April

State:	Oregon
Name of Test:	Oregon Statewide Assessment, Benchmark 3
Subjects Tested:	Writing, Math, Reading/Literature, Mathematics, Science, Extended Career and Life Role Assessment
Month Given:	January, February, March, April

State:	Pennsylvania
Name of Test:	Pennsylvania System of School Assessment (PSSA)
Subjects Tested:	Reading, Mathematics
Month Given:	N/A

State:	Rhode Island
Name of Test:	*New Standards* Mathematics Reference Exam, *New Standards* English Language Arts Reference Exam, National Assessment of Educational Progress (NAEP)
Subjects Tested:	Mathematics, English Language Arts, Reading, Science, History, The Arts
Month Given:	N/A

State:	South Carolina
Name of Test:	Palmetto Achievement Challenge Test (PACT)
Subjects Tested:	Language Arts, Mathematics (Science to be added in 2002)
Month Given:	April, May

State:	Tennessee
Name of Test:	Tennessee Comprehensive Assessment Program (TCAP)
Subjects Tested:	Reading, Language Arts, Math, Science, Social Studies
Month Given:	March, April

State: Texas
Name of Test: Texas Assessment of Academic Skills (TAAS)
Subjects Tested: Reading, Writing, Mathematics, Science, Social Studies
Month Given: March, April

State: Utah
Name of Test: Stanford Achievement Test, 9th Edition (SAT 9)
Subjects Tested: Reading, Language Arts, Mathematics
Month Given: N/A

State: Vermont
Name of Test: New Standards Reference Exam, Written Language Portfolio, Mathematics Problem Solving
                  and Communication Portfolio
Subjects Tested: English/Language Arts, Mathematics, Writing
Month Given: N/A

State: Virginia
Name of Test: Standards of Learning Assessment (SOL)
Subjects Tested: English, Math, History, Social Science, Science
Month Given: October, March

State: Washington
Name of Test: Washington Assessment of Student Learning (WASL)
Subjects Tested: Science
Month Given: April, May

State: Wisconsin
Name of Test: Wisconsin Knowledge and Concepts Examinations (WKCE)
Subjects Tested: Reading, Language Arts, Writing, Mathematics, Science, Social Studies
Month Given: February

State: Wyoming
Name of Test: Wyoming Comprehensive Assessment System (WyCAS)
Subjects Tested: Reading, Writing, Mathematics
Month Given: April

3

Learning—It's Not All Academic

It is the goal of most parents—whether they opt to home-school or to send their children to public school—to raise well-rounded, happy children who will go on to become productive and happy adults. These children are not necessarily well-rounded solely because of their academic proficiency, but possibly more because they have had enriching childhoods. This is not to say that a child who is extremely successful academically, attains high grades, and exceeds expectations is not or cannot be a productive adult citizen. Nor should the importance of academics be minimized. But imagine if this academic high-achiever is also exposed to others of his own age, learns to appreciate the arts, experiences the challenges of the world around him, and pursues his interests whole-heartedly. This child now has a memory bank full not only of academic information but also real-life experiences. As an adult, the child will draw on the experiences and lessons of childhood to make good decisions, relate well with others, and enjoy the world around him. Remember, no matter what choice a parent makes regarding his or her child's education, that child will benefit from being exposed to the world around him outside of the "school" setting.

► PUPPIES AND KIDS

One of the most-voiced concerns surrounding homeschooling includes a word so overused that it has almost lost its meaning: socialization. While researching this book, I typed "What does socialization mean?" into a well-known search engine. Of course I knew what the word meant, but I wanted to learn more about what the rest of the world thought it meant.

The number one match to my question took me to a page explaining how to train a puppy. The article went on to explain that the more "socialized" a puppy was, the more happy and confident it would be when it grew up to be a big dog. At first, I chuckled to myself, but then I stepped back for a moment. Let's think about this puppy for a while. To ensure this puppy's future happiness, the author suggested that we enhance his day-to-day routine of eating, sleeping, sleeping, and eating to include trips to the park, visiting others, and learning about the world around him. Nowhere in the article did it mention enrolling the puppy in a "puppy school."

As with the puppy, the socialization of a child is best achieved when the child is exposed to a variety of experiences, people, and philosophies. A child can be taught at school, and can socialize, but true socialization is an ongoing process that often occurs outside the brick and mortar of institutional walls.

To attain this type of socialization, parents often look to civic groups and organizations for help. Within most communities—regardless of size, religion, or affluence—there exists a core group of civic-minded organizations. These organizations can include youth organizations, sports leagues, or churches. All children, regardless of where they are educated, are welcome at these establishments where common goals, values, rules, regulations, and teamwork are taught—whether on the trail, the playing field, or in the choir.

Scouting and Other Service-Based Organizations

If you are looking for an activity that teaches a variety of values, including volunteerism, citizenship, and various life skills, you may want to explore the world of Scouting. It is possible that your middle school child became involved as a Cub Scout or Brownie earlier in his or her life, so you may be familiar with or already involved in Scouting. Scouting appeals to many because of the wide variety of skills it teaches—from first aid to boating to basic leadership skills. At the middle school level, your Scout will learn even more about citizenship and will become active in volunteerism and charity. While involved in Scouting, your child will interact with children around her same age group who attend public or private school or are homeschooled.

Even if there is no local Boy or Girl Scout troop in your area, your child may be able to be a Scout. To learn more about Scouting, you can inquire locally or check the group's individual websites:

- ◆ Girl Scouts—www.girlscouts.org
- ◆ Boy Scouts—www.bsa.scouting.org

Also, check out your local 4-H chapter as well as Jane Goodall's Roots and Shoots programs. These are excellent groups to tie into your science and social studies curricula.

Sports and Athletics

There are many opportunities for your child to interact with peers through sports and athletics. Some of the more obvious opportunities present themselves in community baseball/softball, basketball, soccer, and football leagues. If your child is too old for these leagues, check into some of the special leagues formed for older children.

Some sports—such as dance, martial arts, gymnastics, skiing, golf, and tennis—are individual sports that often take place at facilities away from the public school. Because these leagues or sports are independent of the local school district, children from public schools as well as private schools and homeschools are welcome. In these activities, your child will interact with a wide variety of children of different ages, degrees of ability, and backgrounds.

It's a Fact!

The dictionary defines *mentor* as "a trusted counselor or guide; a tutor or coach." Middle schoolers can learn from, and even apprentice with, a variety of mentors:

the research librarian
the soccer coach
the 4-H club sponsor
the Scout leader
the older sister who tutors
the woodworking neighbor
the youth choir leader
the grandparent with family stories

Churches, Mosques, and Synagogues

Churches, mosques, and synagogues provide fruitful, inexpensive places to expose children to fellowship, friendship, and culture. Citizenship is also a hallmark value taught within your place of worship—whether it be how to be a good religious member, a good community member, or a generally good member of the human race. If you are not already involved in a local church, mosque, or synagogue you might want to take this time to learn about what your local places of worship have to offer. Many religious organizations—especially those found in large towns and cities—have someone in charge of children's/teens' programs. Speak with the person who fills this position. Inquire about youth groups, youth activities, and other special programs offered. You may be pleasantly surprised to realize how much your local place of worship can offer you and your family. Some of the programs offered to children may include: youth group, choir, Sunday school, charitable events—such as volunteering at a soup kitchen—and bell choir. A plus associated with religious involvement is that your child will be socializing with others who share the same values and beliefs as your family.

Homeschooling Organizations

If there is a homeschooling organization in your area, your child may have the opportunity to participate in events held by this organization. It is common for these organizations to get together on a regular basis for field trips and sports days. The families involved in these groups will often plan to get together solely for the purpose of interacting and reconnecting. This proves to be as important for the homeschooling parents as it is for the homeschooled children. Parents can share tips, debrief, and enjoy each other's company while the children spend time at the important task of being children. These organizations provide both parents and children with emotional and educational support and the opportunity to enjoy others who share the homeschooling philosophy. They are also very important in their capacity to quash any feelings of "being different."

Resources Around You

Bartering—exchanging goods or services without money—is an ancient custom that some homeschooling families are reinventing. They are bartering among themselves or within their communities; for example:

▶ **Ned's homeschooling support group practices *barter teaching*. In his group, one parent, who has a degree in science, teaches science lab to the other homeschoolers. In exchange, their parents teach writing, Spanish, algebra, and painting, according to their skills.**

▶ **Yvonne's family bartered their sewing talents to make costumes for a ballet company in her area. Yvonne received free ballet lessons for many years and ended up attending—on full scholarship—the American Ballet Theatre in New York!**

And a Plethora of Others

The suggestions above merely scratch the surface of the many resources available to help with the socialization of your child—no matter what their educational situation. Volunteering at a local charity, visiting the park, and simply living in a neighborhood with other children all provide excellent occasions for interaction with others.

Given the chance, many middle-school-aged children quickly become social butterflies. It is almost impossible in today's world of easy communication to keep your pre-teen or teen child from finding opportunities to socialize.

▶ TRANSITIONS

Keep in mind that although you have decided to homeschool this year, you may eventually decide, due to educational or lifestyle changes, to enroll your middle school child in public school. This transition could happen during the middle school years or you may decide to wait until your child is ready to enroll in high school. It is possible that you and your child may thrive so well in the homeschool environment that you never look back, and homeschooling becomes your long-term plan for your child's education. Regardless of what your plans are for your child's educational future, it is important that you lay the groundwork now for such a transition in the event that it happens.

Common Issues that Arise

Children who have spent a portion of time being homeschooled and are later enrolled in public school may experience some difficulties during the transition back to the public school setting. Because of these issues, the mainstreaming process can become very stressful and could be detrimental to the educational process. Although you will not be able to completely avoid some of these difficulties, it is important that you remain aware of them so that you can be optimally prepared.

Social Groups

By the time your child reaches middle school, social groups are often informally organized. These social groups in their most extreme form, sometimes called cliques, can make it difficult for the homeschooled child to find his place in the school setting. You can help your child with this problem by keeping him involved in community activities throughout the middle school years. Undoubtedly, if your child is involved and is socializing with a variety of people, including others of her own age, she will know several of her classmates and will have a headstart creating her own place in the complex social world of high school. Also, the involvement with others that you have facilitated will give your middle schooler the self-confidence to withstand these difficult situations with a level of ease and dignity.

Resources Around You

Some school districts are very welcoming to homeschooling families. If you are interested, call the principal at your local middle school or senior high and encourage the administrators to welcome homeschoolers in such activities as:

drama, speech, or debate groups
spelling bees and geography bees
band or orchestra
after-school clubs (chess, Spanish, and so on)
intramural teams
choir
Junior ROTC
science fairs

Curriculum Differences

Children being mainstreamed from the homeschool to the public school may find that they are either ahead of or behind their classmates academically. This problem is not unique to the homeschooled child. Children who transfer from one school to another may also experience this phenomenon, especially if this transfer involves a move between states. You can ease this transition by being aware of the state and local curriculum standards and adhering to the requirements as closely as possible. Also, your record keeping skills may be put to the test at this time as you engage in discussions with your child's new guidance or curriculum counselor. Do not wait until summer to initiate discussions with your local school personnel about your child's future enrollment. Begin talking to school administrators and personnel before the prior school year ends. Waiting later than that can result in delays as the curriculum counselor assesses your child's abilities and educational history.

Culture

Culturally, your child may feel a bit lost in the regimented world of public school. These cultural differences are apparent across the curriculum as well as in the hallways of the public school. Simple actions, such as raising a hand to ask or answer a question, are foreign to the child who has spent considerable time in independent study and learning in the home setting. Your child may feel a bit like a fish out of water while learning the social and academic expectations of the public school world. She may struggle as she adjusts to working at a pace that is suitable to the entire class, rather than racing ahead where she excels, or spending more time on skills that she has had difficulty mastering. There may be stretches of time, especially during the early transition period, where she may yearn for the familiarity of the homeschooling environment that you had previously shared.

Again, ensuring that your child spends time getting to know other children, including those in public school, will help ease any social problems that may arise. One way that you can help your child is by arranging a tour of the school in late spring or summer. Talk to as many teachers as you can prior to the school year so that you can build relationships with the other educators who will play a role in your child's education. With relationships in place, your child will feel more secure while learning her way around this new world.

Trust Yourself

It is amazing how quickly parents forget that they are their child's first and best teacher. No matter where your child receives her education—public school, private school, homeschool—your attitude, guidance, and support are keys to her educational success. There are days during your homeschooling adventure that you may doubt yourself, but self-doubt is not unique to homeschooling parents. All parents are susceptible to moments where they wonder if they are indeed doing all that they can and should be doing to ensure their child's success. You will have your bad days. You will have your good days. There will be days that you celebrate milestones and others where you and your child will experience frustration. The methods that you use to pull yourself from these difficult days will set the tone for your homeschooling experience.

No one expects you to be perfect, as perfection is unattainable. All that is expected is that you provide your child with the tools necessary to grow into a healthy happy citizen. Listen to your child; understand your child.

If you try homeschooling and it does not prove to be the best fit for you and your family, then do not consider yourself a failure. Failure is to ignore your child's needs. If your child's needs were not met within the homeschooling environment, then you would have failed him by continuing down an unsuccessful path.

How to Use This Book

Within these upcoming chapters, we will provide ample information to help your child become educationally successful. Please understand that the purpose of this book is to provide you with basic lessons, facts, exercises, and activities for homeschooling as they pertain to the middle-school-aged child. While we do not mean for this book to be your sole homeschooling resource, we anticipate that you will be provided with a clear overview of homeschooling a middle school child as well as a supplemental math and language arts resource.

Rather than assign specific grade levels, we have divided the middle school years into basic, intermediate, and advanced levels. If you are the parent of a middle-school-aged child, and you are planning on or are considering homeschooling your sixth through eighth grader, then this book is for you. We understand that middle school may encompass children in fifth grade, or in ninth grade, and if your child fits that group, you will find a lot of helpful information within these covers. If you take nothing else away from this book, welcome the feeling of empowerment in your child's education, and enjoy the journey.

PART

II

Language Arts

by
Lee Wherry Brainerd

► GO FOR THE GOALS

Language arts is defined as reading, writing, listening, speaking, and the study of literature. That may seem to cover everything, but we may also add research, problem-solving, and reasoning skills; vocabulary and etymology; and the conventions of the English language, such as grammar, punctuation, and usage. For good measure, let's throw in proofreading, revising, and editing. All such competencies may stand under the language arts umbrella.

The beautiful thing about the study of language arts is that it touches all subjects: literature, history, current events, science, information technology, math, the social sciences, the arts, and so on. Keep in mind then, while considering the language arts standards defined in this chapter, that you and your homeschooler have the freedom to draw upon all subjects and many modes of study.

By the way, if the idea of "standards" bothers you, think of the standards presented here as goals for your middle schooler's mastery of reading, writing, listening, and speaking—and *Go for the Goals!*

It's a Fact!

Many homeschoolers teach with a *multi-discipline* or *unit studies* approach. For example, when studying the Navajo Nation, these homeschoolers might

read Navajo history	**listen to their songs and stories**
compare Navajo and Hopi weaving	**bake Navajo bread**
build a model hogan	**write Navajo-style poetry**
learn Native American dances	**visit a Navajo fairground**

Unit studies add versatility, especially when homeschooling a family with several kids. Your students share resources and learning, yet each child works at his or her own ability level.

► STANDARDS AS LIFELONG GOALS

Consider standards for language arts to be real-life and lifelong goals. As a matter of fact, Connecticut's Common Core of Learning Program puts it this way:

"We want our children to

◆ read, write, speak, listen, and view to construct meaning of visual, oral, and written texts
◆ read with understanding and respond thoughtfully to a variety of texts
◆ write and speak English proficiently to communicate ideas clearly
◆ create works using the language arts in visual, oral, and written texts
◆ choose and apply strategies that enhance the fluent and proficient use of language arts
◆ understand and appreciate texts from many historical periods and cultures
◆ employ language arts for **lifelong learning**, work, and enjoyment."

General Middle School Language Arts Standards

While standards may vary from state to state, in general terms, language arts standards should include these competencies for middle-school-age mastery:

1. Construct, examine, and extend the meaning of literary, informative, and technical texts through listening, reading, and viewing.

2. Use written and oral English appropriate for various purposes and audiences.

3. Research, organize, and evaluate information gained through listening, reading, and viewing.

4. Use literary knowledge accessed through print and visual media to connect herself or himself to society and culture.

5. Apply the conventions of standard written English to compose and revise text.

6. Revise and edit text for organization, clarity, sentence variety, and word choice.

▶ WHY CARE ABOUT LANGUAGE ARTS STANDARDS AND GOALS?

Why do we care to set goals and standards for our children? Here are six reasons. You may know of others.

Loving Learning. The love of discovery often drives success in schooling, in the workplace, and in the world. As learners demonstrate and deepen their understanding across academic disciplines, the ability to use skills such as analysis and self-expression greatly enhances the joy of learning.

Solving Problems. People who are able to recognize and investigate problems, then formulate and propose solutions—supported by reason and evidence, of course—become problem solvers for life. Solving problems demands that students read and listen, comprehend, ask and answer questions, convey their own ideas clearly through written and oral means, and explain their reasoning. In fact, comprehending reading materials and editing and revising are all forms of complex problem solving. The ability to locate, acquire, and organize information from print and electronic sources, is essential to solving problems in research. In all fields—language arts, math, science, social studies, and others—the command of language is essential to reason through problems and convey results.

Communicating. Communication is the essence of language arts, and communication surrounds us in this Information Age. Individuals and groups exchange ideas and information—oral and written—face-to-face, in newspapers and magazines, through radio and television, and online. From the simplest "Yes, ma'am" to the most complex technical manuals, language is the basis and the joy of all human communication.

Using Technology. From farmers to scientists to auto mechanics—it seems that everyone today is "wired," or online. Language arts proficiency helps each of us explore technology—using computers and networks to access information, be in touch with the experts, prepare documents, process ideas, and communicate results.

Working in Teams. In sports, the workplace, family, and around the world, teamwork requires skill in the use of language. People must speak with clarity and listen well as they share ideas, plans, instructions, and evaluations. In researching and bringing outside information to a team, individuals must be able to search, select, and understand a variety of sources. Documenting progress and reporting results demand the ability to organize information and convey it clearly. Those who can read, write, speak, and listen well are valuable contributors in any setting where people are working together to achieve shared goals.

Making Connections. The parts of language arts are closely interconnected: reading and writing provide the means to receive and send written messages. Likewise, listening and speaking enable people to receive and send oral information. Speaking and writing are the creative components, while listening and reading are the receptive components of language. Proficiency clearly supports learning in all academic areas.

Now let's explore how to measure your middle schooler's progress in reaching the goals of language arts studies.

4

Measurements and Assessment

Whatever approach to homeschooling you exercise, you will want to keep records of measurement. Records provide an overall picture of your student's progress and the satisfaction that progress brings. There are multiple ways to assess your child's work, as you will read below. You may want to evaluate your child's work considering:

- ◆ effort put into the project (the student's honest appraisal on this one may be more appropriate than the parent's)
- ◆ mastery of the material
- ◆ the finished project
- ◆ ability to apply or translate what is learned
- ◆ progress toward the family's academic goals

Some families combine traditional measurements with less conventional "thinking out of the box" methods.

Traditional Assessments

Traditional assessments include:

Grades

A, B, C, D, F and Incomplete; or Excellent, Good, Satisfactory, Not Satisfactory; or a percentage (95%); or a fraction ($\frac{17}{20}$). Homeschoolers usually keep traditional grades in a file. Some homeschoolers give weight to this kind of grading and some do not. Interestingly, state education codes usually do *not* require grades, just an assessment of progress.

- ◆ **Test scores:** Scores from quizzes and tests found online, in workbooks and textbooks, in courses, software programs, and standardized tests.
- ◆ **Teacher or mentor evaluations:** Subjective evaluations of the student's effort, outlook, work, progress, goals, and final projects.

Standardized Testing

Standardized testing is only one method—and as we've discussed, not a perfect method—of evaluation. As school districts adjust to the reality of homeschooling and distance learning, they sometimes offer choices for test taking that may suit your homeschooler better than sitting in a huge classroom of test takers. For example, some standardized tests can be taken online, in support groups or community centers, at community colleges, or in prep courses. Some tests can be taken in the home and sent off for grading. Some standardized tests can be given orally. Standardized testing may be **objective** (based on facts; only one right answer for each problem) or **subjective** (based on personal observations, such as short- or long-answer essays, with a range of viable answers). Many tests have both objective and subjective questions.

Standardized testing can include the following question types. The questions may follow the student's reading of texts; viewing films, graphs, charts, maps, and photographs; or listening to speeches and excerpts from literature.

1. **Multiple choice** in response to print and non-print media
2. **Short constructed responses** to print and non-print media using details and interpreting, making predictions, and drawing conclusions
3. **Extended constructed responses** to print and non-print media using details and interpreting, making predictions, and drawing conclusions

Objective questions are scored by machine or with a grid. Scoring for subjective questions is called **holistic scoring,** a method where a teacher or professional reader evaluates a piece of writing for its overall quality. Generally, the grade is based on:

- ◆ content
- ◆ development
- ◆ organization
- ◆ mechanics—conventions of standard written English, such as correct grammar, punctuation, and usage

You, as a homeschooling family, may choose to keep files of problem sets, practice tests, standardized test results, and work samples—such as your child's reports, essays, poetry, short stories, plays, and speeches. You may archive these items for a multitude of reasons: to mainstream back into institutional schools, for college or the workforce, to polish a life skill, or simply for your student's sense of accomplishment.

Carschooling® Tricks

Does your family like trivia and problem solving? *Brain Quest: Be a Know-It-All* (Workman Publishing) **is a wonderful series of flip books, each with 1,000 questions and answers for ages seven to adult. These very portable decks cover math, history, English, and science;** *Brain Quest Extra for the Car* **includes travel games.** *Brain Quest* **decks can be found at bookstores and toy stores, or visit www.brainquest.com for more information.**

Out-of-the-Box Measurements

Homeschoolers are experts at finding imaginative, unorthodox methods of assessing their kids' achievements. Included are subjective assessments and acknowledgment of mastery, such as this homeschooling mom's journal entry: "Kathryn researched, read, and proved her understanding of Egyptian pyramids. She built a model of a pyramid and wrote an essay on mummification." Another consideration is the learning style of your middle schooler, which may not lend itself to traditional assessment (see Chapter 2 on learning styles). Therefore, to measure progress in the basic skills of reading, writing, speaking, and listening, you might pick from among the following creative methods:

1. **Conversation and discussion.** An informal method of measurement, but excellent experience for listening and speaking skills. Listen to your child talk about what she has learned and "reflect back" what has been said, to verify it. Then have your child listen to your observations and reflect them back to you.

2. **Scrapbooking, journals, and diaries.** Help middle schoolers keep records and comments of what they do and learn. Scrapbooks can hold photos, postcards, souvenirs, and brochures from field trips, travel, and special projects. Journals and diaries can be kept by the parent, the homeschooler, or both.

3. **Reading lists.** Students keep lists of the books they read, the audio tapes they hear, and the videos they watch. "Amy" loves to categorize things, including the books and poetry she reads.

4. **Calendars and lesson plan books.** These tools should list tasks completed and ongoing. "The Bartletts," homeschoolers for many years, keep a lesson plan book for each child.

5. Portfolio of work. Some parents include a certified teacher's evaluation of the portfolio, which may include:

- writings—essays, poems, letters, short stories, speeches, Web design and text
- certificates and awards
- photojournalism
- drawings
- audio/video tapes and photographs of projects
- mentor comments

6. Self analysis. Your child can learn to honestly judge his best effort and the results of that effort—a lifelong skill. Compare and discuss with your child your assessments and his assessments in three areas:

- effort put into the project
- mastery of the material
- the finished project

▶ INFINITE RESOURCES

In this cyber age, learners are lucky to have an infinite wealth of resources to draw upon for inspiration and research. These include:

Print resources: books, newspapers, magazines, photos, plays, essays, graphics, recipes, poetry

Cyber resources: websites, search engines, e-mail, software programs

Electronic resources: TV, video, radio, audio cassettes, DVDs, CD-ROMs

Human resources: oral history, interviews, folk tales, songs, speeches, and epic poems—told by relatives, friends, mentors, reference librarians, elders, and peers

Physical resources: nature, sports, games, and manipulatives

Performing and fine arts: works of music, voice, film, dance, theater, photography, painting, sculpture, crafts, and architecture

Now let's take a look at each of the basic skills that will be addressed in the next four chapters, starting with reading.

▶ THE BASIC SKILLS: READING

Reading is often referred to as a key to freedom—the person who masters and enjoys reading will have adventures and make friends and discoveries as close as the nearest bookstore or library. Studies show that reading aloud to your children and having reading materials around the house are the two best indicators of future avid readers.

Because it is such an influential skill, we will spend some time looking at reading. First, what purposes does reading serve?

Why Do We Read?

According to an assessment website called "The Nation's Report Card," people read for three reasons—reasons that also embrace reading for the joy of it.

Reading for literary experience. Readers explore the human condition and human emotions and events by reading novels, short stories, poems, plays, and essays. In reading for literary experience, readers are guided by what and how an author might write a specific genre and by the expectations of how the writing will be organized. Readers make connections to their lives and to other literature. For example, your homeschooler may be enjoying *The Chronicles of Narnia* or *Huckleberry Finn* without really being aware of making discoveries and engaging in vicarious experiences through the texts.

Reading to be informed. Readers gain information by reading books, magazines, newspapers, websites, textbooks, encyclopedias, and catalogs. For instance, your middle schooler may be researching for a project on orangutans or just absorbing general knowledge in *Time* magazine.

Reading to perform a task. Readers apply what they learn from reading materials such as bus or train schedules, recipes, directions for assembly or repairs, games, lab procedures, tax forms, maps, office memos, applications, and so on. To perform a task—for example, replacing an ink-jet cartridge—your child will have to understand the purpose of the document, which guides him or her in selecting, understanding, and manipulating the pertinent information. Readers must be able to *apply* the information—not merely understand it, as is usually the case in reading to be informed. Furthermore, readers are not likely to savor the style or thought in these texts, as they would in reading for literary experience.

How Do We Respond to What We Read?

Experts say we follow these steps—though not necessarily in this order—in our response to what we have read:

1. **Forming an initial understanding:** What is the overall meaning and purpose of what we read?
2. **Developing an interpretation:** What meanings do the relationships among the different parts of the text have? What relationships are there to other readings?
3. **Personal reflection and response:** How does what we read relate to or compare with our personal knowledge and experience?
4. **Critical stance:** How well does what we read communicate information or express ideas?

General Goals for Reading

General goals for reading at any skill level or age are:

1. To read with understanding and fluency
2. To read and understand literature representing diverse societies, eras, and ideas
3. To read for the enjoyment of it

How can you help your middle schooler reach these goals? You can practice skills that are often found in tests, from a first English test through college entrance exams and beyond.

Ten Reading Comprehension Skills To Practice

Identifying the main idea

Recognizing supporting details

Drawing inferences from text

Distinguishing fact from opinion

Recognizing author's purpose

Reading and interpreting graphs, charts, and other visual texts

Making predictions and drawing conclusions

Comparing and contrasting ideas

Recognizing and interpreting the use of literary devices in literature

Interpreting and using information from consumer and workplace documents

A Sample Standardized Test Problem Set

Middle-school reading tests typically consist of several reading passages up to two pages in length. They are followed by multiple-choice or written response questions that usually cover the reading comprehension skills just listed, as well as vocabulary—both words in context and word knowledge.

The reading passages in tests cover many genres, including fiction, poetry, narrative, and expository prose (such as argumentative essays), and excerpts from textbooks or newspapers. Have your homeschooler try this sample problem set of four multiple-choice questions, following an informational passage. The answer key can be found in Appendix A on page 293.

TREATING BURNS

There are three different kinds of burns: first degree, second degree, and third degree. Each type of burn requires a different type of medical treatment.

The least serious burn is the first degree burn. This burn causes the skin to turn red but does not cause blistering. A mild sunburn is a good example of a first degree burn, and, like a mild sunburn, first degree burns generally do not require medical treatment other than a gentle cooling of the burned skin with ice or cold tap water.

Second degree burns, on the other hand, do cause blistering of the skin and should be treated immediately. These burns should be immersed in warm water and then wrapped in a sterile dressing or bandage. (Do not apply butter or grease to these burns. Despite the old wives' tale, butter does

not help burns heal and actually increases the chances of infection.) If a second degree burn covers a large part of the body, then the victim should be taken to the hospital immediately for medical care.

Third degree burns are those that char the skin and turn it black or burn so deeply that the skin shows white. These burns usually result from direct contact with flames and have a great chance of becoming infected. All third degree burn victims should receive immediate hospital care. Burns should not be immersed in water, and charred clothing should not be removed from the victim as it may also remove the skin. If possible, a sterile dressing or bandage should be applied to burns before the victim is transported to the hospital.

1. The main idea of this passage is best expressed in which sentence?
   a. Third degree burns are very serious.
   b. There are three different kinds of burns.
   c. Some burns require medical treatment.
   d. Each type of burn requires a different type of treatment.

2. This passage uses which of the following patterns of organization?
   a. cause and effect, comparison and contrast, and order of importance
   b. cause and effect, chronology, and order of importance
   c. comparison and contrast only
   d. cause and effect and comparison and contrast only

3. A mild sunburn should be treated by:
   a. removing charred clothing.
   b. immersing it in warm water and wrapping it in a sterile bandage.
   c. getting immediate medical attention.
   d. gently cooling the burned skin with cool water.

4. This passage uses the third person point of view because:
   a. The author wants to create a personal and friendly tone.
   b. The author wants to present important information objectively.
   c. The author wants to put readers in his shoes.
   d. The author does not have a specific audience.

▶ THE BASIC SKILLS: WRITING

Luisa knows how to turn her 4-H club's monthly meeting notes into clear, concise, and accurate minutes. Jarron writes a gracious thank-you note to his aunt. Mike keeps a journal of his thoughts and poetry. How will these skills translate into future success for Luisa and Jarron and Mike? The ability to write well is essential to any person's effective communications. Students with high-level writing skills can produce documents that show planning and organization and can effectively convey the intended message and meaning.

Writing clearly is critical to employment and production in today's world. Individuals must be capable of writing for a variety of audiences in differing styles, including standard rhetoric themes, business letters and reports, financial proposals, e-mails, and technical and professional communications. Students should also be able to use computers to enhance their writing proficiency and improve career opportunities as well as writing pleasure.

Dive into the Web

Writing stories, poems, or personal essays is a great way for your middle-schooler to get excited about writing and become comfortable using words to express herself. At Creative Writing for Teens (teenwriting.about.com), thousands of links to writing sites have been collected and sorted by subject. A few of the topics addressed include:

▶ **Curing writer's block**
▶ **Editing and revision**
▶ **Self-publishing**
▶ **Character and plot development**
▶ **Story starter ideas**

A wealth of practical information on grammar, spelling, and vocabulary is also available.

Why Do We Write?

People write for a variety of purposes, which fall into three large categories: narrative, informative, and persuasive.

Narrative writing involves the production of stories, poems, or personal essays. It encourages writers to exercise their powers of observation and creativity to develop stories that can capture a reader's imagination. A narrative writing test item might call for finishing a story.

Informative writing communicates information to the reader, to share knowledge or to convey messages, instructions, and ideas. Informative writing encompasses a variety of formats, such as reports, letters, e-mails, memos, speeches, and articles. An informative writing test item might be to write directions to the town hall.

Persuasive writing seeks to convince or influence the reader to take some action or bring about change. It may contain factual information, such as reasons, examples, or comparisons. However, its main purpose is not to inform but to persuade. Examples of persuasive writing might be letters to the editor or to friends, a video game review, or taking sides in a debate. A persuasive writing test item might be to refute this statement: "Cigarette ads should be allowed in magazines."

General Goals for Writing

The general goals for writing, at any skill level and any age, are:

1. To write to communicate for a variety of purposes to a variety of readers.

2. To write for the enjoyment of it, even for oneself alone.

In all forms of writing, however, the writer should be looking to

◆ Establish **focus** by asserting a main or controlling idea
◆ Develop **content** using sufficient and appropriate supporting details
◆ Provide a logical pattern of **organization**
◆ Convey a sense of **style** with the use of varied vocabulary and sentences
◆ Demonstrate control of the **conventions** of standard written English

Now let's look at how to evaluate short or long essay answers that result from a standardized test prompt.

The Writing Prompt

In standardized testing, students are usually asked to write short or extended answers and sometimes longer pieces, such as letters or essays. The request comes in the form of a prompt. A **prompt** is a statement or question that requires a writer to think and respond—such as "Why do you think it was difficult for Juliet in William Shakespeare's *Romeo and Juliet* to disobey her parents?" or "Write a letter to the relative who influenced you most, explaining why you are writing and how you were influenced." There is no right or wrong answer for a prompt. However, a good piece of writing is well-developed, comprehensible, and abides by the conventions of the English language (grammar, punctuation, and usage).

Chapters 2 through 5 will highlight essential writing skills and tips for teachers and learners. The scoring chart (rubric) that follows defines writing (and speaking) criteria skills, along with the range of mastery of these skills, from unsatisfactory to exemplary.

Rubrics and Exemplars (Also Known as Scoring Charts and Samples)

A **rubric,** or *scoring chart,* is used to score writing samples. Typically, it is a grid that lists the levels of achievement, such as content, development, organization, and conventions, as well as the varying degrees of quality within those categories. "Grades" are usually a range of numbers—for example, 0–4, a score of 4 being the highest.

The chart on the next page is a rubric your family can use to analyze writing, from short answers to short stories. (Note: You may apply the same evaluative standards to a verbal response as you do to a written one.) Don't let these categories intimidate you; the rubric is just a tool. Use a rubric as a guide to help your student grow as a writer, while learning techniques to (see the following chart):

Category	Knowledge and Understanding	Organization	Use of Support Material	Sentence Structure	Vocabulary	Grammar
Description:	The writing exhibits understanding and interpretation of the task.	The writing develops ideas with a coherent, logical, and orderly approach.	The writing exhibits use of relevant and accurate examples to support ideas.	The writing uses varied and accurate sentence structure.	The writing uses effective language and challenging vocabulary.	The writing uses conventional spelling, punctuation, paragraphing, capitalization, grammar, and usage.
4.0	Your child has a good understanding of the topic and writes about it in an imaginative and creative way.	Your child has organized and developed his/her ideas in a coherent and well-defined manner.	Your child purposely uses support material from the story that is relevant and appropriate.	Your child shows the ability to vary sentence structure.	Your child uses sophisticated vocabulary.	Your child makes few mechanical errors, if any.
3.0	Your child shows an understanding of the topic and writes about it in a logical, practical way.	Your child had an obvious plan to develop his/her ideas that was satisfactory.	Your child has used some support material in an organized form.	Your child has used correct sentence structure, but there is little sentence variety.	Your child shows an average range of vocabulary.	Your child makes some mechanical errors, but they do not interfere with communication.
2.0	Your child tries to develop the topic but digresses and writes about other topics as well.	Your child shows little organization and development of content.	Your child does not use relevant support material from the narrative.	Your child shows some knowledge of sentence structure but also writes in fragments or run-on sentences.	Your child uses inaccurate, inexact, or vague language.	Your child makes many mechanical errors that interfere with communication.
1.0	Your child only addresses the topic minimally.	Your child shows no ability to organize or develop ideas.	Your child has not included or organized support material.	Your child does not have a sense of structure.	Your child uses inexact or immature language.	Your child makes mechanical errors that make the paper impossible to understand.
0.0	A ZERO paper would be one that shows no relation to the topic, is illegible, incoherent, or blank.	A ZERO paper would be one that shows no relation to the topic, is illegible, incoherent, or blank.	A ZERO paper would be one that shows no relation to the topic, is illegible, incoherent, or blank.	A ZERO paper would be one that shows no relation to the topic, is illegible, incoherent, or blank.	A ZERO paper would be one that shows no relation to the topic, is illegible, incoherent, or blank.	A ZERO paper would be one that shows no relation to the topic, is illegible, incoherent, or blank.

This scoring rubric has been adapted from the New York State standards.

An **exemplar** is a writing sample or an example. Sometimes exemplars are written to demonstrate a variety of sample answers, from UNSATISFACTORY to SATISFACTORY to EXEMPLARY. In addition, exemplars may illustrate a range of *mastery* for a range of *ages*, such as BASIC, INTERMEDIATE, and ADVANCED. We will include a variety of exemplars, both in the chapters and in Appendix A.

A Sample Standardized Test Problem

Sample answers for the following test questions can be found in Appendix A.

[Form: Narrative]

1. Finish a story that begins "The castle appeared again the next morning."

_____

_____

_____

_____

_____

[Form: Persuasive]

2. You are to write a letter to a television producer trying to convince her to produce a documentary on one of the following topics:

Great Latina Women in History   Animals with Natural Camouflage
The Story of Celtic Dance   Submarines

_____

_____

_____

_____

_____

▶ SPEAKING AND LISTENING

Of all the language arts, listening and speaking are those most often used. Skill in speaking is universally recognized as a primary indicator of a person's knowledge, competence, and credibility. Whether in person, on the phone or via video, good listening and speaking skills are essential to sending, receiving, and understanding messages. To understand messages spoken by others, students must be able to listen carefully and use specific techniques to clarify what they have heard. Grammar, sentence structure, tone, expression, and emphasis must be part of a student's repertoire both to speak properly and to make messages understandable. Why do we listen and speak? For basically the same reasons we read and write—to communicate, pass information back and forth, and partake in narration, creativity, and persuasion. In fact, go back to the sections entitled Why Do We Read? and How Do We Respond to Reading? and substitute *listen* for *read*; go back to the sections entitled Why Do We Write? and How Do We Respond to Writing? and substitute *speak* for *write* and see how well those substitutions work!

General Goals for Speaking and Listening

The general goals for speaking and listening, at any skill level and any age, are:

1. To speak clearly and correctly—using appropriate vocabulary, grammar, tone, expression, and usage—in a variety of situations.

2. To listen attentively, clarifying that what was said was heard correctly, in a variety of situations.

3. To develop a critical ear—being able to understand what has been said and what has not been said.

Practicing and Testing Speaking and Listening

There are many indicators of how well your homeschooler listens and speaks. Here are a few ideas; many more activities will be suggested in the next four chapters:

◆ Accurately and orally paraphrase a speech, sermon, or folk tale
◆ Follow directions that involve many steps; teach the directions to someone else
◆ Tell a story, a joke, or a personal anecdote
◆ Ask specific questions to clarify and extend meaning
◆ Present information orally that you have learned through interviews

▶ RESEARCH, REVISING, AND EDITING

Good reading, writing, speaking, and listening requires research, revising, and editing to reach a level of mastery that is the student's goal.

Research

Homeschoolers are usually big project and report producers, so they are no strangers to research. To be successful and satisfied in schooling and in the world of work, your homeschooler should learn how to find a wide variety of resources (written, visual, and electronic). These competencies include:

- Identifying questions to ask and possibly writing a research plan
- Gathering information
- Locating other sources (library, Internet, video, CD-ROMs, experts)
- Selecting and organizing information from various sources for a specific purpose
- Determining the accuracy and reliability of a source and of materials found
- Citing sources used
- Writing or speaking based on acquired information

As research is a pre-writing skill, revising and editing (or proofreading) are skills that come into play after the writing has begun.

Revising, Editing, and Proofreading

Revising and editing are the two last steps of writing that often get "left out." Nita's brother convinced Nita that even though her review of the fourth Harry Potter book was wonderful, she would not impress their mom if she left the three spelling errors and the subject–verb disagreement in her paper. Also, couldn't that last paragraph be worded more clearly? Nita's brother is right—mistakes in grammar, usage, punctuation, spelling, and clarity color a reader's perception of your work, no matter how fine the research or thought process is.

Revising involves taking a first, or rough, draft and "tightening" it:

- improving the organization
- sharpening the focus
- clarifying fuzzy logic
- unifying tone
- adding detail and example
- refining the vocabulary
- eliminating extraneous material or ideas
- editing and proofreading for errors in vocabulary, grammar, punctuation, and usage

Practicing Revising

Your learner should practice revising all of his writing, even short pieces, so that it becomes second nature. Here are revising tips to be mindful of during the revision stage:

1. Observe basic writing conventions, such as correct spelling, punctuation, and capitalization, as the first draft is written.

2. Check over sentences and paragraphs to see if they are clear and logical.

3. Check for variety of vocabulary and sentence structure.

4. Revise and improve early drafts by correcting errors, restructuring weak sentences, and looking for clarity and effect.

5. Proofread the final draft to be sure no new mistakes were made in the rewrites.

Editing and proofreading, which can be parts of revising, are best begun following a break from writing. Your learner will be able to concentrate and conserve energy better. When editing, look for specific errors, not the general meaning. Editing is not a substitute for, but a supplement to, reading for meaning. Different editing and proofreading strategies work for different learners at different times. They include:

- Cover your writing with a piece of paper and work your way down, line by line.
- Read your writing aloud or ask someone to read it to you, in order to *hear* mistakes.
- Proofread backward for spelling and spacing errors.
- Use a spellchecker when writing on a computer, but also reread, as spellcheckers miss usage errors.
- Identify typical errors (for example, problems with subject–verb agreement).
- Look for your own personal, recurring mistakes.
- Try to understand why you made errors.
- Develop a plan to learn the rule and correction for each error.
- Get a parent or friend to read your writing and make constructive comments.

Your homeschooler's writing (and speaking) will improve slowly but surely with conscientious editing. Both revising and proofreading take lots of practice and habit. The best thing you can do is to revise and edit *with* your homeschooler, so he or she can ask questions and make immediate repairs.

In addition, short and long answers on standardized tests will be easier to revise and improve under pressure if your learner already has the habit of rechecking his or her work in less-stressful situations.

Resources Around You

Guess what? Practicing communication skills and career building can go on at the same time. Homeschoolers have the advantage of having the flexibility to see and try out the real work world in these ways:

- **apprenticing with an adult mentor**
- **visiting Mom's or Dad's workplace for a day or longer**
- **evaluating a variety of workplaces via fieldtrips**
- **working in the family business**

▶ How the Next Four Chapters Will Unfold

The next four chapters are divided into generic standards that are nationally accepted by institutional and homeschooling teachers as important for a student's mastery of language arts.

Each of the next four chapters:

- addresses and defines one language arts standard
- explores how to gauge progress and success
- provides a sample problem set with answers and explanations
- discusses how to teach and practice involved skills
- offers a good many fun and appropriate activities for all levels of mastery and for all learning styles
- presents practice sets of different skill levels, with keys and sample answers (exemplars) in Appendix A

Each chapter addresses reading, writing, listening, speaking, research, revising, editing, and other competencies for a particular purpose such as:

- Social Interaction
- Information and Understanding
- Critical Analysis and Evaluation
- Literary Response and Expression

Since your homeschooler will likely have a range of mastery throughout his or her middle school years, three levels of mastery will be discussed: basic, intermediate, and advanced. Learning styles will be referred to when possible.

Chapter 5: Social Interaction

Goal of the Standard: *Students will read, write, listen, and speak for social interaction.* Students will use oral and written language that follows the accepted conventions of the English language for effective social communication with a wide variety of people. As readers and listeners, they will use the social communications of others to enrich their understanding of people and their views.

Chapter 6: Information and Understanding

Goal of the Standard: *Students will read, write, listen, and speak for information and understanding.* As listeners and readers, students will collect data, facts, and ideas; discover relationships, concepts, and generalizations; and use knowledge generated from oral, written, and electronically produced texts. As speakers and writers, they will use oral and written language that follows the accepted conventions of the English language to acquire, interpret, apply, and transmit information.

Chapter 7: Critical Analysis and Evaluation

Goal of the Standard: *Students will read, write, listen, and speak for critical analysis and evaluation.* As listeners and readers, students will analyze experiences, ideas, information, and issues presented by others using a variety of established criteria. As speakers and writers, they will use oral and written language that follows the accepted conventions of the English language to present, from a variety of perspectives, their opinions and judgments on experiences, ideas, information, and issues.

Chapter 8: Literary Response and Expression

Goal of the Standard: *Students will read, write, listen, and speak for literary response and expression.* Students will read and listen to oral, written, and electronically produced texts and performances from American and world literature; relate texts and performances to their own lives; and develop an understanding of the diverse social, historical, and cultural dimensions the texts and performances represent. As speakers and writers, students will use oral and written language that follows the accepted conventions of the English language for self-expression and artistic creation.

For further language arts terms and definitions, please visit the language arts glossary of terms in Appendix B.

5

Reading, Writing, Listening, and Speaking for Social Interaction

Goal of the Standard: *Students read, write, listen, and speak for social interaction.* Students use oral and written language that follows the accepted conventions of the English language for effective social communications with a wide variety of people. As readers and listeners, they use the communications of others to enrich their understanding of people and their views.

▶ WHAT DO WE MEAN BY SOCIAL INTERACTION?

Writing an e-mail to a pen pal, reading and discussing a brother's journal, listening to and building on a friend's story, and giving directions are examples of social interaction. **Social interaction** means participating in our culture. As parents, we want our children to participate in the satisfying exchange of ideas and feelings.

You probably know that today's job ads often demand "excellent communication skills." Storyteller and teacher Heather Forest adds that social interaction skills "are essential to participating in adult culture. The ability to articulate thoughts, feelings, and needs can contribute to academic, interpersonal, and professional success. For safety's sake, children need to be able to express their thoughts so they can ask for help and get what they need from adults. Good listeners learn more efficiently."

▶ ACTIVITIES FOR SOCIAL INTERACTION

Activities appropriate to this standard include

- **Reading** personal letters, e-mails, cards, notes, postcards, electronic discussions, instructions, directions, and invitations
- **Writing** letters, e-mails, cards, thank-you notes, postcards, instructions, directions, invitations, opinions, and personal essays
- **Listening** to conversation, group discussions, personal reviews, speeches, directions, foreign languages, and meetings
- **Speaking** to give instructions, directions, messages, opinions, greetings, introductions, announcements, and for conversation, group discussion, foreign language, interviewing, presentations, and conducting a meeting

▶ WHAT SKILLS ARE WE LOOKING FOR HERE?

We are guiding our middle schoolers to eventually master these language arts skills:

- Using written and spoken messages to establish, maintain, and enhance personal relationships (*Lisa writes Aunt Maria, asking to work on the farm for the summer.*)
- Writing/reading cards, notes, letters, and e-mails to/from friends, relatives, and neighbors (*David exchanges e-mails with friends from music camp.*)
- Giving and writing instructions and directions (read more in Chapter 3) (*Marie-Claire explains how to strip varnish from an old dresser.*)
- Writing formal letters to inform or persuade (read more in Chapters 3 and 4) (*Tommy writes a letter to the mayor explaining why he thinks there should be more bike paths.*)
- Revising and editing for correct spelling, grammar, punctuation, and usage (*Evan helps his brother revise and edit a short story.*)
- Developing a personal understanding and perspective of what is read and heard (*Stella presents her impressions of a History Channel show she viewed.*)
- Listening for details and both verbal and non-verbal cues (*Tim listens to and helps a lost child in the supermarket.*)
- Speaking to deliver messages, greetings, and introductions (*Molly introduces her youth group friends to her grandmother.*)

◆ Being comfortable in informal conversation (*At his family reunion, Rob learned that his uncle likes the same card games as he does.*)

▶ EVIDENCE OF SUCCESS

Many homeschooling families resist grade-specific measurement of their children's success ("Kenny reads at a seventh-grade level"). One of the advantages of homeschooling is freeing your learner to work at her own pace, neither having to master any one subject at a specified time, nor to absorb all subjects to the same degree at a specified age.

You know your middle schooler's proficiency and progress best. With your help, your middle schooler will move from *basic* to *intermediate* to *advanced* mastery in these skills. How will you recognize success in reading, writing, listening, and speaking for social interaction? Consider these accomplishments.

BASIC MASTERY includes
   ◆ Reading and understanding a relative's letter
   ◆ Composing a thank-you note or an invitation
   ◆ Relaying a message or a question to another person
   ◆ Writing an e-mail to a pen pal in another country
   ◆ Exchanging messages with friends to commemorate special occasions
   ◆ Beginning to interpret how he feels about a written message
   ◆ Listening to and exchanging ideas with a sibling
   ◆ Acting as a host to a visitor
   ◆ Making introductions

INTERMEDIATE MASTERY includes further development of all of the above and
   ◆ Using a variety of print and electronic forms for social communication with peers and adults
   ◆ Writing letters to distant friends
   ◆ Initiating a conversation
   ◆ Sharing how she feels about a letter or journal entry
   ◆ Sending/receiving e-mail messages on a computer network
   ◆ Sending formal invitations to parties or open houses
   ◆ Exploring communication with members of other groups and cultures
   ◆ Beginning to adjust vocabulary and style to match the reader
   ◆ Participating in family and small group discussions
   ◆ Giving announcements or a short speech at a party
   ◆ Listening to others and building upon their comments
   ◆ Learning some words in another language and using them with speakers of that language

ADVANCED MASTERY includes further development of all of the above and

♦ Participating in electronic discussion groups
♦ Writing personal notes and letters to entertain and interest the reader
♦ Adjusting vocabulary and style to account for the nature of a relationship and the interests and needs of the reader
♦ Writing letters and personal essays as part of a college application
♦ Reading and completing part-time job applications
♦ Communicating effectively with members of other groups and cultures
♦ Responding to a newspaper story with an opinion letter
♦ Participating in and conducting a meeting
♦ Communicating to some degree in another language
♦ Interacting with community members through community service or part-time jobs
♦ Interviewing for a job or community college class

Evidence of Growth

You might ask, "What shows progress in my homeschooler's work, from year to year, especially regarding repetition of the same activity, such as writing a personal letter?" What works well is to evaluate progress by considering the five categories of *range, flexibility, connections, conventions,* and *independence*. As a matter of fact, you can assess progress in these five categories with *every* language arts standard and goal:

1. **Range**—breadth and depth of topics, issues, and treatments
2. **Flexibility**—performance in changing and varied conditions
3. **Connections**—ability to see similarities and bridge themes
4. **Conventions**—rules, protocols, and traditional practices in English
5. **Independence**—ability to perform without direction

For the specific materials covered in this chapter, *social interaction goals*, ask yourself, "Over the years, does my homeschooler show progress in:

1. writing and talking to a diverse RANGE of individuals and groups? in a diverse RANGE of topics of conversation, understanding and giving verbal and non-verbal signals?"
2. adapting with more FLEXIBILITY to people of different ages, genders, cultural groups, and social positions? with more FLEXIBILITY in assuming appropriate roles in conversation?"
3. making stronger CONNECTIONS with the interests, experiences, and feelings of another person or group?"
4. understanding more deeply the CONVENTIONS of behavior, tone and diction, and verbal and nonverbal language?"
5. initiating conversations with a greater INDEPENDENCE? adapting language and personal role to the listener/reader?"

Carschooling® Tricks

"Good Grammar Made Easy" is the subtitle of Liz Buffa's *Grammar Smart Junior*, an engaging way to learn parts of speech and sentence structure. The book contains clever examples of good and bad grammar as well as workbook pages and quizzes perfect for car students. An audio cassette version addresses the needs of auditory learners or students prone to carsickness when reading. Geared for middle schoolers, the program won the Parents' Choice Award. Available at bookstores or www.randomhouse.com.

Now let's examine an actual test problem and sample answers (exemplars). Your student may, of course, practice with any sample problems in this book.

SAMPLE TEST PROBLEM

Write an *acknowledgment* (a public thank you), thanking a family member for helping you complete a project, report, or other goal. (*Note:* Student may write one to three paragraphs, depending on level of proficiency. This exercise extends social interaction skills from an oral "thank you" to a third-person acknowledgement.)

_____

_____

▶ EXEMPLARS AND COMMENTS

The following are three examples of successful answers to the short essay prompt above, along with some comments to help you compare your learner's writing. Essay grading is, of course, somewhat subjective; hence, the reasoning behind the categories. Nevertheless, you have the right to disagree!

Basic Example

I would like to thank my mother for helping me with the spelling, grammar, and set up of this report. Thanks, too, to other people like my grandmother and Danny for helping me to remember the information for this report.

Answers the prompt in an acceptable way; reflects understanding of a simple genre, the acknowledgment; manipulates the basic conventions of spelling, punctuation, capitalization, and usage correctly.

Intermediate Example

I would like to thank my father for taking the time to help me with my science project. He is a great inspiration to me. I want to thank him for his time, patience, and efforts extended to make my project look great. Thanks, Dad, for all your help and love. I could not have done it without you.

In addition to the comments given above: combines formal and colloquial language ("efforts extended," and "I would like to thank," and "thanks, Dad,"), recognizing the dual audiences for the text: a general audience and a specific person; shows an appreciation of social interaction customs.

Advanced Example

I did most of this report by myself, but I nevertheless will need to thank my aunt Kay-Kay, because without her teaching me to write well since I was a young tyke, I wouldn't have the skills I have today.

    I do well on reports precisely because my auntie motivates me. She is kind enough to help me out with my terrible spelling too.

    I'd also like to thank my grandfather, Poppi, for reminding me that I was just like my brother and sister are, so I should not treat them like aliens.

In addition to the comments given above: adds humor; uses personal references to reinforce the nature of the relationship between the writer and the person being thanked; uses advanced syntax and vocabulary; uses correct paragraphing.

▶ HOW DO WE TEACH AND PRACTICE THESE SKILLS?

What Is Social Language?

Let's consider the question: What forms a **social language**, the language that we use for interaction with others? Discuss this question with your learner. You may come to a definition something like *"Social language focuses on establishing trust and harmony and growth between people."* If you would like to guide this discussion with your learner, here are three words key to an understanding of social language:

1. **Interpersonal.** Social language seeks to know another person or being together with others.

2. **Immediate.** Social language is primarily the language of face-to-face sharing. Even written or electronic social messages strive to capture the tone of friendly conversation.

3. **Appropriate.** Social language demands selecting the language and behavior appropriate for the relationship, taking into account age, gender, intimacy, and cultural traditions of the other person or people. Appropriateness must extend to verbal and non-verbal signals.

    Now for some tips on how to teach and practice language arts for social interaction. You may find some of the following ideas for teaching and practicing social interaction goals do not fit your teaching style or your student's learning style. Feel free to adapt them as you see fit. Many are suggestions made by storyteller and teacher Heather Forest on her website, www.storyarts.org.

Listening for Social Interaction

1. Ask your child to write a list of the qualities of a good listener. Read and discuss the list. Listen to each other's comment on the art of listening!

2. Assess your own listening skills, learner and parent. Do you always pay complete mental attention to speakers or does your mind stray?

3. Practice showing encouragement to friends or family in nonverbal terms with your eyes, facial expressions, body stance, and touching, to show that you are listening. Kinesthetic learners excel at exercises like this one.

Public Speaking

1. Share stories by retelling jokes, folk tales, or reading a folk tale out loud. While storytelling is often one of the verbal/linguistic learner's strengths, visual learners also enjoy retelling a story after illustrating it.

2. Have your student give an oral book report.

3. Have your learner write and present a first-person monologue, pretending to be someone famous she has been studying or saw a film about.

4. Your co-op learning group can write a radio show, including family news reports, live interviews, poetry, or headline news.

Share Your Values Through Book Talks

1. Read a short story or book aloud to each other, or choose a book you've both enjoyed reading silently.

2. Enter the world of the story together, discussing tough issues, sharing how you both feel about the characters, the plot, and the values in the book.

3. Have your learner identify the themes and conflicts in the story. Have your learner compare the characters to those in other readings.

Dive into the Web

Local schools or public libraries in your area may organize book groups for teens or middle-schoolers. If these groups are not available or don't work with your schedule, an *online book group* can be a great alternative. Most online groups operate as e-mail lists, where members read a book by a specified deadline and then share discussion and opinions through e-mail. Other groups may use a Web-based "message board" format.

You can start your own book group with friends, or see whether a suitable group already exists, at any of these sites:

- Yahoo! Groups: groups.yahoo.com (for existing groups, try searching for "adbooks," "youngadultlit," or "sankofabird")
- Book Clique Café: www.readinggroupsonline.com
- Open Directory: www.dmoz.org/Arts/Literature/Reading_Groups

Practicing the Art of Conversation

1. Choose a news event you have read about. Pair up your student with a friend or sibling to discuss, one-on-one, that particular event or issue. Are the kids aware of their ability to take turns speaking and listening?

2. Small group members can discuss doing a co-op project, such as a short skit based on a folk tale. Kinesthetic and visual learners usually go for acting!

3. Try to sensitize those at the breakfast or dinner table to good listening manners. Mention whenever a speaker is interrupted by others before a communication has been completed. A pause during a speaker's statement may not constitute an opportunity for another person to cut in and speak. Ask the group, "When does a pause allow another person to speak?"

Resources Around You

A repairperson or a tradesperson can offer a window to the working world, if he or she is open to answering questions. Your student can conduct an interview and report back to the family in either oral or written form. Questions might include:

▶ **How did you become a repairperson (or plumber, electrician, etc.)?**

▶ **What training did you need?**

▶ **Do you like it? Why or why not?**

▶ **What's the best/worst thing about your job?**

▶ **What is the strangest/funniest/kindest thing that ever happened to you on the job?**

Telephone Skills

1. Practice (with an unplugged phone receiver) how you would speak on the telephone in the following scenarios. Ask your learner, "Would you speak differently in these calls? How?"

◆ Call a friend's family and ask the mom if your friend is at home

◆ Call your great uncle to ask how his new puppy is doing

◆ Call a tech support number to ask for a replacement game disk

◆ Call the police for medical help

2. Discuss the social courtesies expected in answering a phone:

◆ at home

◆ as a guest at your cousin's house

◆ as if your homeschooler were a receptionist at a business, taking a message

3. Discuss: Do we listen more attentively to the tone of a person's voice if we cannot see their facial expressions?

It's a Fact!

In our rapidly changing world, shaped by emerging technologies, the *skill to learn* may be more important than individual facts. Being a lifelong learner has become more than a tool for employment and excellence. It has become a path to a richer life.

▶ ACTIVITIES, ACTIVITIES, ACTIVITIES

The following activities have been selected because they are fun and also enhance the development of social interaction skills. In addition, they are purposeful, practical, and not simply "busy work." Of course, feel free to adapt these activities to your middle schooler's maturity and abilities.

Advice Columnist. Cover up or cut out the answers to questions written to an Ann Landers or Dear Abby newspaper column. Ask your learner to write her own replies and then compare them with the printed replies.

The Talking Stick Tradition. Practice the Talking Stick Tradition when having a family meeting or small group discussion. The speaker holds a Talking Stick while speaking. (Decorate the Talking Stick with ribbons and feathers as Native Americans did or substitute a treasured shell or stone if you prefer.) Only the person holding the stick may speak; others may not interrupt—it's harder than it sounds! When finished, the speaker either places the object in the center of the group or passes it on to the next speaker. This pause provides a moment of silence between comments in the discussion.

Letter of Persuasion. Ask your middle schooler to write a letter to a member of the family. The letter should try to convince the family member to do something for the learner.

The Demonstration. Have your learner watch a video or live demonstration or read a how-to explanation. Then ask him or her to teach it to someone else.

Hold a Salon. A *salon* is a conversation party, when an invited group of friends gathers socially to discuss an interesting topic. The first meeting of the salon could be to develop a good list of discussion topics such as ethics, current events, novels, or films.

Attend a Play. Educator Jennifer Richard Jacobson suggests, "Plays have predictable structures that are very similar to stories. At intermission, discuss what you've seen so far. Have all the characters been introduced? Has the rising action reached the climax (the most exciting part) yet? What do you think will happen when the curtain goes up again? How do you think the problem will be solved? If the play is a mystery, discuss how the author creates tension and who might be the red herring— a character who is an obvious suspect but is not likely to be the final culprit."

A Wish List. Ask your homeschooler to fill out a wish list before your next trip to the library or bookstore. She can then explain to you why she is interested in a particular magazine or book and how she wants to apply it to her studies. (If it's in the budget, you can buy your child the item she explains the most eloquently.)

Play the Dictionary Game. A game of words and whimsy, bluff and bluster! The Dictionary Game promotes understanding of definitions, roots, and writing tone. You will need pencils and paper for four to six players and one dictionary.

1. The host for this round flips through the dictionary and finds a word he thinks no one else knows. He checks with the group, for instance, "Does anyone know the word *peruke?*"

2. The other players have to answer honestly. If one or more knows the word, that word is disqualified and the host continues searching until he comes up with a word for which no one knows the definition.

3. The chosen word is spelled aloud for everyone to write on their papers. The players are then given a time limit, usually five or six minutes, to concoct and write a plausible definition for that word—a definition that *sounds* like a real dictionary definition. (Each player is trying to fool the other players into voting for his or her phony definition.)

4. Meanwhile, the host is writing down the *real* definition, or a reasonable part of the real definition, from the dictionary onto his paper.

5. The host collects all the papers from the group and shuffles them. He then numbers and reads aloud each definition (the whole batch is read through twice), while the other players listen, trying to discern the one correct definition among the fakes.

6. Everyone writes down a vote (e.g., definition number 3) and, when all have voted, each person announces his vote to the group. People laugh at who fooled whom and how. The real definition is read aloud by the host.

7. Scoring is complex, so it's a good idea to have one scorekeeper for the entire game. Each player who fooled someone else with a phony definition gets a point. Each player who guessed the real definition gets two points. If no one chose the real definition, the host gets three points. The dictionary then moves to the person on the right for a new host and a new word in a new round.

▶ PRACTICE

(The keys, exemplars, and rubrics may be found in Appendix A)

I. AN INVISIBLE FRIEND

Note: This essay practices social interaction with a "wide variety of people," or, in this case, with an invisible person! It requires skills in persuasion, in teaching understanding, and in presentation of example and detail to fit the argument. As always, the letters may be read/answered/discussed aloud.

This morning you found a magic letter on your dresser. It's from an imaginary friend that you have had since you were five years old. Read the letter and think about what you could say that would help your invisible friend decide to become visible.

> *To my best friend,*
> *You are my best and only friend because only you can see and hear me. To everyone else I am invisible.*
> *Last night on my 12th birthday, I figured out how to make myself visible. But I am afraid. I like living in your imagination. I'm not too sure I'd like living in the real world. Who would take care of me? What would I do for fun?*
> *Do you think I should become visible? Besides being with you, what is so great about being visible?*
> *Fondly,*
> *Your confused friend*

Write a letter trying to convince your friend to become visible. Use details and examples.

_____

_____

_____

_____

_____

II. AN OBJECT

Note: The answer to this prompt requires social interaction with the reader in explaining one's own feelings, attitude, bias, and experience. An extension to the writing might be reading aloud and then discussing several answers.

Read the following excerpt by Walt Whitman from "There Was A Child Went Forth," in *Leaves of Grass,* 1855.

There was a child who went forth every day,
And the first object he look'd upon, that object he became,
And that object became part of him for the day or a certain part of the day,
Or for many years or stretching cycles of years.

Whitman's poem suggests that certain objects become important to us and remain important to us even if we no longer have them. Write a story in which you tell about an object that remains important to the main character over a period of years. The main character could be you or someone you know.

In your story, describe the main character's first encounter with the object, why the object is so important to the character, and how, over the years, it remains a part of the character's life.

6

Reading, Writing, Listening, and Speaking for Information and Understanding

> **Goal of the Standard:** *Students read, write, listen, and speak for information and understanding.* As listeners and readers, students collect data and ideas; discover relationship, concepts, and generalizations; and use knowledge generated from oral, written, and electronic texts. As speakers and writers, learners use oral and written language to acquire, interpret, apply, and transmit information.

▶ WHAT DO WE MEAN BY INFORMATION AND UNDERSTANDING?

We live in what is called "the Information Age," although sometimes it seems like the information *overload* age! Data, facts, details, theories, opinions, and conclusions—all types of information bombard us. Ideally, we process, compare, evaluate, and understand the information we each need for our lives to run smoothly. We absorb **information and understanding** from so many sources—printed, visual, verbal, and electronic—and it can truly be exhausting.

Of course, we understand that quality reading and listening are essential to successful information intake. We also want our children to be able to receive and transmit facts and ideas from all the sources the Information Age has to offer: books, newspapers, manuals, letters, contracts, advertisements, software, TV, videos, radio, cassettes, the Internet, and a host of other materials.

As parents, we want our children to read well and widely, building a strong foundation for learning in all areas of life. We want them to differentiate between fact and fiction and opinion and bias.

In the arenas of schooling and work, we want our learners to be able to research and use a wide variety of resources. They also need to know how to frame questions for inquiry, to identify and organize relevant information, and to communicate it effectively in a variety of formats.

▶ ACTIVITIES FOR INFORMATION AND UNDERSTANDING

Activities appropriate to this standard include

- **Reading** essays, speeches, sermons, textbooks, newspapers and magazines, encyclopedias, history, and other fiction and nonfiction text
- **Writing** research reports, essays, lists, outlines, summaries, paraphrases, directions, and instructions
- **Listening** to speeches, sermons, fiction and nonfiction excerpts, lectures, documentaries, films, news broadcasts, and identifying details and fact, bias and propaganda
- **Speaking** to present research findings, give speeches, instructions, and directions

▶ WHAT SKILLS ARE WE LOOKING FOR HERE?

We are guiding our middle schoolers to eventually master these language arts skills:

- Listening and reading to acquire information and understanding (*Ian paraphrases a documentary on preying mantises.*)
- Writing and speaking to transmit information and understanding (*Daria composes an e-mail memo on the agenda for the next conference.*)
- Giving and writing instructions and directions (*Malcolm explains how to get to the amphitheater from work.*)
- Asking questions to probe and clarify (*Reverend Barker requests clarification at the city planning meeting.*)
- Revising and editing for correct spelling, grammar, punctuation, and usage (*Fred helps his dad revise and edit the rough draft of a recommendation for a coworker.*)
- Listening for significant detail or specific facts (*Carter turns on the nightly news and focuses in on the sports report.*)

- Differentiating fact from bias (*Theodora scans an editorial to determine where and how the writer supports his opinions with data.*)
- Applying information from one context to another (*Noi sews a long dress, adapting a blouse pattern.*)
- Speaking to teach, explain, or instruct (*Meg teaches her youth group how to build a compost holder.*)
- Participating in family discussions (*Scotty learns from his dad how to install the printer software and teaches his sister how to change the toner cartridge.*)
- Conduct basic research (*Tomoyuki uses a both printed encyclopedia and the electronic Encarta to write a report with pictures on Easter Island.*)
- Using the library (*Kris finds a reference book and retrieves information on African masks.*)
- Using the computer (*Kevin manipulates the search engine to find a tutorial on making pictographs in Excel.*)

Criteria for Informational Language

When considering speaking and writing for information and understanding, ask "What is the message being communicated?' and "What is the purpose of the information?" Use these criteria:

1. **Public**—The information must be clear and understandable to a public audience.
2. **Efficient**—The information should be presented concisely.
3. **Valid**—The facts and data must be accurate, precise, and relevant to the purpose.
4. **Verifiable**—Information must be well founded and able to be traced to a reliable source.

Study Skills

To handle the challenge of absorbing and transmitting information and understanding, your middle schooler will need to eventually master his or her study skills. During the middle school years, your teen should be able to:

- **Manage time** effectively by creating and following a schedule for completing work.
- **Take effective notes** by differentiating between main and supporting ideas, between key facts and specific examples and details.
- **Manage projects** by breaking them down into manageable tasks.
- **Solve problems** creatively by identifying the problem, brainstorming solutions, evaluating the possible solutions, and assessing the success of the chosen solution.

▶ EVIDENCE OF SUCCESS

Remember, you know your middle schooler's proficiency and progress best. With your help, your middle schooler will move from *basic* to *intermediate* to *advanced* mastery in the skills for information and understanding.

BASIC MASTERY includes

- Paraphrasing what has been read or heard
- Following directions that involve a few steps
- Asking for clarification of an idea
- Beginning to organize information they have collected (maybe through mapping, drawing, or outlining)
- Writing a short report in social studies using at least two sources
- Demonstrating how to care for a pet using props as well as oral explanation
- Writing brief summaries of texts
- Revising an early draft of a report to make it clearer

INTERMEDIATE MASTERY includes further development of all of the above and

- Producing a summary of information about a famous person
- Using facts from news articles and TV reports in an oral report on a current event
- Taking notes that record the main ideas and most significant details of a lecture or speech
- Writing an essay for science that contains information from interviews, magazines, and the Internet
- Participating in a group discussion, citing the sources of information
- Using technical terms correctly
- Surveying friends or family on an issue and reporting the findings

ADVANCED MASTERY includes further development of all of the above and

- Assembling notes for a science or social studies project or exhibit
- Using an electronic database to find evidence of trends in society
- Producing flowcharts or diagrams to show relationships among information
- Determining the relative value of different resources
- Demonstrating how to perform an intricate task
- Writing a science lab report
- Producing program notes for an art exhibit or concert with background information on the artists

Evidence of Growth

Please refer back to Chapter 2 to review the five categories of growth: *range, flexibility, connections, conventions,* and *independence.*

These five categories can be benchmarks for your student's growth over time. Concerning the goals of *information and understanding,* ask yourself, "Over the years, does my homeschooler show progress in:

1. exploring a RANGE of source materials? of strategies for recording, organizing, and transmitting information?"

2. showing FLEXIBILITY in delivering information, adjusting to purpose and audience and when switching from one subject to another?"

3. making stronger CONNECTIONS between familiar information and new information and in understanding the general and the particular in a text?"

4. understanding more deeply the CONVENTIONS of forms and formats for informational texts and those associated with grammar, usage, punctuation, and spelling?

5. demonstrating INDEPENDENCE in establishing purpose, locating resources, deciding what's significant, selecting from available options, and achieving an individual style?

Carschooling® Tricks

As you chauffeur your learners, you can play *License Plate Scrabble*. The basic game and its variations aid spelling, vocabulary, and word order. The idea is to take three letters of a license plate and make them into a word, using the first letter as the first letter of the word, the second letter as any letter in the middle of the word and the last letter as, well, the last letter. For example, DSY can become "daisy" or "Disney" or "discovery."

Scoring: Each person getting a correctly spelled word earns a point. Or, the person making the longest word scores three points and the others score one point. In tournament play, the person forming the longest word gets the sum of the numbers on the license plate. You keep these totals on paper, and the first to reach 100 points wins.

License Plate Scrabble Variations:

▶ Allow the letters to be scrambled first and then make them into a word. Thus, if you see GHL, you could scramble it to LHG and come up with "laughing."

▶ Acronyms: Invent a real-sounding government agency or company with the three letters. For instance, OPA transforms into "Office of Pets Administration" or "Office of Peculiar Acronyms." If you get either a chuckle or groan from other participants, you score!

Forming an Initial Understanding

Forming an initial understanding precedes processing and evaluation of, and response to, what we read or hear. Initial understanding means your learner has a first impression or holistic understanding of what has been read or heard. It involves considering the text as a whole or in a broad perspective. Questions to ask your learner regarding initial understanding might include:

1. After reading this, what do you think is the most important information?

2. What do you think is the best theme of this story/article?

3. What is this piece supposed to help you do or learn?

Self-Correcting Methods

Growth and progress in the language arts are also measured through the eventual mastery of "self-correcting methods." The more experimenting and practice your learner has, the better he or she will coordinate these skills into a method that works best:

- skimming
- scanning
- reading ahead
- rereading
- using resources
- summarizing
- retelling
- readjusting speed

It's a Fact!

Did you know that most everyday texts—like newspaper and magazine articles, websites, and brochures—are written at the *8th-grade reading level*? Homeschoolers may have even higher reading-level goals.

▶ READING COMPREHENSION QUESTIONS

At some time or another, your learner will encounter reading comprehension questions. This form of testing consists of reading a passage and then answering true-false, multiple-choice, and/or essay questions about that passage. Let's examine multiple-choice questions first.

The multiple-choice question offers an advantage for test-takers: They don't need to know anything about the topic of the passage beforehand, because they are being questioned on the information the passage provides.

The test taker does need to know where and how to find the pertinent information quickly in an unfamiliar text. Time limits pressure the test taker to pick a wrong answer, especially since wrong choices are crafted as specific distractors—certain wrong choices included to tempt the impulsive chooser.

The best way to succeed in a passage-questions format is to be familiar with four kinds of questions typically asked. (Other types of questions are referred to in other chapters.)

By the way, these questions may apply to either fiction or nonfiction passages:

1. identify a specific **fact or detail** in the passage
2. note the **main idea** of the passage
3. make an **inference** based on the passage
4. define a **vocabulary** word from the passage

Review with your homeschooler that **facts and details** are the specific pieces of information supporting the passage's **main idea**. The main idea is the thought, opinion, or attitude that governs the whole paragraph or passage. Generally speaking, facts and details are indisputable—they don't need to be proven—such as statistics (*182 people preferred chocolate-chip ice cream*) or descriptions (*a solid gold Cadillac*).

Let's look at the following paragraph from a story on colonial America by author Barbara Cole.

> Early Americans did not bathe as often as we do. When they did, their "bathroom" was the kitchen, in that toasty space by the hearth. They partially filled a tub with cold water and then warmed it up with water heated in the fireplace. A blanket draped from chairs for privacy also let the fire's warmth surround the bather.

The **main idea** of a passage may be *stated* (often it's the first or last sentence.) or *implied*, based on facts and details given. Which is it in this case? Test the first sentence: Does the thought "Early Americans did not bathe as often as we did" govern the whole paragraph? No. It is one of many details supporting an implied main idea such as "Early Americans had different bathing habits than we do." Now test this sentence: It is, in fact, supported by all the other sentences in the passage, so it is the main idea.

Other **inferences**—besides a main idea—can be drawn from a passage, based on fact or evidence. For example, you can infer—based on the fact that "Early Americans did not bathe as often as we do," that they were smellier than we are now! It may not be true, but it is a reasonable inference. If Cole had added, "Also, early Americans did not use sweet-smelling soap or deodorant or perfumes," we would have even more evidence for the inference that they were smellier than we are now!

As you might expect, **vocabulary** questions ask you to determine the meaning of a particular word or phrase *as it is used in the passage*. In your daily lessons, you and your learner probably often guess the meaning of words from their context or how they are used in the sentence. For example, in Cole's passage, a reader who does not understand what a *hearth* is may gather that it has to do with a fireplace from clues within the passage, such as *toasty space* and *the fire's warmth*.

Now let's examine an actual standardized test problem, four multiple-choice questions, and their answers. Encourage your student to practice on any sample problem in this book.

SAMPLE TEST PROBLEM

Directions: Read the following passage; then read the questions and select the best answer. Then refer to the list above and note which type of question has been asked.

In the past two decades, community policing has been frequently touted as the best way to reform urban law enforcement. The idea of putting more officers on foot patrol in high crime areas, where relations with police have frequently been strained, was initiated in Houston in 1983 under the leadership of then Commissioner Lee Brown. He believed that officers should be accessible to the community at the street level. If officers were assigned to the same area over a period of time, those officers would eventually build a network of trust with neighborhood residents. That trust would mean that merchants and residents in the community would let officers know about criminal activities in the area and would support police intervention. Since then, many large cities have experimented with Community-Oriented Policing (COP) with mixed results. Some have found that police and citizens are grateful for the opportunity to work together. Others have found that unrealistic expectations by citizens and resistance from officers have combined to hinder the effectiveness of COP. It seems possible, therefore, that a good idea may need improvement before it can truly be considered a reform.

1. Community-Oriented Policing has been used in law enforcement since
   a. the late 1970s.
   b. the early 1980s.
   c. the Carter administration.
   d. Lee Brown was New York City police commissioner.

   Question type: _____

2. The phrase "a network of trust" in this passage suggests that
   a. police officers can rely only on each other for support.
   b. community members rely on the police to protect them.
   c. police and community members rely on each other.
   d. community members trust only Spider-Man.

   Question type: _____

3. The best title for this passage would be
   a. Community Policing: The Solution to the Drug Problem.
   b. Houston Sets the Pace in Community Policing.
   c. Communities and Cops: Partners for Peace.
   d. Community Policing: An Uncertain Future?

   Question type: _____

4. The word *touted* in the first sentence of the passage most nearly means
   a. praised.
   b. denied.
   c. exposed.
   d. criticized.

   Question type: _____

▶ ANSWERS AND COMMENTS

1. b. Question type: fact or detail

The passage says that community policing began "in the past two decades." A decade is 10 years. In addition, the passage identifies 1983 as the first large-scale use of community policing in Houston. Don't be misled by trying to figure out when Carter was president. Also, if you happen to know that Lee Brown was once New York City's police commissioner, don't let that information lead you away from the information contained in the passage alone. Brown was commissioner in Houston when he initiated community policing.

2. c. Question type: inference

The "network of trust" referred to in this passage is between the community and the police, as you can see from the sentence where the phrase appears. The key phrase in the question is *in this passage.* You may believe that police can rely only on each other, or one of the other answer choices may appear equally plausible to you. But your choice of answers must be limited to the one suggested *in this passage.* Another tip for questions like this: Beware of absolutes! In other words, be suspicious of an answer containing words like *only, always,* or *never.*

3. d. Question type: main idea

The title always expresses the main idea. In this passage, the main idea comes at the end. The sum of all the details in the passage suggests that community policing is not without its critics and that, therefore, its future is uncertain. Another key phrase is "mixed results," which means that some communities haven't had full success.

4. a. Question type: vocabulary

The word *touted* is linked in this passage with the phrase "the best way to reform." Most people would think that a good way to reform something is praiseworthy. In addition, the next few sentences in the passage describe the benefits of community policing. Criticism or a negative response to the subject doesn't come until later in the passage.

▶ HOW DO WE TEACH AND PRACTICE THESE SKILLS?

The very best way to practice exploring themes, main ideas, inferences, details, and vocabulary in context—whether you are preparing for future standardized testing or facility in reading comprehension—is to discuss what you've read. By the way, reading aloud to each other is a natural and pleasurable way to lead into talking about what you've read.

Reading aloud does not need to stop when your child is a pre-teen or teen. The Pallay family of four, for example, reads aloud on a king-size bed several nights a week. And Drew reads a book of his choosing to his dad, as they drive to a co-op sign language class. Reading to each other reinforces your learner's interest in reading and underscores your commitment to reading.

For the visual learner, discussing movies or videos accomplishes the identical reading comprehension goals: understanding, appreciating similarities among people and their concerns, exploring ideas, comparing/contrasting themes, and drawing conclusions.

Prompt your homeschooler with questions such as:

◆ What do you think this is about? (*main idea/theme*)
◆ Have we seen this theme/main idea elsewhere? (*main idea/theme*)
◆ What proof do you read here that _____? (*details/facts*)
◆ What information does the author share with us about _____? (*details/facts*)
◆ What do you think the author means to say here, between the lines? (*inference*)
◆ What can we infer from _____? (*inference*)
◆ Can you guess what this word, _____, means? (*vocabulary*)
◆ What clues are there to its meaning? (*vocabulary*)

Now let's look more specifically at standardized testing for information and understanding. Later, Chapter 4 extends the scope of comprehension to critical analysis and evaluation, while Chapter 5 covers a reader-writer's response and expression.

Fact or Detail Questions

Main idea questions and fact or detail questions both ask readers for information on the page before them. A fact/detail question is usually the simplest kind of question in a problem set. Your reader needs to be able to separate important information from less important information. However, the choices may be similar or tricky.

Test prep experts suggest one of these two methods:

1. Skim the passage for the general idea; read the questions; then read the passage completely.
2. Read the questions first to be prepared to look out for certain details; then read the passage thoroughly once or twice.

Main Idea Questions

The main idea of a passage, like that of a paragraph or a book, is what the material is *mostly* about. Like an umbrella, the main idea covers all of the ideas and details in the passage, so it is usually a more general theme.

As you saw in the practice above, question 3 asked what the best title for the passage would be. The answer is "Community Policing: An Uncertain Future." Why is this the best answer? It is the only choice encompassing both the positive and negative sides to community policing as presented in the passage.

Tell your learner that sometimes the main idea is stated clearly, often in the first or last sentence of a passage (regardless of how many paragraphs it has). In the practice passage, the last sentence expresses the main idea. The sentence that exactly states the main idea is often called the **topic sentence.**

At other times, the main idea cannot be found in a topic sentence, but is *implied* in the overall passage, and your reader will need to determine the main idea by inference. Because a passage may include a great deal of information, the trick is to grasp what all that information adds up to—the gist of what the author wants the reader to know. Often the wrong answers (called **distractors**) on a main-idea test question will be specific facts or details from the passage. A good question for your student to ask is *Can this answer serve as a net to hold the whole passage together?* If not, chances are the answer is a fact or detail, but not the main idea.

Continue answering main idea and detail questions in the practice sets at the end of this chapter. Now let's look at inference and vocabulary questions.

Items asking word meanings (vocabulary questions) and those asking what a passage *suggests* or *implies* (inference questions) differ from detail or main idea questions because you usually have to deduce meaning—sometimes drawing on ideas from more than one place in the passage.

Inference

"What do you think the author meant by . . . ?" "This passage suggests that . . . " Inference questions challenge your learner because he or she will need to recognize implied—rather than directly stated—meanings, to reach a conclusion. Encourage your student to be a detective, looking for such clues as word choice, tone, and specific details that suggest a certain conclusion, attitude, or point of view.

Your learner might ask this question: "What evidence do I have for this inference?" If she can't find any evidence in the passage, she probably has the wrong answer. In other words, the answer choice your middle schooler selects must be logical and based on facts, details, or something clearly implied—not on his or her opinion or hunch.

For example, if your reader picked an answer choice such as "Ludwig seemed sad after his meeting with Clara," can he show evidence that Ludwig was sad? Did the writer use words such as *weepy* and *despondent* or describe Ludwig wiping away a tear?

Vocabulary Questions

Vocabulary questions measure how well you discover the meaning of an unfamiliar word from its component parts, its context, or a nearby synonym or antonym.

Component parts. If you're familiar with prefixes, suffixes, and word roots, your knowledge helps determine the meaning of an unfamiliar word. For example, if you don't know the meaning of *interstellar*, you might know that *inter* is a prefix meaning "between or among" and *stellar* looks like the Latin for star, *stella*. Sure enough, *interstellar* means "between or among the stars."

Context. The words and ideas surrounding a vocabulary word are its context. If the context is clear, you should be able to substitute a nonsense word for the unknown word and still make the right answer choice. For example:

The speaker noted that it gave him great *tervinix* to award the trophy to his best friend. In this sentence, *tervinix* most likely means

    a. pain.
    b. sympathy.
    c. pleasure.
    d. anxiety.

Clearly, the context makes **c**, *pleasure,* the best choice. Giving a trophy to your best friend probably wouldn't bring pain, sympathy, or anxiety.

Consider the context carefully, so that you don't confuse one word with a similar one. For instance, the word *taut* means *tight,* but if you read too quickly or don't check the context, you might mistakenly assume that it means "to publicize or praise" (*tout*) or "to tease" (*taunt*).

Synonyms or antonyms. Search for nearby clues that may be synonyms (same meaning) or antonyms (opposite meaning) of the unknown word:

    ◆ Dave called his roommate **ubiquitous** because he seemed to be everywhere on campus at once. (*ubiquitous* is synonymous with "seemingly everywhere at the same time")
    ◆ Clyde had expected Trisha to be sorry, but she was **unrepentant.** (*sorry* and *unrepentant* are antonyms, or opposites)

▶ PRACTICING THESE SKILLS

A great way to solidify what your homeschooler has learned about the reading comprehension questions discussed in this chapter is to ask her to *create questions and answers!* Try this exercise together; sample answers follow.

Read the passage below and then write your own questions and answer choices. Write one of each of the four types of questions discussed in this chapter: detail, main idea, inference, and vocabulary.

Who is Autherine Lucy? On February 3, 1956, Autherine Lucy became the first African-American student to attend the University of Alabama, although the dean of women refused to allow Autherine to live in a university dormitory. White students rioted in protest of her admission, and the federal government had to assume command of the Alabama National Guard in order to protect her. Nonetheless, on her first day in class, Autherine bravely took a seat in the front row. She remembers being surprised that the professor of the class appeared not to notice she was even in class. Later she would appreciate his seeming indifference, as he was one of only a few professors to speak out in favor of her right to attend the university. Autherine was later expelled due to unrest on campus.

1. Fact or detail question:

_____

a. _____

b. _____

c. _____

d. _____

2. Main idea question:

_____

a. _____

b. _____

c. _____

d. _____

3. Inference question:

_____

a. _____

b. _____

c. _____

d. _____

4. Vocabulary question:

_____

a. _____

b. _____

c. _____

d. _____

Possible Questions and Answer Choices

While your student's questions may be very different, here are some sample question and answer choices for you two to study.

Fact or detail question:

1. According to the passage, Autherine Lucy
   a. lived in a dormitory.
   b. sat in the front row of her class.
   c. became a lawyer.
   d. majored in history.

Main idea question:

2. This passage would most likely be from a book called
   a. *20th Century African-American History.*
   b. *A Collection of Favorite Children's Stories.*
   c. *A History of the Civil War.*
   d. *How to Choose the College That Is Right for You.*

Inference question:

3. The phrase "bravely took a seat in the front row" suggests that
   a. Autherine was used to riding on buses.
   b. Autherine was usually afraid.
   c. There were not enough chairs in the back of the classroom.
   d. Autherine was doing something that was probably shocking to the white students.

Vocabulary question:

4. The word *seeming* in this passage most nearly means
   a. apparent
   b. angry
   c. useless
   d. likely

Answers

   1. **b.**
   2. **a.**
   3. **d.**
   4. **a.**

▶ WRITING PRACTICE

To promote gathering, selecting, organizing, and analyzing information, you and your homeschooler can try these exercises:

1. Write down the exact ingredients and directions for making a favorite recipe; listen to the feedback of someone who tries making your recipe.

2. Follow the directions for assembly of something; then make suggestions for how to improve the instructions.

3. Examine newspaper or magazine articles and interview people to create a documentary showing the various sides of an issue.

4. Fill out a job or college application. Ask a partner to pretend to be the person evaluating you via your application and listen to the critique.

▶ UNIT STUDYING

Unit studies are perfectly adapted to information and understanding goals. Unit studies focus on a topic of interest to the student and follow that topic on as many paths and activities as possible—a cross-disciplinary journey.

Unit studies easily incorporate listening, reading, writing, speaking, and research skills by virtue of the limitless avenues open to exploration: books, field trips, oral history, Internet, and so forth. In addition, learners who follow unit studies are apparently more self-motivated and retain more of what they learn.

For example, one day Arnell visited the Egyptian wing at the Metropolitan Museum of Art and became enamored of mummies! He and his parents selected several ways to explore the topic of mummies, which naturally led to other related topics. Eventually, the mummy unit study took on a life of its own. Arnell's activities soon included:

◆ Reading books on mummification

◆ Watching (and discussing) a PBS series on ancient Egypt

◆ Making flash cards with new vocabulary and meanings

◆ Building a model pyramid, complete with tunnels, chambers, and sarcophagi

◆ Listening to an audio biography of King Tut

◆ Writing essays on mummies and on Cleopatra's life

◆ Creating a translation key for hieroglyphics and English

◆ Teaching his brother some hieroglyphics so they could write to each other in code

◆ Baking the kind of flat bread that was eaten in ancient Egypt

Unit studies lend themselves to adaptation for all ages of children within the homeschooling family—therefore, resources and enthusiasm can be shared. Sibling teaching happens—which means understanding of information is reinforced and passed on. And children promote their own ideas for expanding a topic, which may include reading, writing, research, giving presentations, and taking field trips.

You can also find unit studies in purchased packages or on the Internet—for example, Laura just finished a cyber unit on bats after her Uncle Ted brought her photos of his trip to the Carlsbad Caverns batcaves. The bat unit included vocabulary, biology, physics, drawing, geography, and research.

Dive into the Web

If you are new to homeschooling, the idea of creating a unit study all by yourself may be overwhelming. For help, take a look at the links below.

- Educational Units and Lesson Plans: www.coollessons.org
- About.com's index of unit studies by grade level (also searchable by subject): www.homeschooling.about.com/cs/units/index.htm
- A to Z Teacher Themes: www.atozteacherstuff.com/themes

Sites compiled by homeschooling parents:

- The Four Wheelers' Unit Study Directory: www.thefourwheelers.com/units
- The Milstids' Unit Study for Everyone: www.gulftel.com/~lvhmskl/unit.htm
- Free Unit Study Links: www.home.pacbell.net/ransom/unitstudies.htm

Whether the materials you choose are designed with teachers or homeschoolers in mind, remember that you are free to adapt them to suit your learner's needs—and your own!

▶ ACTIVITIES, ACTIVITIES, ACTIVITIES

We have chosen several fun activities that enhance the development of the information and understanding skills. Of course, feel free to adapt these activities to your middle schooler's maturity and abilities:

Journaling or Scrapbooking. Keep a journal of your current study unit or subject. Sample entries:

- ◆ Traced the routes Captain Cook sailed in the Pacific
- ◆ Read a book about Captain Cook in Hawaii
- ◆ Wrote a short story about the natives at the cove where Captain Cook was murdered
- ◆ Saw a video on the Big Island

Scrapbooking means creatively compiling your writings, drawings, favorite clippings and pictures, photos, and e-mails into a scrapbook. Read some of your best writings or favorite clippings out loud at the dinner table, sharing information and your understanding of it.

Online Games, Quizzes, and Websites. Do a search for any topic you are studying, and you will most likely find a myriad of websites with information, games, quizzes, and links to other sites.

Designing Websites. Design your own family website (learning from software or from the family propeller-head). Post your own and your friends' poetry, art, jokes, short stories, games, photographs, or other information. Add links to sites you admire and explain why you like them.

An Investment Club. Use fake money or commodities and divide up into teams with your family or co-op. Take weekly buy and sell orders, record them, figure commissions, and do company research in the newspapers and on the Internet. Share what you understand from what you've read and heard and ask questions.

Academic Clubs. These clubs unify around a specific academic skill or subject, such as math, history, or environmental science. Some homeschoolers form their own clubs or, in some supportive school districts, homeschoolers join regular schoolers' clubs. One middle school, for example, offers a Weather Club. Students create daily weather maps using data from their own weather station and then broadcast their forecast on the local radio station. Competitive debate clubs help teens develop their public speaking, critical thinking, and language facility, and may lead to competitions around the country. Your child may create a homework club for co-op studying or an honors club that rewards and encourages students of outstanding academic achievement.

Publications. Homeschoolers and homeschooling support groups often produce student-created publications: newsletters, self-published books, yearbooks, newspapers, and literary magazines. They spread information among homeschoolers and their communities. These publications need people to write, edit, photograph, design covers, create page layouts, raise funds, and promote the publication.

Resources Around You

Look for natural science classes in "your own backyard:" your garden, a community park, a pond or stream, the woods, the beach, a desert, the mountains. Grab a pair of binoculars, a compass, a blank book and some drawing and writing pencils, a nature journal, and a portable guidebook exploring animals, insects, plants, birds, or minerals. You can observe and write, draw, memorize poetry while sitting under a shady tree, journal, or enjoy the writings of naturalists such as John Muir and Rachel Carson.

▶ PRACTICE

(The keys, exemplars, and rubrics may be found in Appendix A)

Note: These exercises provide additional practice in mastery of the main idea, inference, facts or details, and vocabulary. Rereading a passage, as in Practice Problem 1, also allows experience in gleaning more information from a second reading of something. A further exercise for Practice 1 might be researching a related subject (EMT workers, firefighting, burn centers, arson, and so on) and giving a report or speech on that topic.

I. *Reread the sample passage in Chapter 4 on pages 56–57, entitled "Treating Burns." Then choose the best answer for these questions.*

1. Which of the following would be a more accurate title for this passage?
   a. Dealing with Third-Degree Burns
   b. How to Recognize and Treat Different Burns
   c. Burn Categories
   d. Preventing Infection in Burns

2. Second-degree burns should be treated with
   a. butter.
   b. nothing.
   c. cold water.
   d. warm water.

3. First-degree burns turn the skin
   a. red.
   b. blue.
   c. black.
   d. white.

4. Why is it important for rescue workers to be able to recognize each type of burn?
   a. Rescue workers are under a lot of stress.
   b. Rescue workers may need to put burn victims into separate rescue vehicles.
   c. They can then be sure that burn victims are given the proper medical treatment.
   d. Rescue workers can tell the victim's family what kind of burn it is.

II. *Read the following passage and questions, selecting the best answers.*

Dealing with irritable customers—either on the phone or in person—poses a challenge for you, our software company's customer service representative. It is critical that you do not lose your patience when confronted by such a customer. When handling irate customers, be sure to remember that they are not angry with you; they are simply projecting their anger against a certain software *onto you*. Remember that if you respond to these customers as irritably as they act with you, you will only increase their hostility, making it much more difficult to complete your job. The best thing to do is to remain calm and ignore any imprecations customers may hurl your way. Some customers will try to anger you just to get some sort of reaction; sometimes they are understandably frustrated. If you react to their anger or sarcasm in kind, the results will be unproductive for both of you.

1. The word *irate* as it is used in the passage most nearly means
   a. irregular, odd.
   b. happy, cheerful.
   c. ill-tempered, angry.
   d. sloppy, lazy.

2. The passage suggests that customer service representatives
   a. easily lose control of their emotions.
   b. are better off not talking with customers.
   c. must be careful with irate customers because the customers might sue the company.
   d. may provide inadequate service if they let themselves become angry at customers.

3. Which of the following best expresses one of the writer's views about irate customers?
   a. Some irate customers just want a reaction.
   b. Irate customers are always miserable.
   c. Irate customers should be made to wait for service.
   d. Managing irate customers is the key to successful career advancement.

4. An imprecation is most likely
   a. an object.
   b. a curse.
   c. a joke.
   d. a software box.

5. Which title would be best for this piece?
   a. Controlling Your Temper
   b. Handling Angry Customers
   c. Why Customers Might Hate Our Product
   d. Anger in the Workplace

III. *Research and write about how the Iroquois and their way of life appreciated and protected nature. Find information about such activities as*

- ◆ farming
- ◆ hunting
- ◆ ceremonies
- ◆ building shelter
- ◆ making tools

Note: More advanced students can write about how the above activities protected or harmed nature compared to the way most Americans do things today.

IV. *Write an essay that describes in an engaging way how to perform a complex task.*

7

Reading, Writing, Listening, and Speaking for Critical Analysis and Evaluation

Goal of the Standard: *Students read, write, listen, and speak for critical analysis and evaluation. As listeners and readers, students analyze experiences, ideas, information, and issues presented by others. As speakers and writers, they use oral and written language following the accepted conventions of the English language to present, from a variety of perspectives, their opinions and judgments on experiences, ideas, information, and issues.*

▶ WHAT DO WE MEAN BY CRITICAL ANALYSIS AND EVALUATION?

"I give it a six out of ten!" Have you ever said something like that? Most of us are continually evaluating our experiences—as we read the newspaper, as we watch a commercial, as we select a movie to rent, and as we listen to our senator's campaign speech. We listen, we read, and we analyze to make judgments and decisions. In a world flooded with media, we want our youth to be discriminating. We want them to be especially skilled in separating fact from rumor and in recognizing bias, propaganda, and point of view. In order to make wise decisions, they need to gather information and to analyze experiences and ideas. Finally, our learners need to present their opinions and defend their judgments—for example, to deliver a cogent argument supported with detail (simultaneously a parent's trial and pride). Summing up, mastering **critical analysis and evaluation** nurtures the skills necessary to sort information, to problem solve, and to construct informed choices.

It's a Fact!

 Standardized tests are given at different times of the year, depending on state requirements. If your homeschooler plans on taking standardized tests, the tests might be taken on a website, at a community college, in a support group, or at home. Investigate within your local support group or at your state Board of Education's website.

▶ ACTIVITIES FOR CRITICAL ANALYSIS AND EVALUATION

Activities appropriate to practicing critical analysis and evaluation include:

- ◆ **Reading** literature, advertisements, editorials, book and movie reviews, literary criticism, political speeches, position papers, and professional journals
- ◆ **Writing** persuasive essays, book and movie reviews, literary critiques, editorials, thesis/support papers, analyses of issues, and college application essays
- ◆ **Listening** to advertising/commercials, political speeches, and debates
- ◆ **Speaking** to present oral book and movie reviews, persuasive speeches, and opinion surveys and to conduct debates and interviews

▶ WHAT SKILLS ARE WE LOOKING FOR HERE?

We are guiding our middle schoolers to eventually master the following language arts skills:

- ◆ Listening, reading, writing, and speaking to analyze and evaluate experiences, ideas, information, and issues within oral and written experiences. (*Teresa critiqued her best friend's speech, using specific examples.*)
- ◆ Using evaluative criteria from different points of view. (*Although Katrina didn't agree with the article, she claimed her cousin Mark would.*)
- ◆ Recognizing the differences in evaluations. (*For the kind of slapstick comedy it wants to be, Carl thinks the movie is great.*)

- Making decisions about the quality of texts and events. (*Ricky appreciates the beauty of the illustrations and appeal of the characters in* The Lion, the Witch and the Wardrobe. *Lisa rejects the subtle persuasion of a running shoe commercial.*)
- Recognizing bias, propaganda, or false claims—in ourselves and others. (*After reading about Auden's life, Douglas revised his opinions of the man's poetry.*)
- Understanding and expressing the difference between fact and opinion. (*"The TV judge was biased and hadn't studied the evidence," Kelley wrote.*)
- Using detail and evidence to support opinions. (*We will research the census statistics before evaluating the necessity of a new clinic.*)
- Presenting arguments with appropriate support. (*Kara and Sara continue to debate the pros and cons of buying the Daisy-Do swing set, based on safety, appeal to children, durability, and cost.*)
- Applying the rules of grammar, usage, spelling, and punctuation in persuasive writing. (*Clint eliminated the double negatives.*)
- Using the best oratory techniques in speech and debate. (*Annabel Lee always seems to end her speeches with a persuasive fact.*)

Dive Into the Web

A great source of analytical and opinionated writing is one you probably see every day: the newspaper. At The Write Site (www. writesite.org), your middle-schooler can learn all about what goes into writing a newspaper article: research, story ideas, and advice on developing a voice and style. The site also provides links, tools, and resources for instructors.

To find examples and inspiration, your learner can read articles online from Children's Express (www.cenews.org), an award-winning international media organization. For over 25 years, Children's Express has worked to publish articles written and edited by children (ages 8–18) in mainstream adult media.

▶ EVIDENCE OF SUCCESS!

How can you measure your homeschooler's mastery of analytical skills? Here are some examples of mastery.

BASIC MASTERY includes
- Giving an opinion in a book discussion, with specific reference to the text and to what makes a good book
- Reading several versions of a fairy tale or myth and recognizing the differences in the versions

- Pointing out examples of false advertising
- Identifying fact versus opinion in a magazine article
- Comparing a nonfiction article with the entries in an encyclopedia or with online research to judge the accuracy and comprehensiveness of the article
- Giving an oral report comparing several versions of the Cinderella story, pointing out similarities and differences

INTERMEDIATE MASTERY includes further development of all of the above and
- Writing a letter to a sports center director recommending that the cafeteria serve pizza, citing that it is a nutritious and appealing food
- Using the standards of scientific investigation to evaluate a science lab experiment
- Reading two conflicting reviews of a popular movie and recognizing the different points of view
- In a poetry group, selecting the most important word of a poem and explaining its significance
- Writing about the effects of a major snowstorm from the perspectives of a working parent, a snowplow operator, and a mail carrier
- Writing a position paper on a current event
- Presenting an oral review of a film—referring to character development, plot, pacing, and cinematography
- Debating a social issue while following the rules for formal debate

ADVANCED MASTERY includes further development of all of the above and
- Comparing the majority decision and the dissenting opinions on a Supreme Court case
- Listening to speeches of two political candidates and comparing their positions
- Reading the writing of two or more critics on the same author and determining what literary criteria each used
- Reading a current article on a scientific issue, such as the greenhouse effect, and comparing it to an earlier article on the same issue
- In a supportive group, critiquing each other's writing; then revising text based on the group's suggestions
- Writing two analyses of a Supreme Court decision—from the perspectives of a strict constructionist and a judicial activist
- Delivering a campaign speech, using a variety of persuasive strategies
- Comparing critiques of a Shakespeare play from two different centuries

Evidence of Growth

Please refer to Chapter 5 to review the five categories of growth: *range, flexibility, connections, conventions,* and *independence.*

These five categories can be benchmarks for your student's growth over time. Keeping in mind the goals of *critical analysis and evaluation,* ask yourself, "Over the years, does my homeschooler show progress in . . .

1. exploring a RANGE of points of view, issues, and criteria?"
2. showing FLEXIBILITY in selecting and applying standards for analysis? in adopting different points of view? in adapting arguments to the audience?"
3. making stronger CONNECTIONS between points of view? between arguments?"
4. understanding more clearly the CONVENTIONS of genre, oral and written analysis, and formal debate?"
5. demonstrating INDEPENDENCE in establishing a point of view? in applying criteria? in selecting effective language?"

SAMPLE PROBLEM

Read the following situation.

You are amazed to read in the local paper about a major incidence of vandalism near your house. This vandalism included graffiti, broken windows, and fence damage at the factory that has recently closed. Discuss what you think may be reasons why people commit vandalism, either in this situation or in general.

_____

_____

_____

_____

▶ EXEMPLARS AND COMMENTS

The following are two examples of successful answers to the short essay prompt above, along with some comments to help you compare your learner's writing. Essay grading is, of course, somewhat subjective; hence, the reasoning behind the categories. Remember, your evaluation may differ.

BASIC EXAMPLE

I don't understand vandalism. Why would somebody hurt someone else's property? I guess they are angry or hurt or feel left out. Maybe they are thinking they are having fun. Some people like a scary feeling (I am not one of them), so maybe this was a thrill for them. I am trying to put myself in the person's shoes, but it's not something my friends or I would think of. We don't dare each other to jump off buildings either!

Answers the prompt in an acceptable way; tries for point of view; uses personal references and humor; manipulates the basic conventions of spelling, punctuation, capitalization, and usage correctly.

ADVANCED EXAMPLE

While vandalism is inappropriate behavior without valid reason, I can try to understand the point of view of a vandal. I believe that the main reason for vandalism is kids who are looking for a good time and think it might be fun to graffiti the walls of the deserted factory. These kids may lack activities after school or the role models to do positive things in the community.

On the other hand, it might be someone who is angry at a parent or teacher and feels that expressing his anger this way is better than violence against a person. That's *almost* an acceptable reason, but not an acceptable excuse!

However, maybe the deserted factory is the clue to why this happened. Some kids might have thought "Since the factory is deserted, what difference does it make if I break the remaining windows?"

Finally, another theory is that the vandals were workers who were put out of jobs when the factory closed. If that is the case, it could be a political statement. Reading what the graffiti says could provide clues to this mystery.

In addition to the comments given above: reflects understanding of a simple genre, the personal essay; proposes many points of view; draws connections between events and results (workers being "put out of jobs"); uses advanced syntax and vocabulary; uses correct paragraphing.

▶ HOW DO WE TEACH AND PRACTICE THESE SKILLS?

Fortunately, opportunities for critical analysis are ever-present at home and work and in the community. You probably have already nurtured a thoughtful, analytical learner. In fact, homeschoolers are known for their sophistication in decision-making and in taking initiative—that is why hundreds of colleges are actively recruiting homeschooled applicants.

Let's look at additional methods for improving analytical skills in your learner.

Demonstrating a Critical Stance

Demonstrating a critical stance requires readers and listeners to stand apart from the text and consider it objectively. What tasks are involved in this?

- ◆ comparing and contrasting
- ◆ recognizing the organization of ideas
- ◆ discovering bias
- ◆ understanding irony and humor
- ◆ making connections between texts

What questions might you ask your learner to promote a critical stance?

1. Can you compare this text to that one?
2. How useful would this text be for _____? Why?

3. Does the author use humor (images, language)? Explain.

4. Do you think the author has a bias?

5. What information could be added to improve the author's argument? Explain.

Practicing Critical Analysis

The following ideas provide an opportunity to practice critical analysis skills. As always, adjust activities to match the learning style and mastery level of your homeschooler.

◆ Evaluate what you read, write, and hear, especially looking for clarity and good logic, supporting detail, comprehensiveness, and originality.

◆ Discuss differences in perspective in the world around us. For example, in considering whether to allow a new industry into your community, one group might be enthusiastic about the additional jobs that will be created, while others are concerned about the air and noise pollution that could result.

◆ Read a sports editorial and evaluate it together, talking about the criteria of accuracy, objectivity, comprehensiveness, and understanding of the game.

◆ Point out examples of propaganda techniques (such as "bandwagon," "plain folks" language, and "sweeping generalities") in public documents and speeches.

◆ Analyze points of view—for example, one critic condemns a biography for its length, while another praises its accuracy and never mentions its length.

◆ Compare two different literary forms expressing the same theme, such as music lyrics and a story about the loss of a love.

◆ Change a first-person account to a textbooklike description of an event or vice versa.

Expressing Opinion

When your learner looks to persuade others, he or she should ask these guiding questions:

1. Who is my audience?

2. What message do I want to communicate?

3. What is my point of view, my bias?

4. What evidence supports my opinion?

5. What is the best way to convince this particular audience?

6. What kind of response or action am I seeking?

7. How will I evaluate my own writing or speaking?

Influences on Writers

Examine with your middle schooler the ways that readers and writers are influenced by individual, social, cultural, and historical context. For example, during the study of pre-Revolutionary America, you could read sermons of the period, then determine which issues of the time shape the sermons and which arise from the author's own experience. Ask, "Which sermon topics would be relevant these days and which topics would be of little interest to today's listeners?"

Developing a Point of View

Ask your learner to choose a narrative written in the first person (or the third person).

1. Have your learner change the point of view to third person (or first person).

2. Discuss the strengths and weaknesses of each point of view.

Resources Around You

Homeschooler: If you are the volunteer type, use your language arts skills to create a *community service portfolio*—a record of volunteerism, church work, and activism. Include community service photos that you have taken or have been taken of you—such as reading to seniors, peer-tutoring, animal shelter work, cleaning up the beaches/highways, planting a neighborhood garden, whatever. Include letters or e-mails you wrote to Congress or to your local newspaper editor (or wished you had written!).

Include a list of "take action" websites, such as www.thehungersite.com. Include newspaper and magazine clippings covering the projects you believe in.

Parents: Creating a portfolio gives your child experience in reading, writing, organization, thinking skills, subject matter, and artistic expression.

Rhetorical Devices

Discuss with your homeschooler—literary learners love these—some of the more common rhetorical devices:

- ◆ alliteration
- ◆ allusion
- ◆ metaphor
- ◆ simile
- ◆ hyperbole
- ◆ personification
- ◆ parallelism
- ◆ understatement

1. One idea to pursue is to have your homeschooler select a rhetorical device, define it, create examples, and hunt for examples in literature, newspapers, and speeches.

2. Discuss how these devices might persuade or influence an audience. Find examples of persuasion; for instance:
- ◆ Listen to an audiotape of Martin Luther King Jr.'s "I Have a Dream" speech.
- ◆ Ask "What features of King's speech appeal to you?" "Why do you think so?"
- ◆ Ask "What are the rhetorical devices that make his speech so powerful?"

Carschooling® Tricks

Don't forget the value of story-telling as a way to nurture your middle schooler's verbal and narrative growth. Here are three story-creation games that kids love, especially those oral and musical/rhythmic learners:

1. **Complete-the-Story**—A simple game that improves listening skills, comprehension, vocabulary, and creative writing. One person begins to tell a story about any subject. After a few descriptive sentences, that person says, "And then . . . " Anyone listening for the "and then" can jump in, adding a few more details or events to the story, until he or she says, "And then . . . " That's when someone else picks up the story. One rule can be that the story must come to a satisfying conclusion at the end of three rounds of play.

2. **The Minister's Cat**—An old parlor game where one person starts with "The minister's cat is an *adorable* cat." The second player continues, substituting another adjective that begins with *a*: "The minister's cat is an *aggressive* cat." Play continues until someone cannot think of another *a* word/adjective. If you are playing in a large group, the stumped player exits the game and play continues with *b* words, then *c* words, and so on, until only one player is left. In a small group or with young children, the stumped player remains in the game, but loses a turn, and the play continues through each letter (round) of the alphabet. Or, you can give an M&M® or a penny to each player who makes it through a round, and if a player runs out of adjectives, he doesn't get the treat for that round.

3. **"I went on a trip . . . "**—This memory-building game begins with a player saying something like "I went on a trip and in my suitcase I took a bald terrier." The next person has to repeat everything said before and add something new: "I went on a trip and in my suitcase, I took a bald terrier and six snowflakes." The third player might say: "I went on a trip and in my suitcase, I took a bald terrier, six snowflakes, and a tuba." If a player can't remember the list or mangles it, that player is out of the game and play continues until the one with the sharpest memory is left!

▶ ACTIVITIES, ACTIVITIES, ACTIVITIES

Author Studies. Each group member reads a biography of a famous author, noting which people and events influenced that author.

1. Learners then determine, discuss, and compare the various influences on their authors' writings.

2. Learners follow up with reading the authors who pique their interest.

Reading by Theme. Some readers find it interesting to choose reading materials by theme or subject. For example, a homeschooler we know has zipped through all of the *Star Wars* and *Jedi Academy* (youth science fiction) series.

Another popular theme is coming-of-age stories, where adolescent characters face issues and decisions that help determine who they are and who they will become. Some examples among many:

To Kill a Mockingbird by Harper Lee

The House on Mango Street by Sandra Cisneros

Little House on the Prairie series by Laura Ingalls Wilder

Johnny Tremain by Esther Forbes

My Friend Flicka and *Thunderhead* by Mary O'Hara

His Dark Materials series by Philip Pullman

The Yearling by Marjorie K. Rawlings

The *Harry Potter* series by J. K. Rowling

Harriet the Spy by Louise Fitzhugh

Treasure Island and *Kidnapped* by Robert Louis Stevenson

Little Women and *Little Men* by Louisa May Alcott

Evaluating Community Values. Ask your learner to develop a list of generally accepted standards of communal behavior—such as cooperation, honesty, and sharing—encouraging people to live together in a peaceful, productive way. Analyze stories, folk tales, and myths to see which ones express social values that might still be relevant today.

Literature on a Shoestring. Buy or swap used and discounted literature at these sites:

◆ library sales
◆ homeschooling conferences
◆ used bookstores
◆ curriculum sales
◆ "Park Day" swaps
◆ remainders sales at nationwide bookstores
◆ garage sales
◆ through newsletter and websites for homeschoolers

Stories with Music. Cassettes or CDs that showcase music history can invigorate musical/rhythmic and verbal/linguistic learners to listen, and then analyze what they've heard. Audio stories such as *Beethoven Lives Upstairs* highlight Beethoven's music between chapters. *Beethoven Lives Upstairs* is also available as a video to visually reinforce the lessons heard. Some evaluative prompts for *Beethoven Lives Upstairs* might be:

- Describe the personality of the girl in the story.
- How does she feel about Beethoven at the beginning, in the middle, and at the end of the story?
- What experiences have you had with an eccentric person?

Analyze Multicultural Aspects. Roy's family goes to the local Renaissance Faire every year. During the day's events, they have plenty of opportunities to learn about and to compare costumes, food, crafts, music, dances, games, and theater representing various cultures. Both the Faire's actors and its attendees show diversity: Scottish bagpipers and Cockney commoners meet Spanish pirates and French royalty!

Produce an Ad. Today's consumer-savvy kids will have fun creating their own video or print advertising for a product, tailoring the text and visuals to a particular audience. Members of a family or co-op group can create ads for the same or for different products, and compare them.

Read Shakespeare! Families or co-op groups can read Elizabethan classics aloud, such as Shakespeare's *Romeo and Juliet,* and discuss the context within the story and the verse (to help them comprehend Elizabethan usage and phrases). Watching and comparing/contrasting Zeffirelli's *Romeo and Juliet* to *West Side Story* to *Romeo + Juliet* adds a visual context.

Analyze a Commercial or a Political Speech. Sammy's dad talks about the power of words to influence our thoughts and actions, so their family makes a game of analyzing commercials or political speeches on TV or the radio. They ask each other:

- What do you like/dislike about it?
- What words or phrases have enough bang to influence the targeted audience?
- What kind of strategy drives the message?
- What about tone and delivery? background music and images?
- Am I convinced? why or why not?

It's a Fact!

Reading *living books,* or original writings, instead of textbooks, is a method championed by early twentieth-century educator Charlotte Mason. Mason believed that living books, or firsthand information—such as essays *by* Thomas Paine instead of commentaries *about* Thomas Paine—brings a person or a subject alive for the reader. Many homeschooling families incorporate the living books method into their program by investigating the books and websites that describe Mason's philosophy and methods (which were radical for her day).

► PRACTICE

(The keys, exemplars, and rubrics may be found in Appendix A.)

I. *Read the passage and then select the best answer among the choices.*

Note: The objective answers following the passage require evaluation of mood, theme, and detail. The short-answer questions require the reader to differentiate fact from opinion and connect the story to his experiences and knowledge. Of course, this story and its questions may be read/answered/ discussed aloud.

A DAY AT THE NATURE CENTER

Emma stared sadly out the window of the bus. The farm was only fifty miles outside of town. She thought about the farm all the time, remembering the breathtaking view from her bedroom window, the creaky wooden floors of the old farmhouse, and especially the animals.

When Emma's parents sold their hundred-acre farm and moved to the nearby town of DeKalb, Emma had been enthusiastic. But when she got to the new school, she felt overwhelmingly shy around so many strangers.

With a sigh, Emma turned her attention back to the present. The bus came to a stop, and Emma climbed off with the rest of her Earth Studies classmates. "Welcome to the Leinweber Nature Center," her teacher, Mrs. Bowes, announced. "In a few minutes, a guide will give us a presentation about the area's native animals and habitat. After the presentation, you'll have a worksheet to complete while you explore the rest of the center. Now, I want everyone to find a partner."

Emma looked around apprehensively as her classmates began to pair up. She didn't have any friends yet—who would be her partner? Emma hesitated for a moment and then approached Julia, a talkative and outgoing girl who sat near her in class. "Could I be your partner?" Emma asked tentatively.

"Sure," said Julia warmly. "Let's go get the worksheet from Mrs. Bowes."

Together, the girls walked into the Leinweber Nature Center. They listened to the guide talk about how the workers at the center cared for injured and orphaned animals and how the center tried to recreate the animals' natural habitats as much as possible. Emma listened intently. She thought it would be wonderful to have a job that involved nurturing and caring for animals all day.

After the presentation, the girls examined their worksheets. "Let's see," said Julia, "One of the things we're supposed to do is locate the rodent area and assist with feeding the baby squirrels. How big is a baby squirrel? Do you think we actually have to hold one? Maybe you should let me feed it while you watch." Julia was so excited that she fired off one question after another and didn't wait for a response from Emma.

Emma and Julia walked into the rodent area and stood there, looking around at all of the rats, mice, chipmunks, and squirrels. "Hi there!" boomed an enthusiastic voice from behind them. "I'm Josh Headly, the keeper in charge of rodents. Did you come to see the squirrels?"

"Yes," said Emma, turning around with an eager smile on her face. "Do we actually get to feed the babies?"

"You sure do. Here—let me demonstrate the feeding procedure for you."

Josh showed them how to wrap a baby squirrel in a towel and hold the bottle of warm milk. Emma settled back into a chair, enjoying the warmth of the tiny ball of fur nestled in her hand. She flashed a smile over at Julia, but Julia, who was suddenly silent, was focusing on her own baby squirrel.

After the babies were finished eating, Josh asked, "Would you like to help feed the adult squirrels, too?"

Emma was quick to volunteer, but when Josh opened the first cage, the squirrel inside leaped out. Julia shrieked and tried to jump out of the way. Emma, who maintained her composure, bent down, held out her hand, and made quiet, soothing sounds. The runaway squirrel cocked its head to one side and seemed to listen to her. Quickly, while the squirrel was distracted by Emma, Josh reached over and scooped it up.

He smiled appreciatively. "Good job, Emma! It's not easy to remain calm when a wild animal gets out of its cage. I'm impressed!"

"Wow!" Julia chimed in. "You're always so quiet. I thought you were shy and scared of everything, but you're braver than I am if you can get close to a wild animal, even if it is just a squirrel."

"I'm only shy around people, not animals. And I used to live on a farm, so I know that when animals are scared or excited, you have to stay calm—even when you don't feel calm—if you want to help them."

Josh nodded in agreement. "You know," he began, "we've been taking applications for part-time volunteers to help out with the animals. Would you be interested in interviewing for a volunteer position here at the center?"

"Interested? I would love to work here! What an opportunity! Where are the application forms? When could I start?" Now it was Emma who was so excited she couldn't wait for a response.

That afternoon, in the bus on the way back to school, Emma sat next to Julia. A rush of newfound contentedness washed over her. Not only had she found a place full of animals to help take care of, but she had also made a new friend.

1. In which of the following ways are Emma and Julia *alike?*
   a. They both are very outgoing and talkative.
   b. They both feel comfortable around animals.
   c. They both have a class called Earth Studies.
   d. They both live on farms outside of DeKalb.

2. Which words best describe how Emma feels when her classmates first begin to pair up?
   a. angry and disappointed
   b. anxious and uncertain
   c. enthusiastic and joyful
   d. jealous and hurt

3. Reread the following excerpt from the story:

Emma hesitated for a moment and then approached Julia, a talkative and outgoing girl who sat near her in class. "Could I be your partner?" Emma asked tentatively.

As it is used in the story, what does the word *tentatively* mean?
- **a.** carelessly
- **b.** eagerly
- **c.** forcefully
- **d.** cautiously

4. The author presents Julia as someone who:
- **a.** makes friends easily.
- **b.** is fun-loving but a poor student.
- **c.** knows a lot about animals.
- **d.** treats her friends badly.

5. Arrange the following events in the order that they took place in the story:
  1. Julia and Emma sat together on the bus.
  2. A guide spoke about the nature center.
  3. Emma and Julia fed some baby squirrels.
  4. Josh introduced himself to the two girls.
- **a.** 3, 4, 2, 1
- **b.** 2, 4, 3, 1
- **c.** 1, 2, 4, 3
- **d.** 1, 4, 3, 2

6. Which word best describes Julia's tone in the following paragraph?

"Wow!" Julia chimed in. "You're always so quiet. I thought you were shy and scared of every-thing, but you're braver than I am if you can get close to a wild animal, even if it is just a squirrel."
- **a.** impressed
- **b.** jealous
- **c.** disbelieving
- **d.** embarrassed

7. Reread Emma's reaction to Josh's offer below:

"Interested? I would love to work here! What an opportunity! Where are the application forms? When could I start?"

The style of Emma's response:
- **a.** helps create an excited tone.
- **b.** is repetitive and dull.
- **c.** shows that she is unsure about what to do.
- **d.** reflects her shy nature.

8. Emma is happy at the end of the story because:
   a. She is no longer shy.
   b. She will be paid well for her work at the nature center.
   c. She has a new job and a new friend.
   d. She thinks Josh has a crush on her.

9. What words or phrases does the author choose to show the reader that Emma is unhappy at the beginning of the story?

_____

_____

10. List two facts and two opinions in this passage.
   Fact 1: _____
   Fact 2: _____
   Opinion 1: _____
   Opinion 2: _____

11. Do you like this story? Why or why not? (Give your opinion and support it with detail or proof.)

_____

_____

II. *For this cross-cultural assignment, examine a book of art from Africa, China, or some other non-Western culture.*

Note: All level students may augment this with further research into the art and philosophies of the culture they have chosen. In your essay, discuss any of the following:

   ◆ What are some of the significant features of this culture's art? Some of the typical elements and styles? Common themes?
   ◆ Can you describe some of the works in this book?
   ◆ How do particular works illustrate this culture's themes and styles?
   ◆ What connections can you make with Western art, with other artists, and with other artistic themes?
   ◆ What are some of your personal reactions to this culture's art?

8

Reading, Writing, Listening, and Speaking for Literary Response and Expression

Goal of the Standard: *Students read, write, listen, and speak for literary response and expression.* Students read and listen to oral, written, and electronically produced texts and performances from American and world literature; relate texts and performances to their own lives; and develop an understanding of diverse social, historical, and cultural dimensions. As speakers and writers, students use oral and written language, following accepted conventions of English, for self-expression and artistic creation.

▶ WHAT DO WE MEAN BY LITERARY RESPONSE AND EXPRESSION?

Overheard at intermission:

"What do you think of this play?"

"Oh, I don't know, Corky. It's fine. What do you think?"

"Well, I laughed at every reference to Ebenezer Scrooge! And the character of Cecile pulls one surprise after another, doesn't she? Yet when you think about it, we had clues in the first scene that she longed to change boyfriends. But I *don't* like being tortured with the butler's stupid puns—I could write better jokes for him!"

The expressive Corky seems to enjoy plays and certainly knows something about the conventions of literature—in this case, allusion and metaphor, character arcs, plot, and wordplay. Corky knows how to analyze and appreciate this play.

Appreciating literature, responding to it, and creating literature—**literary response and expression**—are truly among the great joys of life. Really, literature does no less than transmit human thought across cultures and centuries, reflecting the differences and similarities among societies and eras. It expresses the human imagination and the human condition.

Often parents hope that, beyond learning to read, children will grow up to absorb and connect with literary works, drawing from their expanding personal knowledge and experience, loving to interpret, analyze, and create literature as well. In the dual role as both parent and teacher, they can instill a love of reading in their children.

Personal Reflection and Response

Personal reflection and response requires readers to merge understanding of a text with prior knowledge and experience. Questions that ask learners to reflect and respond from a personal point of view might include the following:

- How did this character change your ideas of _____?
- Do you think that a grandparent and a five-year-old would interpret this passage the same way? Explain.
- What current event does this remind you of? Explain.
- Does this description fit what you already know about _____?

▶ ACTIVITIES FOR LITERARY RESPONSE AND EXPRESSION

Activities appropriate to practicing critical analysis and evaluation include

- **Reading** picture books, stories, myths, fables, legends, poems, literary essays and criticism, plays, and novels
- **Writing** personal responses, interpretations, literary analyses, critiques, explications of texts, original stories, sketches, poems, and plays
- **Listening** to oral readings of literature; attending stage plays and films
- **Speaking** for recitations of literary passages, dramatic presentations, and group discussions of literature

▶ WHAT SKILLS ARE WE LOOKING FOR HERE?

We are guiding our middle schoolers to eventually master the following language arts skills:

◆ Reading and viewing texts and performances from a broad range of authors, subjects, and genres, periods and traditions, and cultures (*Chris appreciated the local staging of* Man of La Mancha, *having read an excerpt of* Don Quixote.)

◆ Identifying the features of major literary genres, using those features to interpret works (*Omar prefers to classify* The Old Man and the Sea *as a novella, rather than a novel.*)

◆ Recognizing features that distinguish literary genres (*Tina likes the formal structure of a Shakespearean sonnet.*)

◆ Understanding the literary elements of setting, character, plot, theme, and point of view and comparing those features to other works and to their own lives (*Emily selected a movie told from more than one character's point of view.*)

◆ Using inference and deduction to understand text (*The clues in Chapter 13 led John to deduce who the murderer was.*)

◆ Identifying significant literary elements: metaphor, symbolism, foreshadowing, dialect, rhyme, meter, irony, climax, and so forth (*When Bette read that the door had been left unlocked, she realized the door would be important in a later chapter.*)

◆ Recognizing different levels of meaning (*"Allegories and fables have lessons within them," said Jamie.*)

◆ Reading aloud with expression, conveying the meaning and mood of a work (*Harold recites Macbeth's dagger speech perfectly.*)

◆ Evaluating literary merit and presenting personal responses to literature, making reference to plot, characters, ideas, vocabulary, and structure (*The characters in the play didn't have clear or consistent motivations, thought Paul.*)

◆ Explaining the meaning of literary works with attention to meanings beyond the literal level (*Tyrone describes how the poet Keats seems to say just one thing, while conveying several ideas.*)

◆ Creating their own stories, poems, essays, plays, and songs using the elements of the literature they have read, with appropriate vocabulary (*Marie composes a song every year to celebrate Earth Day.*)

Criteria for the Language of Literary Response and Expression

When speaking and writing for this goal, consider these special criteria:

Personal—Literary response and expression should be connected to the individual's personal knowledge and experience. The style and diction of literary writing should be distinctive; in fact, in the best literary expression, a writer's style is as unique as a fingerprint.

Textual—Literary language depends on the exact words, lines, images, and structures of the text. Conventions must be appropriate to the genre and the literary tradition to which the work belongs. For example, meaning is found in the language of the poem, not in a paraphrase of it.

Multilayered—Meanings of literature and writings about literature may be explicit and literal, implied and symbolic.

▶ EVIDENCE OF SUCCESS

How can you measure your homeschooler's mastery of literary response and expression? Here are some examples of mastery.

BASIC MASTERY includes

- ◆ reciting a favorite poem and telling why it's a favorite
- ◆ choosing which books to read from a broad palette and keeping a reading inventory
- ◆ retelling a familiar fairy tale or myth
- ◆ reading a picture book, pointing out how the pictures add meaning
- ◆ performing dramatic readings or recitations of stories, poems, or plays
- ◆ writing a review of a book to recommend it
- ◆ creating a picture book or fable
- ◆ writing new endings or sequels to familiar stories
- ◆ pretending to be a character in a historical story and writing letters about the character's life

INTERMEDIATE MASTERY includes further development of all of the above and

- ◆ reading or reciting a poem, conveying the meaning of the poem and the effect of the rhythm and rhyme patterns
- ◆ producing a list of recommended readings for peers, grouping the works according to some common element (e.g., theme, setting, type of characters)
- ◆ using references to literature to support a position
- ◆ taking part in family or co-op productions of short plays
- ◆ writing a sequel to a story, continuing the development of the characters, plot, and themes
- ◆ writing reviews of one work from different cultural points of view
- ◆ writing stories or poems for peers or siblings

ADVANCED MASTERY includes further development of all of the above and

- ◆ reading poems of different forms, including sonnets, lyrics, elegies, narrative poems, and odes; recognizing the effect of the structure and form on the meaning
- ◆ acting out scenes from a full-length play

- reading literary pieces on a common theme from several literary periods (such as Renaissance, Neo-Classical, Romantic, Realistic, Naturalistic, and Contemporary) and comparing the treatments of the theme
- reading and interpreting works from several world cultures and recognizing the distinguishing features of those cultural traditions
- viewing stage or film productions of a major play or novel and discussing the interpretation of the work
- writing stories or poems using stanzas and chapters, metaphors, foreshadowing, symbolism, and different forms of dialogue and narration
- writing interpretations, including a discussion of the principal features of the genre, the period, and the tradition.

Evidence of Growth

Please refer to Chapter 2 to review the five categories of growth: *range, flexibility, connections, conventions,* and *independence.*

These five categories can be benchmarks for your student's growth over time. Keeping in mind the goals of *literary analysis and expression,* ask yourself, "Over the years, does my homeschooler show progress in . . .

1. exploring a RANGE of literary genres, authors, periods, traditions, and cultures? Of literary elements? Of critical approaches to literature?"

2. showing FLEXIBILITY in adapting to the genres? In accommodating diverse cultural traditions?"

3. making stronger CONNECTIONS in relating new texts to others? In using prior knowledge to interpret literature? In using metaphor?"

4. understanding more clearly the CONVENTIONS of genre, period, and tradition? Of standard English?"

5. demonstrating INDEPENDENCE in selecting literature? In adopting an interpretive approach? In producing imaginative texts, while achieving an individual style?"

► SAMPLE ADVANCED LITERARY ESSAY

While the following is a challenging assignment for advanced readers and writers, analyzing the use of symbols—such as light and darkness in *Macbeth*, or "jumping" in *Lord Jim*—begins with analyzing symbols verbally, based on a simpler play or book or movie. Start with questions such as "Is there more than one meaning for the mirror in the Harry Potter books?" or "Why do you think Darth Vader's name sounds like *dark;* is he from the dark side?"

Advanced Essay Assignment: *Analyze Shakespeare's use of images of darkness and light in a scene from Macbeth.*

► EXEMPLARS AND COMMENTS

Here are two excerpts from literary essays for the above advanced assignment in analysis, demonstrating poor and good analytical approaches, respectively.

Example of Poor Development

Before the murderers enter to kill Banquo, Macbeth makes a speech like the one Lady Macbeth makes in Act 1 when she gets Macbeth's letter. This speech is another good example of light and dark imagery. Macbeth asks night to come quickly:

> *Come, seeling night,*
> *Scarf up the tender eye of pitiful day,*
> *And with thy bloody and invisible hand*
> *Cancel and tear to pieces that great bond*
> *Which keeps me pale! Light thickens, and the crow*
> *Makes wing to the rooky wood.*
> *Good things of day begin to droop and drowse,*
> *While night's black agents to their preys do rouse.*
> *(3.2.46–53)*

Here Macbeth seems to be saying that day is associated with good things, and night with bad ones. Another example of this idea is . . .

This essay emphasizes plot rather than analysis. Notice that this writer fills up space with a long quotation, but only paraphrases the last two lines in his/her commentary before going on.

Dive into the Web

Where can you find Shakespeare's complete works, Mary Shelley's *Frankenstein*, Louisa May Alcott's *Little Women*, and Herman Melville's *Moby Dick*? If you thought of a bookstore or library, you're right, but did you know that you can also get them without ever leaving home? These and over 14,000 other titles are available online at no charge through the University of Pennsylvania's On-Line Books Page (onlinebooks.library.upenn.edu). A smaller collection of fiction, nonfiction, and poetry (also free!) is accessible at www.Bartleby.com.

Example of Strong Development and Advanced Writing

The idea that Macbeth is an evil creature who stalks his prey in the dark is reinforced by his call to night in Act 3, Scene 2. Like Lady Macbeth's call to "thick night" in Act 1, Scene 5, his speech is an attempt to strengthen his resolve and to drive away fear. By asking night to "scarf up the tender eye of pitiful day" (line 47), Macbeth tries to repress his conscience, but he will learn all too painfully that "that great bond/That keeps me pale" (ll. 49–50) is also the sense of moral limits that ties him to other people. Equally ominous is his statement that

> . . . *Light thickens, and the crow*
> *Makes wing to the rooky wood.*
> *Good things of day begin to droop and drowse,*
> *While night's black agents to their preys do rouse.*

Literally, "night's black agents" means the animals and birds of prey who hunt in the "rooky wood" at night. As a metaphor, it suggests that Macbeth has become an agent of evil, less than human.

This advanced essay clearly gives an analytic approach, supported with examples and details.

▶ How Do We Teach and Practice These Skills?

How do we teach planning what we write and reviewing what we write? The Nation's Report Card website includes an excellent two-paneled brochure, which graphically illustrates universal tips for planning and reviewing writing. Go to page 303 in Appendix A to view the brochure.

Writing About Literature
You might consider adapting some of these helpful tips for writing or speaking about literature to your learner:

Prewriting
- ◆ Remember that **your purpose is to give your readers insights** that might not occur to them or to give them a well-developed opinion.
- ◆ In preparation for your writing, **reread the text with your topic in mind.** Make a list of key passages to discuss and important points to make.
- ◆ **Refine your thoughts to clearly state your central idea(s)**. Note that a good theme is *very specific* about what you are trying to communicate. For example:

VAGUE: "Shakespeare uses a great many images of darkness and light in *Macbeth*."

CLEAR AND SPECIFIC: "Shakespeare uses images of darkness and light in *Macbeth* not only to establish the time and mood of scenes, but also to suggest the way that Macbeth and Lady Macbeth are identified with evil."

- ◆ **Let your first draft sit** a few days, and then come back to it to make revisions.

Five Tips for Good Literature Papers

As your homeschooler drafts his essay, make sure it follows these guidelines:

1. **Be straightforward and specific.** Introduce the topic in a straightforward, natural way, not as an answer to a given assignment. In the first few sentences suggest why the subject is significant or interesting. Do not make claims that are too sweeping. *End the first paragraph with a strong and clear statement.*

Compare the following examples of openings from papers on the use of darkness and light in *Macbeth*:

POOR (assumes we know the topic): "In looking at the darkness and light imagery in *Macbeth*, the first thing I noticed was . . . "

POOR (covers too much territory): "Since the beginning of time, poets have used imagery to express their feelings. . . . The English poet William Shakespeare is one of the great masters of dramatic imagery. In his *Macbeth* . . . "

BETTER (*very* specific): "In the troubled world of Shakespeare's *Macbeth*, much of the action takes place either in 'fog and filthy air' or at night. The modern theater would use lighting to set the time and mood of scenes. Shakespeare, however, uses an extensive pattern of light and dark imagery. These images do more than set the scene or tell the time. They also create the moral atmosphere of the play, suggesting a world in which Macbeth and Lady Macbeth become increasingly identified with evil while trying to hide the nature of their deeds from themselves and from others."

Notice that the last example avoids stock formulas such as "First I/We will consider . . . " Note too that it does not merely promise to talk about imagery in *Macbeth*, but indicates quite specifically *which* major points the writer wants to make.

2. **Be clear**. Each paragraph of the paper should develop some aspect of the theme. The aim should be to clarify and illustrate main points as the essay proceeds. Check for clarity by reading in succession the first sentence or two of each paragraph. Do they signal the logical development of the essay? If this quick reading does not show an argument in progress, rewrite the paper.

3. **Analyze, don't paraphrase.** Do not let plot summary or paraphrase substitute for literary analysis. Concentrate instead on *significance* or *how* speeches and actions shape the understanding of events and characters. How are you moved emotionally? How do word choice, imagery, and rhythm communicate more powerfully than statement alone?

Remember that, in great literature,

◆ ideas and issues are usually presented from complex perspectives

◆ conflicts within the writer or the writer's culture may be reflected in the text

◆ form is as important as *content*

4. Support your opinions. Remember to provide evidence for your personal responses by quoting the text. Check that quotations really support your theme. Learn to work short quotations into sentences to enrich the reader's awareness of the significant phrases in the text.

5. Give an interesting conclusion. Do not make the conclusion a needless repetition of previous topic sentences. All too many essays end with a mechanical list of points already made. Instead, use the final paragraph to take your main point farther or to draw out the significance of the topic.

▶ TEACHING IDEAS

The following teaching ideas reference several types of popular readings for middle schoolers. You and your homeschooler can devise similar exercises for your choice of texts as well. Try the Internet: In your search box, enter the title of the book or poem you are studying and search for lesson plans, book reviews, and study guides (Internet study guides are called *cyberguides*) to give you guidance.

Interpreting Literature

1. Discuss interpretations of the symbolism in Maya Angelou's book *I Know Why the Caged Bird Sings*.

2. Read the book, then view the movie version of Lynne Reid Banks's *Indian in the Cupboard*, comparing the representations of character and setting in each.

3. Chart the conflicts among the characters of Edith Wharton's *Ethan Frome*. Or, write an essay explaining what the novel reveals about the author's view of human nature.

4. Write and recite a poem of your own, imitating the theme, structure, or style of a poem/poet you admire.

5. For advanced students: Write an interpretation of a major nineteenth-century novel, discussing the features of the novel that reflect the conventions of the genre in that time period. Explore social realism in Charles Dickens' *Great Expectations* or *David Copperfield,* William Makepeace Thackeray's moral stance in *Vanity Fair*, or Jane Austen's social commentary in *Emma*.

Carschooling® Tricks

Visual/spatial and math/logical learners, listen up. You probably can already list some visual games to play in the car, but have you tried these?

- ▶ **imagining images from cloud shapes**
- ▶ **creating or solving mazes and other puzzles**
- ▶ **drawing with colored pencils or washable markers**
- ▶ **designing a map of where you are going**
- ▶ **interpreting a map for the driver**
- ▶ **identifying constellations and planets at night**

Cross-Cultural Empathy: Farewell to Manzanar

Using *Farewell to Manzanar* by Jeanne Wakatsuki Houston and James D. Houston, your student can use the Internet to explore the themes of racism and the civil and legal rights of Japanese-Americans during World War II in order to respond to this piece of literature.

1. The following questions may prompt oral or written response:

- Who made the decisions about the Japanese-Americans?
- Where were the relocation camps located and what were the conditions?
- Is there significance to the geographical location of these camps?
- How were the families selected to go to the location camps? What happened to their property?
- How were Japanese-Americans treated in the relocation camps? Who was responsible for their welfare?
- What can today's citizens do to attempt to right past or present wrongs committed by the U.S. government?

2. Discuss or write about what the family's life was like before the events described in the novel, supporting inferences with references in the novel. Write a story or journal from one or more points of view.

3. After reviewing different accounts and seeing pictures of internment camps (see http://members.aol.com/Amerwar/justice.htm), give voice to your literary expression by writing a persuasive letter to President Roosevelt discussing reasons for releasing the prisoners.

4. Visit www.sdcoe.k12.ca.us/score/manz/manztg.html for additional activities and resource links.

5. View the films *Farewell to Manzanar* (Universal, made-for-TV, 1976) and *Snow Falling on Cedars* (1999, based on David Guterson's 1994 mystery novel), and compare them to each other and to the books they are based on.

Dialectical Journal as a Literary Response

While reading *Farewell to Manzanar,* learners can create a *dialectical journal* (see example that follows) to help them better understand Japanese-American internment experiences and their feelings about them. With this exercise, students can react and relate *Farewell to Manzanar* to their own lives while developing an understanding of cultural, historical issues.

It's likely that you will want to use a dialectical journal for other texts as well. This tool of literary response allows students to highlight significant ideas in a text, provide support through detailed references, and identify and assess complexities within a text. Here is one dialectical journal format that your learner can copy and fill in.

Dialectical Journal

Quotation	Page	Why do I find this quotation interesting or important?

▶ ACTIVITIES, ACTIVITIES, ACTIVITIES

Literary Debates. Encourage oral debate or even a formal debate about literature. For example, students who have read *Call of the Wild* and *Hatchet* can debate which is a better piece of literature and why.

Fairy Tales. Write and illustrate your own fairy tale or fable or myth, using the conventions of the genre. Especially effective with visual/special learners.

Resources Around You

Why not start a community book club? Educators Jennifer Richard Jacobson and Dottie Raymer note that book clubs are cropping up all over the country because people love talking about and sharing the books they read. Here are some tips adapted from their book *How Is My Sixth Grader Doing in School?*

1. Choose the time, place, and composition of the group. Will it be a father/son or mother/daughter group? Children and parents of either gender? All children with one adult facilitator?
2. Create a democratic method of choosing books. You might take turns, or you might bring books to be introduced, then voted on. It may be a requirement that any book chosen must have garnered at least one good review or book award.
3. Encourage open, nonjudgmental discussion, so that everyone has a chance to speak.
4. Establish some ground rules such as "no interrupting" and "no put-downs."

Short Stories for Young Adults. Well-written short stories make a strong, quick impact and can be readily compared to each other (themes, characters, and writers' styles). The librarians of Tempe, Arizona, recommend the following and other short story collections for youth at www.tempe.gov/library/youth/yashort.htm:

8 Plus 1 by Robert Cormier: Relationships—friend to friend, father to daughter, black to white, young to old—are at the core of these stories.

American Eyes: New Asian-American Short Stories for Young Adults: Stories reflecting the conflict Asian Americans face balancing an ancient heritage and an unknown future.

Baseball in April and Other Stories by Gary Soto: The everyday life of young Hispanics growing up in Fresno, California.

The Bus People by Rachel Anderson: The passengers on a special-education school bus tell the stories of their lives, shaped by the experiences of their disabilities.

Catfantastic: Nine Lives and Fifteen Tales edited by Andre Norton: The fantastic world, seen through feline eyes.

Echoes of War by Robert Westall: These stories examine the lingering effects of war on the lives of the young.

A Fit of Shivers: Tales for Late at Night by Joan Aiken: Ten short stories with elements of horror and the supernatural.

Heartbeats and Other Stories by Peter D. Sieruta: Stories about growing up, with friends, siblings, and first loves.

I Love You, I Hate You, Get Lost by Ellen Conford: Humorous stories about teenage love and life.

Make Your Move and Other Stories by James Watson: Teens challenged by racism, hatred, and violence find strength through hope and humor.

Martian Chronicles by Ray Bradbury: The conquest of Mars, told in a series of loosely connected stories.

Somehow Tenderness Survives: Stories of Southern Africa edited by Hazel Rochman: Stories of growing up under apartheid.

Tales from Gold Mountain: Stories of the Chinese in the New World by Paul Yee: The immigrant experience of the Chinese as they built a unique place for themselves in American life.

A Thief in the Village, and Other Stories of Jamaica by James Berry: The quiet simplicity of Caribbean life, the rage of hurricanes, and the universal need for family.

Things in Corners by Ruth Park: Five tales of the unexpected and the unexplained lurk in these pages.

Where Angels Glide at Dawn: New Stories from Latin America edited by Lori Carlson and Cynthia Ventura: The flavor of Latin America is captured in this set of stories translated into English.

With the Snow Queen by Joanne Greenburg: People, personalities, and relationships intertwine to produce a collection of psychological short stories.

It's a Fact!

Pursuing your hobby with your homeschooler may bring you to a shared interest while you learn and relax:

▶ **Tracy and her daughter read together four evenings a week, sometimes aloud to each other, sometimes each reading her own book. They often discuss favorite passages. They sometimes recommend books to each other.**

▶ **Berta and Hector sew quilts; Hector reads the directions and does the math to cut the geometric shapes that make up each quilt block.**

▶ **Rex and Keely research their family history together. Rex loves genealogy and his daughter is mastering a software program for building family trees.**

Folk Tales Revisited, Part I. As an exercise in literary expression, invent a different written form for telling a folk tale, fairy tale, or myth, such as

◆ a poem.
◆ a journal entry.
◆ a newspaper report.
◆ a letter to a friend.
◆ a play.

Folk Tales Revisited, Part II. Invent a different oral, narrative form for telling a folk or fairy tale or myth, such as

◆ a picture book.
◆ a puppet show.
◆ a play.
◆ a ballad.
◆ a narrated pantomime.

Common-Theme Stories. An exercise for advanced students is to compile a collection of literature from different cultures around a common theme and write an analytic introduction to the collection explaining the similarities and differences.

▶ PRACTICE

(The keys and exemplars may be found in Appendix A.)

Note: These problems demonstrate a range of possibilities for literary response and self-expression. Adapt them to your learner's level of mastery. As always, these prompts may be read/answered/discussed aloud.

I. *Read this advanced-level passage and then choose the best answers to the multiple-choice questions.*

They carried USO stationery and pencils and pens. They carried Sterno, safety pins, trip flares, signal flares, spools of wire, razor blades, chewing tobacco, statuettes of the smiling Buddha, candles, grease pencils, *The Stars and Stripes,* fingernail clippers, bush hats, bolos, and much more. Twice a week, when the resupply choppers came in, they carried hot chow in green mermite cans and large canvas bags filled with iced beer and soda pop. They carried plastic water containers, each with a 2-gallon capacity. Mitchell Sanders carried a set of starched tiger fatigues for special occasions. Henry Dobbins carried Black Flag insecticide. Dave Jensen carried empty sandbags that could be filled at night for added protection. Lee Strunk carried tanning lotion. Some things they carried in common. Taking turns, they carried the big PRC-77 scrambler radio which weighed 30 pounds with its battery. They shared the weight of the memory. They took up what others could no longer bear. Often, they'd carry each other, the wounded or weak. They carried infections. They carried chess sets, basketballs, Vietnamese-English dictionaries, insignia of rank, Bronze Stars and Purple Hearts, plastic cards imprinted with the Code of Conduct. They carried diseases, among them malaria and dysentery. They carried lice and ringworm and leeches and paddy algae and various rots and molds. They carried the land itself. Vietnam, the place, the soil . . . dust that covered their boots and fatigues and faces. They carried the sky . . . the stink of fungus, and decay, all of it, they carried gravity.

—Tim O'Brien
The Things They Carried

1. Throughout this passage, *they* refers to
   a. soldiers.
   b. trains.
   c. civilians.
   d. ambulances.

2. The variety of items the men carried reflects their desire to
   a. make friends.
   b. bribe villagers.
   c. sell products.
   d. maintain morale.

3. The repetition of the expression "They carried" helps establish a feeling of
   a. relentlessness.
   b. monotony.
   c. suspense.
   d. disappointment.

4. The word *gravity* is used to mean
   a. earthly delights.
   b. fond memories.
   c. weighty matters.
   d. unexplained forces.

5. The organization of this passage is characterized by a movement from
   a. literal to figurative.
   b. past to present.
   c. emotion to reason.
   d. far to near.

II. *Write a third-person narrative that incorporates your personal feelings about homeschooling. Be as creative as you like, as long as you follow accepted conventions of English and literary expression.*

_____

_____

III. *Imagine this situation: A noise awakens you one night. You look out the window and see a spaceship. The door of the spaceship opens, and out walks an alien. What does the creature look like? What does it do? What do you do?*

Write a story about what happens next.

_____

_____

IV. *As an interdisciplinary English/Biology project, assume the voice and personality of a living organism and present a view of the world through its eyes. Write creatively for a wide audience, using accurate scientific information. (Note: The learner can also write a formal science research paper on the same organism and compare both writing experiences.)*

_____

_____

PART

III

Mathematics

by
Jessika Sobanski

▶ Go for the Goals

In the middle years, your child will be able to appreciate the relevance of mathematics in her day-to-day life as well as in our technological world. You need not leave behind the games and manipulatives that made math fun in the early years of your child's education. Learning percent decrease is more interesting when predicting and calculating the percent decrease of a ShrinkyDinks™. Probability is much more fun while sketching tree diagrams on a dry-erase board.

The main concerns regarding learning mathematics at home have always been:

- Make it relevant
- Make it fun
- Make it portable
- Make it personalized

Learning a tough subject is made more palatable for both parent and child when the lessons are applied to real life and when they touch on the typical experiences of a middleschooler.

Math, for some homeschooling parents, can present a bit of anxiety if it is not their educational strong suit. Fortunately, good math curricula are available, and using the lessons and practice exercises here as a supplement should provide the homeschooling parent with plenty of information and ideas on skill building. Solid math skills serve every student well in the future—whether that student is college-bound or workforce-bound.

In the Clinton Administration's Goals 2000 education initiative, eighth grade math was listed as one of the Department of Education's seven priorities. Specifically, the Department's goal is for all students to "master challenging mathematics, including the foundations of algebra and geometry, by the end of 8th grade." Therefore, your homeschooler's curriculum will aim to achieve this goal by reinforcing existing skills and teaching several important new math concepts in a way that emphasizes real-life uses of mathematics.

The math curriculum for the middle school years begins with a review of previously learned concepts, as well as an introduction to more complex concepts, including:

- whole numbers, number practice, and basic operations
- decimals and fractions
- percentages, ratios, and proportions
- exponents and roots
- simple interest and compound interest
- translating word problems into expressions and solvable equations
- algebra basics and principles
- geometry basics and principles
- measurement principles, including the metric system

Then, your advanced student may move forward to learn new math skills, such as:

- how to use variables and equations as problem-solving techniques
- how to add, subtract, and multiply polynomials
- how to graph and solve quadratic equations
- how to classify and measure angles
- how to understand and use if-then statements and truth tables
- how to use formulas to determine area and volume of geometric shapes
- how to use length and areas to solve geometric problems
- how to define basic tangent, sine, and cosine ratios
- the Pythagorean Theorem and its applications

When possible, these subjects may incorporate use of computer technology.

This math section is filled with ideas on how to integrate math with other studies. Ideas for car travelers are incorporated and there are plenty of recommendations on taking advantage of computer programs and the Internet. The lessons covered in the next six chapters are designed so that they can be learned in any order you choose, and each lesson comes with three levels of corresponding practice problems—basic, intermediate, and advanced. The suggested quests can easily be studied with the aid of a search engine, a helpful librarian, or an encyclopedia (traditional or CD-ROM).

▶ WHY CARE ABOUT MATHEMATICS STANDARDS AND GOALS?

Why do we care to set mathematics goals and standards for our children? Here are six reasons.

Loving Learning. It's easy to think of math as boring or dry, with no connection to our everyday lives. When your learner begins to see how math skills and problem-solving are already important in the things he does, he will feel empowered to confront and solve the challenges he encounters.

Solving Problems. In the literal sense, it's important to be able to solve math problems for tests or schoolwork. But sharp math and logic skills are useful in all kinds of other places: in the kitchen, at the symphony, or at the grocery store. Being confident in her problem-solving abilities will allow your homeschooler to become self-sufficient in areas beyond just studying math.

Communicating. One of the best ways for your child to show mastery of a math concept or skill is to teach it back to you. It's sometimes not enough just to get the right answer; on tests and in high school and college classes, students are often asked to explain *how* they arrived at those solutions. The ability to explain—in a clear and understandable way—the reasoning behind a step can be as important as doing the calculations correctly.

Using Technology. You may sometimes feel as if your child has a better understanding of technology than you do! Strong problem-solving abilities will increase your child's ability to utilize computer programs, the Internet, and other new technology. Some of tomorrow's fastest-growing careers will also require good math skills: architecture, computer software and support, and healthcare are a few of the fields where math is not just useful—it's essential.

Working in Teams. If you are homeschooling more than one child, math can be an excellent place for your children to work together on a project, honing their problem-solving skills as they gain experience communicating and collaborating with other people toward a common goal. Logical thinking and the ability to solve problems cooperatively are skills that are in demand in any number of fields.

Making Connections. For you and your learner, the trick to enjoying math is to see how much it permeates the things we encounter every day. You can study cooking, music, or sports, and still be practicing existing math skills and sharpening new ones. Emphasizing the real-life applications of math skills that may at first seem abstract will help make mathematics accessible, and more appealing, to your homeschooler.

9

Basic Operations and Number Concepts

For some homeschoolers, basic number operations and number concepts have been covered at great length in previous years. For others, these ideas have been touched on, but need to be practiced and reinforced. For all middle school-aged students, a clear understanding of these basic skills is a necessary foundation on which to build math proficiency.

▶ NUMBER PROPERTIES

Let's jump into math by first discussing the different types of numbers. Numbers with different names have different properties. Some of the terms you should know are listed below.

- **Whole Numbers:** 0, 1, 2, 3, and so on. Notice that *whole numbers* <u>do not</u> include negatives, fractions, or decimals.
- **Counting Numbers (also called "natural numbers"):** Include all whole numbers, with the exception of 0.

- **Integers:** Include <u>all</u> the *whole numbers* and negatives too. Examples are –3, –2, –1, 0, 1, 2, and 3. Note that *integers* <u>do not</u> include fractions, or decimals.
- **Real Numbers:** Include fractions and decimals in addition to the *integers*. Some examples of real numbers are $-\frac{1}{2}$, –8.5, 3, $\frac{3}{4}$, –9.
- **Prime Numbers:** Include numbers that are divisible by only 2 positive factors: 1 and themselves. Note that 1 is <u>not</u> prime. Examples include: 2, 3, 5, 7. Note also that 2 is the only even prime number, and that prime numbers can be negative. For instance, –7 has the factors –7, 1, -1, and 7. Thus, –7 is prime because it has exactly 2 positive factors: 1 and 7.
- **Composite Numbers:** Have more than 2 factors. You can think of *composite* as the opposite of *prime*; however, note that 1 is not composite.

It's A Fact

Any composite number can be written as the product of prime numbers. This simply means that if you break the factors of any composite number down far enough, you will arrive at a set of prime numbers.

For example, try the number 42. It is equal to 21 times 2. Since 21 is not a prime number, divide further: 21 = 7 x 3, so 42 = 2 x 7 x 3. Because 2, 7, and 3 have no factors other than 1 and themselves, they are all prime numbers.

- **Rational Numbers:** Can be written as a fraction or as a decimal that either terminates (ends) or repeats. Some example are –5, $.\overline{3}$, $\frac{1}{2}$. (A bar over a number means that it repeats infinitely.)
- **Irrational Numbers:** Cannot be represented as a ratio (comparison) of 2 numbers because their decimal extensions go on and on without repeating or terminating. π, $\sqrt{2}$, and $\sqrt{11}$ are all irrational.

▶ ABSOLUTE VALUE

The *absolute value* of a number is just its positive distance from zero. For example, $|-3| = 3$. $|5| = 5$, and $\left|\frac{1}{2}\right| = \frac{1}{2}$.

Let's look at $|-8|$.

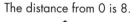
The distance from 0 is 8.
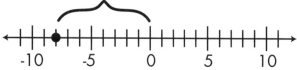

Thus, the absolute value of –8 is 8.

Math and Technology

Research hexadecimal numbers. Here we are dealing with more than 10 digits. How is that possible? Explore and find out!

▶ PLACE VALUE

Numbers have different names for the different places that each digit occupies:

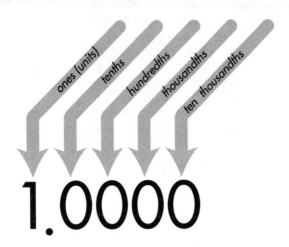

Example: The place values we are accustomed to are for **base 10,** where the *ones* represent $10^0 = 1$, the *tens* represent $10^1 = 10$, the *hundreds* represent $10^2 = 100$, and so forth. There are 10 available digits to fill these places with: 0 1 2 3 4 5 6 7 8 9. Thus, a 9 in the thousands place would equal $9 \times 10^3 = 9 \times 1000 = 9000$.

Base ten:

ten thousands	thousands	hundreds	tens	ones
10^4	10^3	10^2	10^1	10^0
10,000	1000	100	10	1

When working with computers, you have probably heard the term ***binary***. This is because a computer deals with only two possible digits: 0 and 1. The base that only uses two possible digits is **base 2**.

The places in base two with the base ten equivalents marked below:

2^7	2^6	2^5	2^4	2^3	2^2	2^1	2^0
128	64	32	16	8	4	2	1

A 0 or a 1 alone is termed a **_bit_** and 8 bits in a row is termed a **_byte._** Consider the following _byte_:

01100101

What is the base 10 equivalent of the byte above?
   a. 256
   b. 197
   c. 101
   d. 76

First, we can see where each bit falls according to its place value:

2^7	2^6	2^5	2^4	2^3	2^2	2^1	2^0
128	64	32	16	8	4	2	1
0	1	1	0	0	1	0	1

Next, we add up the values that are indicated:

128	64	32	16	8	4	2	1
0	1	1	0	0	1	0	1
	64 +	32			+ 4		+ 1

Thus, 01100101= 64 + 32 + 4 + 1 = 101, and choice **c** is correct. You may have wondered how computers can perform such intricate tasks just by representing data as streams of **zeros** and **ones**. It turns out that even the most complex tasks reduce down to **zeros** and **ones**.

Carschooling® Tricks

Try this guessing game to help strengthen number skills. One person thinks of a number within a range that has been agreed to ahead of time (for example, 1 to 30). The other person has to guess the number by asking "yes or no" questions, for example *Is this an even number? Is it odd? Is it a prime number? Is it divisible by five?*

To make the game more challenging, use a larger range of numbers (like from 1 to 100). For a simpler game, start out with a hint about the number: *I'm thinking of a number that's divisible by 2 . . .* If you are homeschooling more than one child, learners can take turns guessing or have a contest to see which child can guess the most numbers.

▶ ROUNDING

Rounding is a way of changing a number according to the place value specified and bearing one rule in mind: *Only round up if the digit to the right is greater than or equal to 5.*

For example:

1. 188 rounded to the nearest hundred is 200. Look at the *tens place*: 1**8**8. Because 8 ≥ 5, we round the hundreds place up to 200.

2. 140 rounded to the nearest hundred is 100. Look at the *tens place*: 1**4**0. Because 4 < 5, we do not round up.

3. 2,514 rounded to the nearest thousand is 3,000. Look at the *hundreds place*: 2,**5**14. Because 5 ≥ 5, we round up the thousands place to 3,000.

Example:

What is the product of 512 and 320 when rounded to the nearest thousand?

    a. 163,600
    b. 163,000
    c. 164,000
    d. 164,600

512 × 320 = 163,840. Because there is an 8 in the hundreds place, we round the thousands place up to 164,000. Thus, choice **c** is correct.

▶ ORDER OF OPERATIONS

When performing multiple operations in a math question, you need to follow this order:

1. Parentheses
2. Exponents
3. Multiplication/Division
4. Addition/Subtraction

An easy way to remember this order of operations is by remembering the acronym, "**PEMDAS**" or the acrostic, "**P**lease **E**xcuse **M**y **D**ear **A**unt **S**ally."

It's A Fact

 To see if a number is divisible by 4, see if the last two digits in the number are divisible by 4. For example, look at the number 693,412. The last two digits form the number 12. Since 12 is divisible by 4, then 693,412 is also divisible by 4.

Example: Use the chart below to sequentially follow the steps in PEMDAS.

$$2^5 - 7 \times (4 - 12) \div 4$$

Parentheses	$2^5 - 7 \times (\,\boxed{4 - 12}\,) \div 4$
	$2^5 - 7 \times (-8) \div 4$
Exponents	$\boxed{2^5} - 7 \times (-8) \div 4$
	$32 - 7 \times (-8) \div 4$
Multiplication/Division	Multiplication appears first, so we multiply . . .
	$32 - \boxed{7 \times (-8)} \div 4$
	$32 - (-56) \div 4$
	Next, we divide
	$32 - \boxed{(-56) \div 4}$
	$32 - (-14)$
Addition/Subtraction	$32 - (-14)$
	$32 + 14$
	46

▶ PATTERNS WITH NUMBERS

Sometimes you will see a number sequence that is missing a term. It is your job to analyze the numbers and figure out the pattern. You can then fill in the missing piece.

Example:

2 5 4 2 6 –1 8 ___ 10

   a. 12
   b. 6
   c. 1
   d. –4

Do you see the 2, 4, 6, 8, 10? Notice how every other term is a multiple of 2:

②5 ④2 ⑥-1 ⑧ ___ ⑩

Next, let's look at the remaining terms:

2 ⑤ 4 ② 6 ⑴ 8 ⑶ 10

Go from 5 to 2 to –1. Notice that this is just a decrease of 3 from each term to the next. So the missing term will be –1 – 3 = –4. Thus, the answer is **d**.

Integrate

Math and History
Throughout history, mathematicians have studied number patterns. Research Pascal's Triangle, Fibonacci and the Fibonacci Sequence, and the Golden Mean that was used by the Greeks in building the Parthenon.

▶ ESTIMATING

When you are called upon to give an estimate, you just need to come up with an approximate figure. While grocery shopping it is easy to keep a "rough estimate" in your head by rounding to the nearest dollar.

Example:

In the Midwest, one wind turbine can generate electricity for three homes. If a community of 1,162 homes would like to obtain power from wind turbines <u>only</u>, estimate how many turbines the community would need.

    a. 700
    b. 650
    c. 400
    d. 350

You can quickly come up with an estimate by rounding the 1,162 homes up to 1,200. Next, divide the "1,200" homes by 3 to figure out the number of turbines needed. 1,200 ÷ 3 = 400. So, the correct answer is **c**.

Dive into the Web

Figure This: **Math Challenges for Families (www.figurethis.org) is designed for middle school students and their families. Math challenges are brightly illustrated and emphasize practical application of math skills. Kids use step-by-step problem solving to answer questions like, "How fast does my heart beat?" and "How many Fridays are Friday the thirteenths?" Each challenge includes hints, answer explanation, extra questions, and suggestions for further reading, as well as information about how its content relates to the real world. A parents' section includes an article on using children's literature to study math concepts.**

▶ PRACTICE

The questions in this section have been divided into three categories: Basic, Intermediate, and Advanced. Questions 1 – 15 are Basic, questions 16–32 are Intermediate, and questions 33–47 are Advanced. An answer key with explanations can be found in Appendix C.

BASIC

    1. In Edgarton, Marcy is delivering new phone books. At the beginning of the day, there were 470 phone books in her truck. At the end of the day, she knew that she had delivered 378 phone books. How many phone books were left in her truck?
       a. 92
       b. 98
       c. 102
       d. 848

2. Marcus played his favorite video game 4 times. His scores for the 4 games were 576, 731, 542, and 693. What was Marcus's total score from these 4 games?
   a. 2332
   b. 2342
   c. 2532
   d. 2542

3. What number is marked by the **P** on the number line below?

   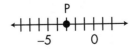

   a. −7
   b. 7
   c. −3
   d. 3

4. Which of the following numbers is evenly divisible by 3?
   a. 235
   b. 236
   c. 237
   d. 238

It's A Fact!

A quick way to see if a number is divisible by 3 is to add up the digits in the number. If this sum is evenly divisible by 3, then so is the original number.

   For example, for 237, 2 + 3 + 7 = 12. 12 is evenly divisible by 3 (12 ÷ 3 = 4), therefore 237 is also divisible by 3.

5. John has a box containing 84 nails and he finds 47 around his workshop. If his current project requires four times the amount he already has, how many more nails does he have to buy?
   a. 131
   b. 524
   c. 393
   d. 84

6. Which expression below shows two million, thirty-seven thousand, eight hundred four in expanded notation?
   a. $(2 \times 10,000) + (3 \times 1,000) + (7 \times 100) + (8 \times 10) + (4 \times 1)$
   b. $(2 \times 100,000) + (3 \times 10,000) + (7 \times 1,000) + (8 \times 100) + (0 \times 10) + (4 \times 1)$
   c. $(2 \times 1,000,000) + (3 \times 100,000) + (7 \times 10,000) + (0 \times 1,000) + (8 \times 100) + (0 \times 10) + (4 \times 1)$
   d. $(2 \times 1,000,000) + (0 \times 100,000) + (3 \times 10,000) + (7 \times 1,000) + (8 \times 100) + (0 \times 10) + (4 \times 1)$

7. What is another name for 20,706?
   a. 200 + 70 + 6
   b. 2,000 + 700 + 6
   c. 20,000 + 70 + 6
   d. 20,000 + 700 + 6

8. What is $|47 - 64|$?
   a. 17
   b. −17
   c. 111
   d. 47

9. Jane is a waitress. She made $153 on Friday, $167 on Saturday, and $103 on Sunday; then she spent $94 on Monday, and $19 on Tuesday. How much did she have left?
   a. $133
   b. $423
   c. $94
   d. $310

10. Find $\left|-\frac{2}{3}\right|$.
    a. $-\frac{2}{3}$
    b. $\frac{3}{2}$
    c. $1\frac{1}{2}$
    d. $\frac{2}{3}$

11. What is $|-423| + |423|$ equal to?
    a. 0
    b. $-|423|$
    c. 846
    d. 423

12. $12(84 - 5) - (3 \times 54) =$
    a. 54,000
    b. 841
    c. 796
    d. 786

13. 4! is equivalent to:
    a. 4×4
    b. $4 \times 3 \times 2 \times 1$
    c. $4 \times 4 \times 4 \times 4$
    d. $4 \times 3 \times 2 \times 1 \times 0$

14. The greatest common factor of 56 and 64 is
- **a.** 4.
- **b.** 6.
- **c.** 8.
- **d.** 9.

15. Choose the expression that corresponds with the following statement:
The quotient of nine divided by three is decreased by one.
- **a.** $9 \div 3 - 1$
- **b.** $9 \div (3 - 1)$
- **c.** $1 - 9 \div 3$
- **d.** $(1 - 9) \div 3$

INTERMEDIATE

16. What are the missing integers on this number line?

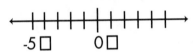

- **a.** −4 and 1
- **b.** −6 and 1
- **c.** −6 and −1
- **d.** 4 and 9

17. The Cohrs Jam Company received 2,052 crates of blackberries for their next shipment of jam.
If they need 12 crates to make a batch of jam, how many total batches of jam can they make?
- **a.** 161
- **b.** 167
- **c.** 170
- **d.** 171

18. $(-5)(-3)(2) - |-20| =$
- **a.** 50
- **b.** 40
- **c.** 20
- **d.** 10

19. Which set represents 4 consecutive even numbers whose sum is 44?
- **a.** {7, 9, 11, 17}
- **b.** {4, 6, 8, 10}
- **c.** {8, 10, 12, 14}
- **d.** none of the above

20. Fill in the missing term in the following sequence:

31 23 17 13 __

a. 12

b. 11

c. 7

d. 5

21. At a baseball game, Deanna bought food for herself and her sister Jamie: 1 jumbo box of pop-corn to share at $7 a box, 2 hot dogs for each of them (4 total) at $3 a dog, and one soda for each at $4 apiece. Jamie paid for their tickets at $13 a ticket. Who spent the most money and by how much?

a. Deanna, by $1

b. Deanna, by $3

c. Jamie, by $2

d. Jamie, by $4

22. 5 ☐ = (10 × 2) + (5 × 3)

a. × (5 + 2)

b. + (5 + 2)

c. × (5 × 2)

d. + (5 × 2)

23. What number is missing from the sequence below?

4 28 __ 62 79

a. 30

b. 45

c. 48

d. 51

24. One evening, Super Tunes 96.6 FM sponsored a phone pledge-a-thon. The average caller pledged a donation of $796. If there were 182 callers, how much money was raised in the pledge-a-thon?

a. $8,756

b. $15,920

c. $144,872

d. $217,882

25. If Brian can run around the block 4 times in 20 minutes, and Jaclyn can run around the block 3 times in 12 minutes, who can make it around the block more times in an hour, and by what amount?

a. Brian, 3 more times

b. Jaclyn, 3 more times

c. They both go around 12 times

d. Brian, 8 more times

26. What is the estimated product when 157 and 817 are rounded to the nearest hundred and multiplied?

    a. 160,000

    b. 180,000

    c. 16,000

    d. 80,000

27. If the product of 253 and 631 is rounded to the nearest hundred, the result is

    a. 100,000

    b. 159,600

    c. 159,643

    d. 160,000

28. At Megan and Nathan's wedding, there will be 23 tables for dinner. Each table has 9 seats. How many people total can be seated for dinner at Megan and Nathan's wedding?

    a. 32

    b. 187

    c. 216

    d. none of the above

29. Which of these is divisible by 6 and 7?

    a. 63

    b. 74

    c. 84

    d. 96

30. Roger earned $24,355 this year, and $23,000 the year before. To the nearest $100, what did Roger earn in the past two years?

    a. $47,300

    b. $47,400

    c. $47,455

    d. $47,500

31. $|5 - 9| - |7 - 1| =$

    a. −10

    b. −2

    c. 1

    d. 2

32. Janice has started a wholesale jewelry making business. She makes 36 bracelets a day, and sells them to local shops for $18.00 a dozen. How much does Janice make per week if she works 5 days a week?
   a. $220
   b. $270
   c. $54
   d. $378

ADVANCED

33. Eric is making cookies. He can bake 1 dozen cookies in 9 minutes, and it will take him 16 minutes to clean up after baking. Which equation could be used to find t, the time that it takes for Eric to bake 4 dozen cookies and clean up afterward?
   a. $t = (9 \times 4) + 16$
   b. $t = (4 \times 16) + 9$
   c. $t = (4 \times 16) \times 9$
   d. $4 = (t + 16) \times 9$

34. Carla has 20 math problems for homework. It takes her between 5 and 7 minutes to do each problem. Which is a reasonable estimate of the total number of minutes it will take her to do her math homework?
   a. 20 min.
   b. 80 min.
   c. 120 min.
   d. 240 min.
   e. 260 min.

35. Which of the following numbers *disproves* the statement "A number that is divisible by 2 and 4 is also divisible by 8"?
   a. 8
   b. 16
   c. 24
   d. 28

36. $|6^2 - (-3)^3| =$
   a. 9
   b. 27
   c. 54
   d. 63

37. Given: $9BA \times 1000 = 932{,}000$ and $BA \div 4 = C$. If A, B, and C represent <u>DIGITS</u> of the numbers in the above equations, what is the value of C?

  a. 2
  b. 4
  c. 6
  d. 8

38. The tens digit of a two-digit number is 8 and the units digit is U. If the two-digit number is divisible by U, which of the following CANNOT be the value of U?

  a. 2
  b. 3
  c. 4
  d. 5

39. Stacey helped direct parking lot traffic at the school carnival. Between noon and 1:00 P.M. the number of cars doubled. In the next two hours the number increased by $\frac{2}{3}$. Between 3:00 P.M. and 4:00 P.M., 37 cars drove away, leaving 123 cars in the lot. How many cars were in the lot at noon?

  a. 41
  b. 48
  c. 82
  d. 96

40. When Mitchell went to bed at 9:30 P.M. the temperature was 68°F. He awoke at 2:00 A.M. and the temperature had dropped 9 degrees. When his mother got up at 5:30 A.M. the temperature had risen 5 degrees since 2:00 A.M. When Mitchell got up at 7:30 A.M. it was 2 degrees warmer than it was when his mother got up. What was the temperature when Mitchell got up?

  a. 70°F
  b. 66°F
  c. 62°F
  d. 56°F

41. At this year's fundraiser for new playground equipment, Mayor Mayfield had whipped cream "pies" tossed at her face. One chance to toss a pie cost $2.75. While Mayor Mayfield was in the pie-tossing booth, $242 was raised. How many pies were tossed at her?

  a. 88
  b. 89
  c. 90
  d. 91

42. A carbon monoxide detector reads 50 ppm at 9 A.M. and 1350 ppm at 12 P.M. This most nearly indicates that the concentration of carbon monoxide
   a. quadrupled every hour.
   b. tripled every hour.
   c. doubled every hour.
   d. remained constant.

43. The square root of 35 is
   a. between 6 and 7.
   b. between 5 and 6.
   c. between 4 and 5.
   d. between 3 and 4.

44. Leah was typing a letter to her grandmother. On average, for every 20 words that she typed, 3 were misspelled. If there were 160 words in the letter she wrote, how many words were probably misspelled?
   a. 8
   b. 16
   c. 24
   d. 53
   e. 60

45. A cafeteria had three different options for lunch.
   ◆ For $2, a customer can get either a sandwich or two pieces of fruit.
   ◆ For $3, a customer can get a sandwich and one piece of fruit.
   ◆ For $4, a customer can get either two sandwiches, or a sandwich and two pieces of fruit.
Jan has $6 to pay for lunch, which of the following is NOT a possible combination?

   a. three sandwiches and one piece of fruit
   b. two sandwiches and two pieces of fruit
   c. one sandwich and four pieces of fruit
   d. three sandwiches and no fruit

46. All pies at the baked-goods booth were cut into eighths. When Justina Hartley's shift in the booth began, there were eight and one-fourth apple pies waiting to be sold. At the end of her shift there were only five pieces of apple pie left. How many pieces of apple pie were sold during Justina's shift?
   a. 60
   b. 61
   c. 63
   d. 64

47. Use the graph below to best approximate the amount of bacteria (in grams) present on day 4.

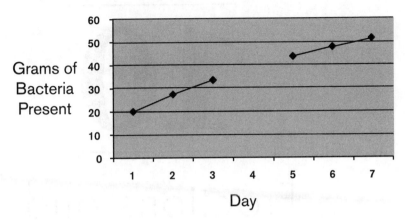

a. 48 g

b. 38 g

c. 28 g

d. 18 g

10

Fractions and Decimals

▶ FRACTIONS

Fractions enter into many different types of math problems. They appear in proportion questions, geometry questions, chart questions, mean questions, ratio questions, and so on. This chapter begins by explaining the anatomy of a fraction, then the lesson is reinforced with fraction questions for all levels.

Fractions represent pieces of a whole. A whole can be divided many ways, for example:

Into halves . . .

Into thirds . . .

Into quarters . . .

Into twelfths . . .

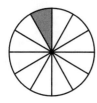

You can divide the whole into any number that you can think of.

Resources Around You

Devise a monthly home budget and determine the fractional part each expense is to the total monthly income. Create a circle graph of this information to illustrate how each expense relates to the whole.

Let's review the anatomy of a fraction. Fractions are always written with the *numerator* on top, and the *denominator* on the bottom:

$$\frac{\text{numerator}}{\text{denominator}}$$

Improper Fractions have a larger numerator than denominator, like $\frac{21}{8}$. To convert this improper fraction into a **proper fraction**, divide: $\frac{21}{8}$ = 21 ÷ 8 = 2 r5. Since you are dealing with *eighths*, simply put the remainder over 8, yielding $2\frac{5}{8}$.

To convert a mixed number like $2\frac{5}{8}$ into an improper fraction, first multiply the 2 times the denominator and add the numerator:

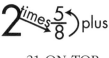

$$= 21 \text{ ON TOP}$$

Because you are dealing with *eighths*, put this value over 8: $\frac{21}{8}$.

Resources Around You

Use the recipe for one of your favorite foods to see how fractions play a big part in cooking. Change the fractions in the recipe to double the amount it would make—or see what would happen to the fractions if you were to cut the recipe in half.

Depending on the situation at hand, you may prefer to deal with improper fractions or proper fractions. Later you will learn how to convert fractions to decimals.

Operations With Fractions:

1. **Addition** and **Subtraction**: In order to add or subtract fractions, you must have the same denominator.

$$\frac{3}{8} + \frac{3}{8} = \frac{\text{numerator} + \text{numerator}}{\text{denominator}} = \frac{6}{8}.$$

$$\frac{3}{8} + \frac{1}{4} =$$

First, convert the $\frac{1}{4}$ into *eighths*:

$$\frac{1 \times 2}{4 \times 2} = \frac{2}{8}$$

$$\frac{3}{8} + \frac{2}{8} = \frac{5}{8}.$$

2. **Multiplication:** You do not need to worry about denominators when you multiply.

$$\frac{1}{8} \times \frac{3}{8} = \frac{\text{numerator} \times \text{numerator}}{\text{denominator} \times \text{denominator}} = \frac{1 \times 3}{8 \times 8} = \frac{3}{64}$$

Sometimes, you can reduce before you multiply:

$$\frac{2}{3} \times \frac{3}{5} =$$

$$\frac{\overset{1}{\cancel{2}}}{3} \times \frac{3}{\underset{1}{\cancel{5}}} = \frac{2}{5}$$

If you are asked to find the fraction *of* a number, *multiply* that number by the fraction:

$$\frac{1}{3} \text{ of } 9 \text{ means } \frac{1}{3} \times 9 = 3.$$

Dive into the Web

From a professor of mathematics comes Cynthia Lanius' Fun Mathematics Lessons (www.math.rice.edu/~lanius/Lessons/index.html), a wonderful collection of creative, practical activities. These lessons address topics ranging from basic math up to calculus and fractals. Whether it's a problem that uses pizza to talk about fractions, or one that teaches math through mapmaking, you and your child will both appreciate the engaging, straightforward tone of the site. Notes for teachers and extensive links to online resources are also available.

3. **Division:** In order to divide one fraction by another, you need to flip the second fraction and then *multiply* the fractions:

$$\frac{2}{3} \div \frac{3}{5} =$$

First, flip the second fraction (take its *reciprocal*):

$$\frac{3}{5} \text{ –reciprocal} \rightarrow \frac{5}{3}$$

$$\frac{2}{3} \times \frac{5}{3} = \frac{10}{9}.$$

Example:

In 1850, Montana's Glacier National Park had 150 glaciers. Today, only $\frac{1}{3}$ of these glaciers still remain. How many glaciers have disappeared since 1850?

    a. 50
    b. 75
    c. 100
    d. 125

$\frac{1}{3}$ of the 150 are still present, so $\frac{2}{3}$ of the 150 must have disappeared. $\frac{2}{3}$ of 150 = $\frac{2}{3}$ × 150 = 100 glaciers disappeared. Thus, answer choice **c** is correct.

Integrate

Math and Music

In music, beats are divided into measures. For example, in standard time, there are 4 beats per measure and a quarter note gets 1 beat. Explore whole notes, half notes, quarter notes, eighth notes, sixteenth notes. Can you make sure that each measure has the right number of beats? If you already play an instrument, try explaining these different notes to someone new to learning music theory.

▶ DECIMALS

Decimals are really fractions in disguise. It is important to be familiar with the names of the places to the right of the decimal point. Look at the number **.1**. Here the one is in the *tenths place*. You can also write this number as $\frac{1}{10}$. Given **.01**, you say the 1 is in the *hundredths place*, and you can express this as $\frac{1}{100}$. Similarly **.001** has a 1 in the *thousandths place*, and is equivalent to $\frac{1}{1000}$.

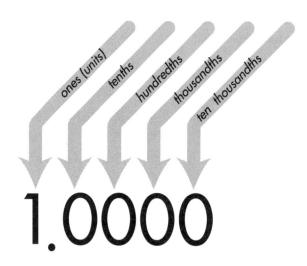

To convert a fraction to a decimal, just divide the top by the bottom. For example, $\frac{5}{8}$ equals 5 ÷ 8, or .625. Memorizing some of the decimal values of the more common fractions can come in handy:

Fraction	Decimal
$\frac{1}{2}$	.5
$\frac{2}{3}$	.3
$\frac{2}{3}$	.6
$\frac{1}{4}$	.25
$\frac{1}{5}$	.2

To convert a decimal into a fraction, first take note of the rightmost place that the number occupies. For example, .423 has a rightmost digit of 3. Because the 3 is in the thousandths place, our fraction has a denominator of 1000. Thus, .423 = $\frac{423}{1000}$. If you can say the name of the decimal, you can easily covert it to a fraction. For example, if you see .325, you can say "325 thousandths," which is the same as $\frac{325}{1000}$.

Addition with decimals: When adding decimals, just line up the decimal points and add. Let's try 8.421 + 7.83562.

$$\begin{array}{r} 8.421 \\ + 7.83562 \\ \hline 16.25662 \end{array}$$

Carschooling® Tricks

Next time you go for a long drive, keep a tally of all of the different types of vehicles you see along the way. You may want to keep track of how many compact cars versus SUVs. You can then research the differences in energy consumption associated with different sized vehicles. How does using gasoline affect global warming? What type of car is easiest on the environment?

Subtraction with decimals: When subtracting decimals, just line up the decimal points and subtract. Let's try 453.9816 − 51.935.

$$\begin{array}{r} 453.9816 \\ - 51.935 \\ \hline 402.0466 \end{array}$$

Multiplying with decimals: When multiplying decimals, first you multiply in the usual fashion, and then count over the proper number of places. Let's try .532 × .81. First we get "43092" and next we need to count over 5 places to the left. Note that the decimal is **3** places to the left in .532 and **2** places to the left in .81, and will thus be **5** places to the left in the answer:

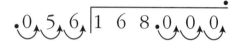

Thus, the answer is .43092.

Dividing with decimals: When dividing with decimals, you move the decimal point of the dividend and divisor the same number of places. (Recall *dividend ÷ divisor = quotient*.) For example, let's divide 168 by .056.

168,000 × 56 = 3,000.

Resources Around You

Choose your favorite sport and determine how math plays a part in the record keeping and statistics of that event. For example, what does it mean to have a softball batting average of .324?

▶ PRACTICE

The questions in this section have been divided into three categories: Basic, Intermediate, and Advanced. Questions 1–15 are Basic, questions 16–31 are Intermediate, and questions 32–45 are Advanced. An answer key with explanations can be found in Appendix C.

BASIC

1. $4\frac{1}{3} + 3\frac{3}{10} =$

    a. $7\frac{2}{15}$

    b. $7\frac{4}{13}$

    c. $7\frac{2}{3}$

    d. $7\frac{19}{30}$

2. Which number sentence is true?

    a. $0.43 < 0.043$

    b. $0.0043 > 0.43$

    c. $0.00043 > 0.043$

    d. $0.043 > 0.0043$

3. $3\frac{5}{6} \times 4\frac{2}{3} =$

    a. $17\frac{8}{9}$

    b. $12\frac{7}{18}$

    c. $16\frac{2}{3}$

    d. $13\frac{3}{5}$

4. Which point best represents $-\frac{1}{3}$ on the number line?

    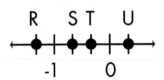

    a. R

    b. S

    c. T

    d. U

5. $2.9 \div 0.8758 =$

    a. 3.31

    b. 0.331

    c. 0.302

    d. 0.0302

6. $\frac{1}{4} \div 2\frac{4}{7} =$

    a. $\frac{9}{14}$

    b. $\frac{7}{72}$

    c. $1\frac{2}{7}$

    d. $\frac{9}{28}$

7. -3.125
     $+\ 0.59$

    a. -3.715
    b. -2.535
    c. 2.535
    d. 3.525

8. Which of the following numbers is the smallest?
    a. 6.03
    b. 6.3
    c. 6.031
    d. 6.005

9. What is 0.716 rounded to the nearest tenth?
    a. 0.7
    b. 0.8
    c. 0.72
    d. 1.0

10. Which of these has a 9 in the thousandths place?
    a. 3.0095
    b. 3.0905
    c. 3.9005
    d. 3.0059

11. Calculate $\left| \frac{3}{4} \div \frac{1}{5} \right|$.

    a. $\frac{3}{20}$

    b. $3\frac{3}{4}$

    c. $\frac{4}{15}$

    d. $3\frac{1}{4}$

12. Which of the following is the equivalent of $\frac{13}{25}$?

 a. 0.38

 b. 0.4

 c. 0.48

 d. 0.52

13. Which of the following fractions is the largest?

 a. $\frac{7}{8}$

 b. $\frac{3}{4}$

 c. $\frac{2}{3}$

 d. $\frac{5}{6}$

14. $-2.9 \times -6.03 =$

 a. 17.487

 b. -17.487

 c. -6.633

 d. 6.633

15. Which of the following numbers is NOT between -0.02 and 1.02?

 a. -0.15

 b. -0.015

 c. 0

 d. 0.02

INTERMEDIATE

16. Dr. Drake charges $36.00 for an office visit, which is $\frac{3}{4}$ of what Dr. Jean charges. How much does Dr. Jean charge?

 a. $48.00

 b. $27.00

 c. $38.00

 d. $57.00

17. Which group of fractions below is ordered from greatest to least?

 a. $\frac{29}{12}, \frac{7}{3}, 2\frac{5}{10}, 2\frac{1}{4}$

 b. $2\frac{5}{10}, \frac{29}{12}, 2\frac{1}{4}, \frac{7}{3}$

 c. $2\frac{1}{4}, \frac{29}{12}, 2\frac{5}{10}, \frac{7}{3}$

 d. $2\frac{5}{10}, \frac{29}{12}, \frac{7}{3}, 2\frac{1}{4}$

18. How much is one-eighth of one-sixth?

   a. $\frac{1}{48}$

   b. $\frac{1}{2}$

   c. $\frac{1}{12}$

   d. $\frac{1}{6}$

19. Ross and his friends want to buy 14 snow cones. If they have $31.00 to spend, which is the best estimate of the highest price that they can pay for each snow cone?

   a. $1.00

   b. $1.25

   c. $2.00

   d. $3.00

20. Marvelous Maids pledged $5.25 to their favorite charity for each house they cleaned during the third week of May. Their total donation to the charity was $1,291.50. How many houses did they clean during the third week of May?

   a. 25

   b. 245

   c. 246

   d. 6,780

21. Jesse ate $\frac{1}{2}$ of a pizza and left the other half in his dorm room. Dennis came by and ate $\frac{1}{4}$ of what was left there. How much of the original pizza did Dennis eat?

   a. $\frac{1}{16}$

   b. $\frac{1}{6}$

   c. $\frac{1}{4}$

   d. $\frac{1}{8}$

22. $2\frac{1}{3} \times 1\frac{1}{14} \times 1\frac{4}{5} =$

   a. $1\frac{7}{18}$

   b. $2\frac{1}{2}$

   c. $3\frac{6}{7}$

   d. $4\frac{1}{2}$

23. Six friends agree to evenly split the cost of gasoline on a trip. Each friend paid $37.27. What was the total cost of gas?

    a. $370.27

    b. $223.62

    c. $314.78

    d. $262.78

24. Here is a list of the ingredients needed to make 16 brownies.

Deluxe Brownies

    $\frac{2}{3}$ cup butter

    5 squares (1 ounce each) unsweetened chocolate

    $1\frac{1}{2}$ cups sugar

    2 teaspoons vanilla

    2 eggs

    1 cup flour

How much sugar is needed to make 8 brownies?

    a. $\frac{3}{4}$ cup

    b. 3 cups

    c. $\frac{2}{3}$ cup

    d. $\frac{5}{8}$ cup

25. $4\frac{1}{5} + 1\frac{2}{5} + 3\frac{3}{10} =$

    a. 9

    b. 8

    c. 8

    d. 8

26. Ellen is a traveling saleswoman. She drove 373.5 miles on Monday, 481.6 miles on Tuesday, 392.8 miles on Wednesday, 502 miles on Thursday, and 53.7 miles on Friday. What was the total distance she drove?

    a. 1,351.8 miles

    b. 1,803.6 miles

    c. 1,813.6 miles

    d. 2,286.9 miles

27. The table below shows the number of cases of a particular kind of floor tile in four warehouses for The Home Fixers store.

Warehouse	Cases of Tiles
1	$1\frac{1}{16}$
2	$1\frac{5}{12}$
3	$1\frac{1}{2}$
4	$1\frac{2}{3}$

Hatim needs to fill an order for 3 cases of these floor tiles. From which 2 warehouses should he request tiles to fill this order?

  a. 1 and 2

  b. 1 and 4

  c. 2 and 3

  d. 2 and 4

28. The Rockets Soccer Team bought new uniforms. They bought 18 uniforms for $21.79 each. What was the total cost of the 18 uniforms?

  a. $39.79

  b. $196.11

  c. $381.22

  d. $391.22

  e. none of the above

29. On the number line below, point L is to be located halfway between points M and N. What number will correspond to point L?

  a. $-\frac{1}{4}$

  b. $-\frac{1}{2}$

  c. $-1\frac{1}{4}$

  d. 0

30. Yuri works in the school library. He needs to put away books with these call numbers in order from smallest to largest: 513.26, 513.59, 513.7, 513.514. In which order should Yuri place these books on the shelf?
    a. 513.514, 513.59, 513.26, 513.7
    b. 513.7, 513.26, 513.59, 513.514
    c. 513.7, 513.26, 513.514, 513.59
    d. 513.26, 513.514, 513.59, 513.7

ADVANCED

31. Lu makes $7.75 an hour. He worked $38\frac{1}{5}$ hours last week. How much money did he earn?
    a. $592.10
    b. $296.05
    c. $775.00
    d. $380.25

32. The heights of 8 students were measured in feet and then ordered from least to greatest on a number line. Their heights were as follows: $5\frac{1}{2}$ ft, 5.25 ft, $5\frac{1}{6}$ ft, 5.8 ft, $5\frac{3}{4}$ ft, 5.4 ft, 5.2 ft, and $5\frac{7}{8}$ ft. Which number was third on the number line?

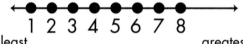

    least   greatest

    a. $5\frac{1}{2}$
    b. 5.25
    c. $5\frac{3}{4}$
    d. 5.4

33. At her party, Mackenzie put out a bowl containing 360 jellybeans. Marina came by and ate $\frac{1}{12}$ of the jellybeans, Christina ate $\frac{1}{4}$, Athena ate $\frac{1}{5}$, and Jade ate $\frac{1}{8}$. How many jellybeans were left?
    a. 120
    b. 240
    c. 237
    d. 123

34. After three days, a group of hikers discovers that they have used $\frac{2}{5}$ of their supplies. At this rate, how many more days can they go forward before they have to turn around?
    a. 0.75 days
    b. 3.75 days
    c. 4.5 days
    d. 7.5 days

35. Each case of Tasty Treat baby food has 24 jars. The case of baby food weighs 8.64 pounds. How much does each jar of baby food weigh?

    a. 0.24 lb

    b. 0.35 lb

    c. 0.36 lb

    d. 0.46 lb

36. $-12\frac{2}{7} - (-3\frac{4}{7}) =$

    a. $-15\frac{6}{7}$

    b. $-15\frac{2}{7}$

    c. $-9\frac{2}{7}$

    d. $-8\frac{5}{7}$

37. Lauren and Jenna want to buy a present for their mom, a bracelet that costs $50. Lauren has $5 from her allowance and $13.73 saved in her piggy bank. Jenna has $2.50 from her allowance and $7.19 in her piggy bank, plus she found $2 outside. If their dad gives them $10 toward the gift, how much more money do they need?

    a. $30.42

    b. $19.58

    c. $40.42

    d. $ 9.58

38. A recipe calls for $\frac{2}{3}$ cup of butter and yields 16 cookies. What is the greatest number of brownies that can be made if the baker has only 1 cup of butter?

    a. 12

    b. 16

    c. 24

    d. 32

39. If the pattern $\frac{1}{2}, \frac{1}{4}, \frac{1}{8}, \frac{1}{16} \ldots$ is continued, what is the denominator of the tenth term?

    a. 64

    b. 212

    c. 512

    d. 1024

40. A recipe calls for $1\frac{1}{4}$ cups of flour. If Larry wants to make $2\frac{1}{2}$ times the recipe, how many cups of flour does he need?

    a. $2\frac{3}{4}$

    b. $3\frac{1}{8}$

    c. $3\frac{1}{4}$

    d. $3\frac{5}{8}$

41. Half of all the nails in a barrel are 2 inches long. Of the remainder, $\frac{1}{3}$ are 3 inches long and $\frac{2}{3}$ are half an inch long. If 300 nails are 3 inches long, how many nails are there in all?

    a. 900

    b. 1,800

    c. 2,700

    d. 3,600

42. What is the missing term in the number pattern below?

240, 120, 60, 30, 15, __, $3\frac{3}{4}$

    a. $7\frac{1}{2}$

    b. $9\frac{1}{4}$

    c. 10

    d. $11\frac{1}{4}$

43. A 600-page book is 1.5 inches thick. What is the thickness of each page?

    a. 0.0010 inches

    b. 0.0030 inches

    c. 0.0025 inches

    d. 0.0600 inches

44. The cost of movie theater tickets is $7.50 for adults and $5 for children ages 12 and under. On Saturday and Sunday afternoons until 4:00 P.M., there is a matinee price: $5.50 for adults and $3 for children ages 12 and under. Special group discounts are available for groups of 30 or more people.

Which of these can be determined from the information given in the passage?

    a. how much it will cost a family of 4 to buy movie theater tickets on Saturday afternoon

    b. the difference between the cost of two movie theater tickets on Tuesday night and the cost of one ticket on Sunday at 3:00 P.M.

    c. how much movie theater tickets will cost each person if he or she is part of a group of 40 people

    d. the difference between the cost of a movie theater ticket for an adult on Friday night and a movie theater ticket for a 13-year-old on Saturday afternoon at 1:00 P.M.

45. Rudy forgot to replace his gas cap the last time he filled up his car with gas. The gas is evaporating out of his 14-gallon tank at a constant rate of $\frac{1}{3}$ gallon per day. How much gas does Rudy lose in 1 week?

    a. 2 gallons

    b. $2\frac{1}{3}$ gallons

    c. $3\frac{1}{3}$ gallons

    d. $4\frac{2}{3}$ gallons

    e. 6 gallons

11

Exponents and Roots

▶ EXPONENTS

Exponents are the method for raising numbers to different powers. Exponents and roots are less likely to be encountered in everyday life, but they are very important in fields such as science, computer programming, and applied mathematics.

Here are a few simple examples of exponents. Note that when a number is raised to a nonzero whole number exponent, you are actually multiplying the number by that many instances of itself:

Ten to the second power = Ten squared = 10^2 = 10 × 10 = 100
Ten to the third power = Ten cubed = 10^3 = 10 × 10 × 10 = 1000
Ten to the fourth power = 10^4 = 10 × 10 ×10 × 10 = 10,000

It's A Fact

Any number, except zero, raised to the zero power is equal to 1.

When looking at 10^4, we call 10 the **base** and 4 the **exponent**.

Things get trickier when we deal with negative exponents. If we have 10^{-4}, we can equate this with $\frac{1}{10^4}$.

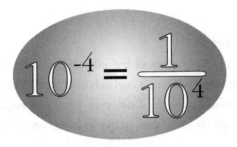

Here are the rules for operations with exponents:

1. When multiplying powers of the same base, add the exponents.

$$4^2 \times 4^3 = 4^{2+3} = 4^5$$

2. When dividing powers of the same base, subtract the exponents.

$$5^8 \div 5^2 = 5^{8-2} = 5^6$$

$$5^{-2} \div 5^3 = 5^{-2-3} = 5^{-5} = \frac{1}{5^5}$$

3. When raising a power to a power, multiply the exponents.

$$(6^3)^4 = 6^{3 \times 4} = 6^{12}$$

4. Always raise everything inside the parentheses by the power outside of the parentheses.

$$(5 \times 6^3)^4 = 5^4 \times 6^{3 \times 4} = 5^4 \times 6^{12}$$

$$(6a^3)^2 = 6^2 \times a^{3 \times 2} = 36a^6$$

5. When you do not have the same base, try to convert to the same base:

$$25^4 \times 5^{12} = (5^2)^4 \times 5^{12} = 5^8 \times 5^{12} = 5^{20}$$

Integrate

Math and Science

Binary fission is the process by which bacteria divide to produce new cells. One cell becomes two cells, which become four cells, and so forth. We call this *exponential growth*. Can you find a graph of bacterial cell growth? What are the phases of cell growth involved and how do they relate to the graph?

▶ SCIENTIFIC NOTATION

Consider the number four hundred and fifty trillion: 450,000,000,000,000. Would you find it easy to work with this number in mathematical equations? Let's say you needed to divide four hundred and fifty trillion by nine thousand. Sounds messy? This is where scientific notation becomes helpful. Instead of writing 450,000,000,000,000, you can write an equivalent value of 4.5 times the appropriate power of 10. Let's look at the powers of ten:

10^0	= 1	
10^1	=10	
10^2	=100	
10^3	=1000	
10^4	=10,000	
10^5	=100,000	
10^6	=1,000,000	one million
10^7	=10,000,000	
10^8	=100,000,000	
10^9	=1,000,000,000	one billion
10^{10}	=10,000,000,000	
10^{11}	=100,000,000,000	
10^{12}	=1,000,000,000,000	one trillion
10^{13}	=10,000,000,000,000	
10^{14}	=100,000,000,000,000	

Fortunately, you do not have to memorize the chart above. The trick to expressing 450,000,000,000,000 as 4.5 times a power of 10 is to start at the current decimal point and then count until you reach the place where you want to insert the new decimal point.

Remember:

$$450,000,000,000,000 = 450,000,000,000,000.$$

$$450,000,000,000,000.$$

There are 14 places counted, so $450,000,000,000,000 = 4.5 \times 10^{14}$.

Now, let's divide 4.5×10^{14} by 9000. It can be expressed 9000 as 9×10^3.

$$\frac{4.5 \times 10^{14}}{9 \times 10^3}$$

Using the rules of exponents, you can subtract $14 - 3$ to get a new power of 10 on top:

$$\frac{4.5 \times 10^{11}}{9}$$

You may not want to divide 4.5 by 9, but wouldn't it be nice to divide 45 by 9? You can *steal* one of those tens from the 10^{11}. Remember $4.5 \times 10^{11} = 4.5 \times 10 \times 10 \times 10 \times 10 \times 10 \times 10 \times 10 \times 10 \times 10 \times 10 \times 10$. If we steal one of those tens to turn 4.5 into $4.5 \times 10 = 45$, then we would have $10 \times 10 \times 10 \times 10 \times 10 \times 10 \times 10 \times 10 \times 10 \times 10$, or 10^{10} left.

$$4.5 \times 10^{11}$$
$$= 4.5 \times 10 \times 10 \times 10 \times 10 \times 10 \times 10 \times 10 \times 10 \times 10 \times 10 \times 10$$
$$= (\mathbf{4.5 \times 10}) \times 10 \times 10 \times 10 \times 10 \times 10 \times 10 \times 10 \times 10 \times 10 \times 10$$
$$= \mathbf{45} \times 10 \times 10 \times 10 \times 10 \times 10 \times 10 \times 10 \times 10 \times 10 \times 10$$
$$45 \times 10^{10}$$

Now, we have $\dfrac{45 \times 10^{10}}{9} = 5 \times 10^{10}$

Remember, when you *steal* (move the decimal to the *right*), you *subtract* from the exponent. What happens if you have $6{,}000 \times 10^{10}$ and you want to make it 6 times to the appropriate power of 10? You can *donate* a power of ten from the 6,000 to the 10^{10}.

$$6{,}000 \times 10^{10}$$
$$= \mathbf{6{,}000} \times 10 \times 10 \times 10 \times 10 \times 10 \times 10 \times 10 \times 10 \times 10 \times 10$$
$$= (\mathbf{6 \times 1{,}000}) \times 10 \times 10 \times 10 \times 10 \times 10 \times 10 \times 10 \times 10 \times 10 \times 10$$
$$= (\mathbf{6 \times 10 \times 10 \times 10}) \times 10 \times 10 \times 10 \times 10 \times 10 \times 10 \times 10 \times 10 \times 10 \times 10$$
$$= \mathbf{6 \times 10 \times 10 \times 10} \times 10 \times 10 \times 10 \times 10 \times 10 \times 10 \times 10 \times 10 \times 10 \times 10$$

Remember, when you *donate* (move the decimal to the left), you *add* to the exponent. Example: Consider the data below:

1997 World Consumption of Resources

Coal	5,200,000,000 tons
Oil	26,400,000,000 barrels
Natural Gas	8,700,000,000,000 ft^3

Rewrite the data in scientific notation:

1997 World Consumption of Resources

Coal	tons
Oil	barrels
Natural Gas	ft³

Answers: Coal = 5.2×10^9 tons, Oil = 2.64×10^{10} barrels, Natural Gas = 8.7×10^{12}.

Integrate

Math and Science

Can you find out the sizes of different cells, bacteria, and viruses and express them in scientific notation? Just how tiny are they? What size particles can get through a cell membrane? How do bigger particles get inside?

▶ ROOTS

Like exponents, roots are often encountered in the world of science, math, and computers. A solid understanding of the basics of roots will help you handle higher levels of these concepts in high school and college courses.

The **index** is the root you are taking, and the **radicand** is the number under the radical. If there is no index labeled, then it is just the square root.

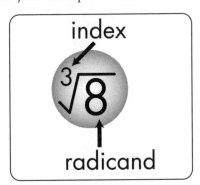

If you ever see a fractional exponent, you are actually taking a root. For example $8^{\frac{1}{3}} = \sqrt[3]{8}$. To solve, just ask yourself: "What number cubed is 8?" or "What number to the third power is 8?" $2 \times 2 \times 2 = 8$, so $\sqrt[3]{8} = 2$.

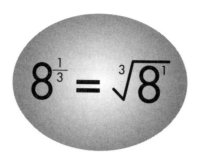

$$8^{\frac{1}{3}} = \sqrt[3]{8^1}$$

Ways to manipulate radicals

1. You can express the number under the radical as the product of other numbers. You can then equate the root of the product of those numbers as the product of separate roots of those numbers.

$$\sqrt{24} = \sqrt{4 \times 6} = \sqrt{4} \times \sqrt{6} = 2\sqrt{6}$$

2. When multiplying 2 roots (with the same index) you can combine them under the same radical:

$$\sqrt{2} \times \sqrt{32} = \sqrt{2 \times 32} = \sqrt{64} = 8$$

3. When dividing 2 roots (with the same index) you can combine them under the same radical:

$$\frac{\sqrt{200}}{\sqrt{2}} = \sqrt{200 \div 2} = \sqrt{100} = 10$$

4. If there is a division bar under the radical (as in $\frac{15}{16}$), you can separate the top from the bottom and place each part under its own radical:

$$\sqrt{\frac{15}{16}} = \frac{\sqrt{15}}{\sqrt{16}} = \frac{\sqrt{15}}{4}$$

The same rule applies for $\sqrt{15 \div 16}$.

5. You can add roots only if they have the same index and radicand.

$$2\sqrt{3} + 3\sqrt{3} = 5\sqrt{3}$$

6. Also, you can subtract roots only if they have the same index and radicand.

$$8\sqrt{5} - 2\sqrt{5} = 3\sqrt{5}$$

The square root of any negative real number is an imaginary number: $\sqrt{-1} = i$. **For example,** $\sqrt{-25} = 5i$.

▶ ADVANCED TOPIC: LOGARITHMS

Logarithms, or logs, can be to different bases. **log$_2$** denotes a log to the base 2, and **log$_{10}$** denotes a log to the base 10. Logarithms are exponents. When you solve a log, you are actually calculating the exponent that the base was raised to.

Look at the problem $\log_2 8 = ?$ Logs can be tackled easily by making a spiral right through the problem . . .

Follow the spiral...

$\log_2 8 = ?$

and say...
"2 to what power is 8?"

$2^? = 8$

You spiral your way through the 2, then the "?" and end on the 8. "Two to what power is 8?" Two to the third power is 8, so $\log_2 8 = 3$.

log$_{10}$ is so common that if you see a question like log 100 = ?, you are taking the log to the base 10. Thus log 100 = $\log_{10}$ 100. To solve, make a spiral . . .

$\log_{10} 100 = ?$

"10 to what power is 100?"

10 to the second power is 100, so $\log_{10} 100 = 2$.

Resources Around You

Imagine that you are going to start saving money starting on the first day of the month, and will double the amount you put away each day until the end of the month. On the first day you will save one penny, on the second day you will save two pennies (for a total of three cents), on the third day you will save four cents (for a total of eleven), and so on.

How much money will you have saved by the 15th of the month? The 20th of the month? The 30th? Would you be able to store that number of pennies in your room? Can you find a shortcut to calculate the total amount of money saved this way?

Logs are used in many branches of math and science. For example, we use logs to describe the intensity of sound waves. First, we compare the intensity of the sound we are hearing to a reference level, and then we take the log of this value and multiply it by 10. (dB = decibels)

$$\mathbf{dB} = 10 \times \log_{10}(\textit{comparison of intensities})$$

For example, the comparison of the sound of traffic to the reference level is 10^7. To find the number of decibels, we put 10^7 into the formula:

$$\mathbf{dB} = 10 \times \log_{10}(10^7)$$

10 to what power is 10^7? 10 to the seventh power is 10^7, so $\log_{10}(10^7) = 7$. We put 7 back into the formula to get:

$$\mathbf{dB} = 10 \times 7 = 70 \text{ dB}.$$

Normal speaking is 60 dB, a loud concert is 120 dB, and a library is 40 dB.

Integrate

Math and Science

Logs are also used to calculate the pH of acids and bases. Acids love to donate a positive charge (a proton), and are called *proton donors*. Water, H_2O, accepts the charge and becomes H_3O+. Can you find the formula that is used to calculate pH? Do acids have high or low pH values?

▶ PRACTICE

The questions in this section have been divided into Basic, Intermediate, and Advanced. Questions 1–12 are Basic, questions 13–25 are Intermediate, and questions 26–43 are Advanced. An answer key with explanations can be found in Appendix C.

BASIC

1. Find the value of -12^2.
   a. 144
   b. -144
   c. 24
   d. -24

2. What is another way to write $4 \times 4 \times 4$?
   a. 3×4
   b. 8×4
   c. 4^3
   d. 3^4

3. 17^2 is equal to
   a. 34
   b. 68
   c. 136
   d. 289

4. Find $(\frac{2}{3})^2$.
   a. $\frac{5}{9}$
   b. $\frac{1}{3}$
   c. $\frac{1}{6}$
   d. $\frac{4}{9}$

5. What is another way to write 3^4?
   a. 12
   b. 24
   c. 27
   d. 81

6. $8^3 =$
   a. 2
   b. 24
   c. 512
   d. 6,561

7. What is the square root of 121?

   a. 242

   b. 12

   c. 11

   d. 14,641

8. What is another way to write 7.25×10^3?

   a. 72.5

   b. 725

   c. 7,250

   d. 72,500

9. Choose the answer to the following problem: $10^5 \div 10^2 =$

   a. 10

   b. 10^3

   c. 10^7

   d. 10^{10}

10. $(-2)^3 + (-3)^2 =$

    a. 35

    b. 19

    c. 17

    d. 1

11. What is another way to write 2.75×100^2?

    a. 275

    b. 2,750

    c. 27,500

    d. 270,000

12. 25^2 is how much greater than 21^2?

    a. 184

    b. 40

    c. 18

    d. 4

INTERMEDIATE

13. What is $(4 + 2)^3$?

    a. 196

    b. 72

    c. 216

    d. 18

14. 5.133 multiplied by 10^{-6} is equal to

    a. 0.0005133

    b. 0.00005133

    c. 0.000005133

    d. 0.0000005133

15. What is $\sqrt{64} + \sqrt{36}$ equal to?

    a. 100

    b. 10

    c. 14

    d. 64

16. Calculate $43^2 \times 4$.

    a. 172

    b. 129

    c. 7,396

    d. 1,849

17. 7.359 multiplied by 10^{-6} is equal to

    a. 0.0007359

    b. 0.00007359

    c. 0.000007359

    d. 0.0000007359

18. Which of the following equations is correct?

    a. $\sqrt{36} + \sqrt{64} = \sqrt{100}$

    b. $\sqrt{25} + \sqrt{16} = \sqrt{41}$

    c. $\sqrt{9} + \sqrt{25} = \sqrt{64}$

    d. None of the above.

19. What is another way to write $5\sqrt{12}$?

    a. $12\sqrt{5}$

    b. $10\sqrt{3}$

    c. $6\sqrt{3}$

    d. 12

20. What is the correct way to write 3,600,000 in scientific notation?

    a. $3,600 \times 100$

    b. 3.6×10^6

    c. 3.6×10^{-6}

    d. 36×10^6

21. Which answer choice is equivalent to the following expression?

$$\frac{18 \div 2}{3(19 + 8)}$$

   a. 3^{-2}
   b. 3^{-3}
   c. 3^{2}
   d. 3^{3}

22. Calculate $(-\frac{1}{5})^3$.

   a. $\frac{1}{125}$
   b. $\frac{1}{5}$
   c. $-\frac{1}{125}$
   d. $-\frac{3}{15}$

23. $(4\sqrt{7})^2 =$
   a. $8\sqrt{7}$
   b. 28
   c. $16\sqrt{7}$
   d. 112

24. Which of these equations is incorrect?
   a. $\sqrt{16} + \sqrt{9} = \sqrt{(16 + 9)}$
   b. $\sqrt{4} \times \sqrt{36} = \sqrt{(4 \times 36)}$
   c. neither is incorrect
   d. both are incorrect

25. What is another way to write 3.0×10^{12}?
   a. 3 billion
   b. 3 trillion
   c. 3 million
   d. 300,000

ADVANCED

26. What is 4.0×10^4 multiplied by 3,000?
   a. 12×10^8
   b. 1.2×10^4
   c. 1200×10^4
   d. 1.2×10^8

27. $(2\sqrt[3]{9})^3 = ?$
  a. 18
  b. 24
  c. 54
  d. 72

28. Pure gold can be hammered to a thickness of only 0.000013 cm. Which is another way to express this measure?
  a. 1.3×10^6 cm
  b. 1.3×10^5 cm
  c. 1.3×10^{-6} cm
  d. 1.3×10^{-5} cm

29. $(7x^3y^2)^2$
  a. $49x^3y^2$
  b. $49x^5y^4$
  c. $49x^6y^4$
  d. $7x^5y^4$

30. Which of the following is equivalent to $2y^2$?
  a. $2(y + y)$
  b. $2y(y)$
  c. $y^2 + 2$
  d. $y + y + y + y$

31. What is $\log_2 128$?
  a. 7
  b. 8
  c. 9
  d. 10

32. Calculate $\sqrt{(97-16)}$ multiplied by $\sqrt{(48 \div 3)}$.
  a. $\sqrt{36}$
  b. 9
  c. 6^2
  d. 4

33. $\dfrac{4^{-2} \times (-2)^3}{2^{-3} \times (-4)^2} = ?$
  a. -4
  b. -1
  c. $-\frac{1}{4}$
  d. $\frac{1}{4}$

34. $\dfrac{6.5 \times 10^{-6}}{3.25 \times 10^3} =$

    a. 2×10^{-9}

    b. 2×10^{-3}

    c. 2×10^{2}

    d. 2×10^{3}

35. $(4.1 \times 10^{-2})(3.8 \times 10^{4}) =$

    a. 1.558×10^{-8}

    b. 15.58×10^{-2}

    c. 1.558×10^{2}

    d. 1.558×10^{3}

36. $\dfrac{(6.5 \times 10^{-6})}{(3.25 \times 10^{-3})}$

    a. 2×10^{-9}

    b. 2×10^{-3}

    c. 2×10^{-2}

    d. 2×10^{2}

    e. 2×10^{3}

37. $\log_{10}(1 \times 10^{5}) =$

    a. .0005

    b. 100

    c. 5000

    d. 100,000

38. Find the product of $7p^{2}q^{5}$ and $3p^{4}q$.

    a. $10p^{8} + 2q^{5}$

    b. $10p^{8}q^{5}$

    c. $10p^{6}q^{6}$

    d. $21p^{6}q^{6}$

39. $\sqrt{51}$ when rounded to the nearest tenth is equivalent to

    a. 6.5

    b. 6.8

    c. 7.1

    d. 8.2

40. Which value is equal to the square root of 64?

    a. $\sqrt[3]{64}$

    b. $4\sqrt{4}$

    c. $4\sqrt{2}$

    d. 8^{2}

41. $\sqrt{1151}$ to the nearest tenth is

    a. 29.7

    b. 33.9

    c. 35.8

    d. 37.2

42. What is $\log_{10}100$?

    a. −2

    b. 2

    c. −10

    d. 10

43. $\log_{10}(10 \times 10^{-6}) =$

    a. 5

    b. 6

    c. −5

    d. −6

12

Ratios and Proportions

***R**atios* and proportions are often found in textbooks and news reports. You will also encounter them in many math word problems. In this chapter, you will learn what ratios and proportions are and how they are represented.

Integrate

Math and Art

You probably already use ratios all the time in the kitchen, so try something new with your homeschooler. Use the ratio of plaster of Paris to water to make different amounts of plaster of Paris that is ready to go. If the bag charts out the amounts, don't peek! See if you and your homeschooler can figure it out. You can hollow out some regular clay as a mold, grease it up, and pour the plaster in to make whatever your imagination desires. This project is the perfect launching pad for science investigations as well: Why does the plaster get hot as you mix it? Why does it harden?

► RATIOS

Ratios are a way of comparing numbers. If an animal shelter has two dogs for every cat, you can express this as a 2 to 1 ratio. You will see ratios expressed in three ways:

- ◆ In sentence form:
  There is a two to one ratio of dogs to cats.
- ◆ By using a colon:
  2:1
- ◆ By using a fraction bar:
  $\frac{2}{1}$

Just like fractions, ratios can be reduced to smaller terms. Someone may count that the shelter has 32 dogs and 16 cats. They would be correct to say that there is a 32 to 16 ratio of dogs to cats. Mathematically, $\frac{32}{16} = \frac{2}{1}$. Notice that when dealing with a 2:1 ratio, the total must be a multiple of 2 + 1 , or 3. Let's check this. The shelter has 32 dogs + 16 cats = 48 dogs and cats. 48 is indeed a multiple of 3.

BASIC RATIOS: WHEN YOU KNOW THE PIECES . . .

Example: If a shelter across town had the same ratio of dogs to cats as the last example, and they had 10 dogs, how many cats would they have?
  - **a.** 20
  - **b.** 15
  - **c.** 10
  - **d.** 5

Since it is still the same 2 dogs to every 1 cat ratio, there must be 5 cats. Thus, choice **d** is correct.

It's A Fact

A special ratio often associated with circles is π. This is the ratio of the circumference of any circle to the length of its diameter. It is an irrational number, but is often approximated to be $\frac{22}{7}$, or 3.14.

INTERMEDIATE RATIOS: WHEN YOU KNOW THE TOTAL . . .

Suppose a garden has 3 pansies for every carnation. If there are 56 flowers in all, how many pansies are there?

Well, here is a 3:1 ratio. Right away, you know that the total will be a multiple of 3 + 1, or 4. You know there are 56 flowers. Fifty-six represents 56 ÷ 4 = 14 groups of 4. So, you now have 14 groups like the one in the picture above. Let P = pansy and C = carnation. You have:

$$\text{PPPC} \quad \text{PPPC} \quad \text{PPPC} \quad \text{PPPC} \quad \text{PPPC} \quad \text{PPPC} \quad \text{PPPC}$$
$$\text{PPPC} \quad \text{PPPC} \quad \text{PPPC} \quad \text{PPPC} \quad \text{PPPC} \quad \text{PPPC} \quad \text{PPPC}$$

Each of the above 14 groups has 3 pansies, so there are a total of 14 × 3 = 42 pansies.

A shortcut would be to utilize the fact that there's a 3:1 ratio, and thus in each group of 4, 3 will be pansies. This means that pansies will be $\frac{3}{4}$ of the total. $\frac{3}{4}$ of 56 = 42.

Example: The ratio of usage of the earth's natural resources today is 3:4:3 for coal, oil, and natural gas, respectively. What fractional part of natural resource usage does coal represent?

    a. $\frac{3}{4}$

    b. $\frac{3}{10}$

    c. $\frac{3}{7}$

    d. $\frac{7}{10}$

The three parts listed in the ratio of coal:oil:natural gas are 3, 4, and 3, respectively. Thus the total (all parts combined) would be 3 + 4 + 3 = 10. So, put the part that coal represents, 3, over the total, 10, yielding $\frac{3}{10}$. Thus, the answer is **b.**

BASIC SKILLS FOR HOMESCHOOLING

Dive Into The Web

Stumped? If you don't know the answer to a question, chances are Dr. Math (www.mathforum.com/dr.math) will. The "Dr. Math" column is a question-and-answer service that examines classic math problems. The Frequently Asked Questions area covers topics ranging from basic (order of operations, fractions, and decimals) to advanced (imaginary numbers and two-column proofs). If you don't see what you're looking for, you can even e-mail Dr. Math for help.

The Dr. Math column is part of the Math Forum (www.mathforum. com), a huge collection of math resources for students and teachers at all skill levels. Software reviews, Internet resources, lesson plans, and forums are grouped by subject area as well as age group. For students, activities include a "problem of the week" challenge and an online math treasure hunt.

ADVANCED RATIOS: WHEN THE RATIO CHANGES OVER TIME . . .

Let's say that in a yoga class there used to be a 2:3 ratio of men to women. Then several men joined, and now there's a 4:3 ratio of men to women. If there are 35 students in the class now, how many people were in the class before the men joined?

To solve a question like this, you need to look at the before and after. *Before* there was a 2:3 ratio. The total was a multiple of 2 + 3, or 5. It is not known how many groups there were, but each group looked like this:

MMWWW

After, there is a 4:3 ratio, and the total is a multiple of 4 + 3, or 7. Since there are 35 students, you must have 35 ÷ 7 = 5 groups:

MMMMWWW   MMMMWWW
MMMMWWW   MMMMWWW
MMMMWWW

Since the number of women didn't change, you can count that there are 15 women in the class now, so there were 15 women in the class *before*. Thus, the before picture is:

MMWWW   MMWWW
MMWWW   MMWWW
MMWWW

And the total number of students *before* was 25.

Before:

The men will be 2*x* and the women will be 3*x*, so that the 2:3 ratio is preserved.

$$men + women = total$$
$$2x + 3x = 5x$$

After:

There is a 4:3 ratio, and the total is a multiple of 4 + 3, or 7. Since there are 35 students, it is known that there must be 5 groups of 7. Each group looks like this:

MMMMWWW

Each of the 5 groups has 3 women, so there must be 3 × 5 = 15 women. Since the number of women did not change, you know that in the *"Before"* equation, 3*x* must equal 15. If 3*x* = 15, *x* = 5. The before total, 5*x* would then be 5 × 5 = 25.

Resources Around You

Another type of special ratio is scale. Create a scale drawing of the floor plan of your home. Use an appropriate scale, a ruler, and graph paper to help you be accurate. Calculate the total square footage of your house, and find out what percentage your room is to the rest of the house.

▶ PROPORTIONS

Proportions are means of relating two ratios to one another; in fact, they are simply two equal ratios. When you set up a proportion, just be sure to align the units correctly.

Example: One gallon of gas ultimately produces 18 pounds of carbon dioxide. If a car used up 8 gallons of gas during a trip, how many pounds of carbon dioxide were produced during the trip?

First, set up the proportion. On the left side of the equals sign, use the factual information presented. On the right side of the equation, use the information relevant to the scenario at hand:

$$\frac{1 \text{ gallon}}{18 \text{ lbs}} = \frac{8 \text{ gallons}}{? \text{ lbs}}$$

Next, cross multiply to get 1 gal × ? lbs = 8 gal × 18 lbs, so ? = 8 × 18 = 144 lbs.

Integrate

Math and Social Studies

How many U.S. dollars is a British pound worth? How about a Japanese yen? You can translate your savings into the currencies of other nations by using proportions.

Harder proportion questions require you to convert units before setting up the proportion.

Example: Underwater ice streams can travel about 3,000 feet per year from their East Antarctic point of origin. About how many miles will they travel in 2.5 years?

   a. 7500 mi

   b. 526 mi

   c. 10 mi

   d. 1.42 mi

First, convert the feet to miles. 1 mile = 5,280 feet, so 3,000 ft/yr = 3,000 ft/yr × 1 mi/5,280 ft = .568$\overline{18}$ mi/yr (the 18 is repeating), which can be approximated as .568 mi/yr. Next, set up the proportion:

$$\frac{.568 \text{ mi}}{1 \text{ yr}} = \frac{? \text{ mi}}{2.5 \text{ yr}}$$

Cross multiply to get .568 × 2.5 = ? × 1, which means 1.42 = ?.

Resources Around You

Measure a tree using proportions. Get out your ruler. Now you can figure out how tall a tree or a building is by using proportions (and shadows). All you have to do is measure your height, the length of your shadow, and the length of the tree's shadow. Can you set up a proportion to calculate the height of the tree?

▶ PRACTICE

The questions in this section have been divided into Basic, Intermediate, and Advanced. Questions 1–14 are Basic, questions 15–31 are Intermediate, and questions 32–45 are Advanced. An answer key with explanations can be found in Appendix C.

BASIC

1. If it takes 27 nails to build 3 boxes, how many nails will it take to build 7 boxes?
    a. 64
    b. 72
    c. 56
    d. 63

2. If Jack always spends $18 on gaming equipment in a week, how much does he spend in 6 weeks?
    a. $60
    b. $48
    c. $108
    d. $180

3. Jessica is having a party and is making a sparkling drink. Her recipe calls for 1 part fruit punch and 2 parts seltzer. If she adds 3 cups of fruit punch, how much seltzer would she need?
    a. 2 cups
    b. 6 cups
    c. 3 cups
    d. 4 cups

4. If it takes 5 workers to build 3 sheds, how many would it take to build 18?
    a. 90
    b. 18
    c. 15
    d. 30

5. The ratio of 20 to 50 can be represented by
    a. 50:20
    b. 1:2
    c. 2:1
    d. 2:5

6. A floor plan is drawn to scale so that one-quarter inch represents 2 feet. If a hall on the plan is 4 inches long, how long will the actual hall be when it is built?
   a. 2 feet
   b. 8 feet
   c. 16 feet
   d. 32 feet

7. A clerk can process 26 forms per hour. If 5,600 forms must be processed in an 8-hour day, how many clerks must you hire for that day?
   a. 24 clerks
   b. 25 clerks
   c. 26 clerks
   d. 27 clerks

8. A large jar of olives costs $5.49 and provides enough olives to garnish 30 salads. What is the approximate cost of the olives used on 11 salads?
   a. $3.50
   b. $3.00
   c. $2.50
   d. $2.00

9. Jeanne's car gets 24.35 miles per gallon. On a tank holding 14 gallons, how many total miles could Jeanne drive?
   a. 121.75
   b. 230.90
   c. 330.90
   d. 336
   e. None of the above

10. A dosage of a certain medication is 12 cc per 100 pounds. What is the dosage for a patient who weighs 175 pounds?
   a. 15 cc
   b. 18 cc
   c. 21 cc
   d. 24 cc

11. Out of 100 shoppers polled, 80 said they buy fresh fruit every week. How many shoppers out of 30,000 could be expected to buy fresh fruit every week?
   a. 2,400
   b. 6,000
   c. 22,000
   d. 24,000

12. A town of 105,000 is served by 3 hospitals. If the same ratio were to be maintained, how many people would be served by 4 hospitals?

    a. 130,000

    b. 135,000

    c. 140,000

    d. 145,000

13. If tofu costs $1.50 a pound, how much will $6\frac{1}{2}$ pounds of tofu cost?

    a. $9.75

    b. $11.25

    c. $12.50

    d. $13.25

14. While on vacation, Carla would like to visit the places labeled Site A and Site B on the map below. How many miles is Site A from Site B?

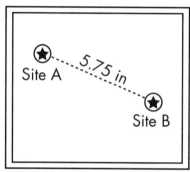

Scale: .25 in = 1 mile

    a. 2.3 miles

    b. 2.5 miles

    c. 23 miles

    d. 25 miles

INTERMEDIATE

15. If one gallon of water weighs 8.35 pounds, a 25-gallon container of water would most nearly weigh

    a. 173 pounds.

    b. 200 pounds.

    c. 209 pounds.

    d. 215 pounds.

16. Carl bought 7 packages of tapioca pudding for $5.53. At this rate, what would be the cost of 3 packages of tapioca pudding?
    a. $0.79
    b. $2.37
    c. $2.67
    d. $7.90

17. A gallon of wiper fluid costs 95¢. How many dollars will 3 gallons cost?
    a. $285
    b. $270
    c. $2.85
    d. $2.70

18. White stones cost $3.59 for 25 pounds. Which proportion can be used to solve for the cost, c, of 100 pounds?
    a. $\frac{25}{100} = \frac{c}{3.59}$
    b. $\frac{3.59}{100} = \frac{25}{c}$
    c. $\frac{3.59}{25} = \frac{c}{100}$
    d. $\frac{c}{3.59} = \frac{25}{100}$

19. A recipe serves four people and calls for $1\frac{1}{2}$ cups of broth. If you want to serve six people, how much broth do you need?
    a. 2 cups
    b. $2\frac{1}{4}$ cups
    c. $2\frac{1}{3}$ cups
    d. $2\frac{1}{2}$ cups

20. For dinner, Louisa is making stuffed green peppers for her guests. She plans to serve herself and each of her 5 guests 2 green peppers each. The recipe calls for 1 cup of rice for 3 green peppers. How many cups of rice will Louisa need?
    a. 2 cups
    b. 4 cups
    c. 6 cups
    d. 12 cups
    e. 36 cups

21. It takes a typist 0.75 seconds to type one word. At this rate, how many words can be typed in 60 seconds?

   a. 4.5

   b. 8

   c. 45

   d. 80

22. Mrs. Hammond's class went to visit a petting zoo. The ratio of students to animals was 5 to 3. Which proportion will give s, the number of students if there were 18 animals?

   a. $\frac{5}{3} = \frac{s}{18}$

   b. $\frac{3}{s} = \frac{18}{5}$

   c. $\frac{5}{3} = \frac{18}{s}$

   d. $\frac{3}{18} = \frac{s}{5}$

   e. $\frac{5}{18} = \frac{s}{3}$

23. 250 pieces of foil are in a stack that is half an inch tall. How thick is each piece?

   a. .25 in

   b. .125 in

   c. .02 in

   d. .002 in

24. The height of the Statue of Liberty from foundation to torch is 305 feet 1 inch. Webster's American Mini-Golf has a 1:60 scale model of the statue. Approximately how tall is the scale model?

   a. 5 inches

   b. 5 feet 1 inch

   c. 6 feet 5 inches

   d. 18,305 feet

25. The table below shows the numbers of male and female students involved in several activities. Which activity has the lowest ratio of males to females?

Activity	Male	Female
Drama	11	13
Journalism	12	10
Science Club	9	11
Debate	12	15

   a. Drama

   b. Journalism

   c. Science Club

   d. Debate

26. If the average woman burns 8.2 calories per minute while riding a bicycle, how many calories will she burn if she rides for 35 minutes?

    a. 286

    b. 287

    c. 387

    d. 980

27. If 100 staples in a stick measure 2″ long, how thick is 1 staple?

    a. .2 in

    b. .02 in

    c. .4 in

    d. .04 in

28. One afternoon, Bonnie read 14 pages of her book in 20 minutes. If she continued at the same rate, which equation could be used to find p, the total number of pages Bonnie read in 50 minutes?

    a. $\frac{14}{50} = \frac{20}{p}$

    b. $\frac{14}{p} = \frac{50}{20}$

    c. $\frac{p}{14} = \frac{14}{50}$

    d. $\frac{14}{20} = \frac{p}{50}$

    e. $\frac{14}{20} = \frac{50}{p}$

29. The student enrollment at Lafayette Technical Institute is given below in the form of a three-dimensional pie chart in which students are grouped according to their course of study. What is the ratio of programming students to multimedia students?

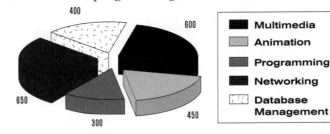

    a. 2:1

    b. 1:2

    c. 4:6

    d. 3:4

30. A recipe calls for $\frac{1}{2}$ tsp of coriander and serves 4 people. If Heather needs to cook for 24 people, how much coriander does she need?

    a. 3 tsp

    b. $3\frac{1}{2}$ tsp

    c. 4 tsp

    d. 6 tsp

31. Suppose that in the question above, Heather needs to prepare enough food for 26 people. How much coriander should she add?

    a. $3\frac{1}{4}$ tsp

    b. $3\frac{1}{2}$ tsp

    c. $4\frac{3}{4}$ tsp

    d. $6\frac{1}{4}$ tsp

ADVANCED

32. Greg completes $\frac{3}{4}$ of his data entry assignment in 45 minutes. How long, in *hours*, does it take him to complete the whole assignment?

    a. 1 hr

    b. 1 hr 20 min

    c. $1\frac{1}{2}$ hr

    d. $1\frac{3}{4}$ hr

33. Michael went to Spain last summer, where the currency is the peseta. While he was there, he bought a hat for 19,237 pesetas. If 1 U.S. dollar is equal to 4,750 pesetas, which is the best estimate of how much the hat cost in U.S. dollars?

    a. $0.30

    b. $3.00

    c. $4.00

    d. $16.00

    e. $40.00

34. This is a picture of Albert under a palm tree. Albert is really 68″ tall, but on the picture he is only $\frac{3}{4}$″ tall. The tree is $5\frac{1}{4}$″ tall in the picture. How many inches tall is the actual palm tree?

   a. 544″

   b. 476″

   c. 9.7″

   d. 0.06″

35. In Mrs. Sam's first grade class, the ratio of boys to girls is 3 to 4. There are 28 students total. How many are girls?

   a. 12

   b. 20

   c. 16

   d. 4

36. A model statue is $4\frac{1}{2}$″ tall. If it was built to scale, such that $\frac{1}{2}$ inch represents 1 foot, which proportion below can be used to solve for the height (in feet) of the actual statue?

   a. $\dfrac{1}{\frac{1}{2}} = \dfrac{4\frac{1}{2}}{height}$

   b. $\dfrac{\frac{1}{2}}{1} = \dfrac{height}{4\frac{1}{2}}$

   c. $\dfrac{\frac{1}{2}}{1} = \dfrac{12}{height}$

   d. $\dfrac{\frac{1}{2}}{1} = \dfrac{4\frac{1}{2}}{height}$

37. White flour and whole wheat flour are mixed together in a ratio of 5 parts white flour to 1 part whole wheat flour. How many pounds of white flour are in 48 pounds of this mixture?

   a. 8 pounds

   b. 9.6 pounds

   c. 20 pounds

   d. 40 pounds

   e. 42 pounds

38. The sum of p and q is twice their difference. What is the ratio of p to q?

   a. 1:1

   b. 1:2

   c. 2:1

   d. 1:3

   e. 3:1

39. If colored paper clips cost $1.25 per 100 count, which proportion can be used to calculate the amount of money (in *dollars*) that 556 paper clips would represent?

   a. $\frac{125}{100} = \frac{x}{556}$

   b. $\frac{100}{125} = \frac{x}{556}$

   c. $\frac{1.25}{100} = \frac{x}{556}$

   d. $\frac{100}{1.25} = \frac{x}{556}$

40. The number of red blood corpuscles in one cubic millimeter is about 5,000,000, and the number of white blood corpuscles in one cubic millimeter is about 8,000. What, then, is the ratio of white blood corpuscles to red blood corpuscles?

   a. 1:625

   b. 1:40

   c. 4:10

   d. 5:1,250

41. At a certain school, half the students are female and one-twelfth of the students are from outside the state. What proportion of the students would you expect to be females from outside the state?

   a. $\frac{1}{12}$

   b. $\frac{1}{24}$

   c. $\frac{1}{6}$

   d. $\frac{1}{3}$

42. Ralph can hike 1.3 miles in 45 minutes. Which equation could be used to find d, the distance in miles that Ralph can hike in 3 hours?

   a. $\frac{d}{3} = \frac{0.75}{1.3}$

   b. $\frac{1.3}{0.75} = \frac{d}{3}$

   c. $\frac{0.75}{d} = \frac{3}{1.3}$

   d. $\frac{0.75}{3} = \frac{d}{1.3}$

   e. $\frac{1.3}{0.75} = \frac{3}{d}$

43. Per 1,000,000 molecules of air there are 78,083 molecules of nitrogen, 20,945 molecules of oxygen, and 35 molecules of carbon dioxide. What is the ratio of carbon dioxide to oxygen?
    a. 20,945:35
    b. 35:78,083
    c. 7:4,189
    d. 945:8,083

44. Use the chart below to calculate the ratio of wet sand to pumice (in pounds per cubic feet).

Substance	Weight (lbs/ft^3)
Pumice	40
Saltpeter	75
Sand, dry	101
Sand, wet	120

    a. 10:4
    b. 1:3
    c. 4:10
    d. 3:1

45. In a study group, the ratio of men to women is 3:4. If there are 21 people in the group, how many men are there?
    a. 3
    b. 6
    c. 9
    d. 12

46. There was a 5:1 ratio of men to women in a karate class. Then, seven women joined the class resulting in the current 3:2 male to female ratio. What is the total number of *people* currently enrolled in the karate class?
    a. 3
    b. 10
    c. 18
    d. 25

47. The ratio of math majors to English majors to chemistry majors is 3:2:1. If there are 12,000 students attaining these majors, how many are English students?
    a. 2,000
    b. 3,000
    c. 4,000
    d. 5,000

13

Percents, Simple Interest, and Compound Interest

P*ercents* and interest are found everywhere. Whether you're spending or saving, you will need to know your percentages and interest rates to manage money.

▶ WHAT IS A PERCENT?

Percents are a way of creating a special ratio. When you see a number followed by a percent symbol, or %, you just write a ratio comparing that number to 100. For example, $40\% = \frac{40}{100}$, $3\% = \frac{3}{100}$, $500\% = \frac{500}{100}$, and so forth.

You can express a percent in two other ways: as a fraction (just put the number over 100), or as a decimal (move the decimal point 2 places to the left). These two options are summarized below:

Let's look at 25%. Put 25 over 100 to get $\frac{25}{100}$. Notice that $\frac{25}{100}$ reduces to $\frac{1}{4}$. It is good to be familiar with some of the common fraction and decimal equivalents of percentages. Some are listed in the chart below.

Percent	Fraction	Decimal
25%	$\frac{1}{4}$	.25
50%	$\frac{1}{2}$	.50
75%	$\frac{3}{4}$	.75

Fill in the chart below. More than one response may be correct.

When I see . . .	I will write . . .
50%	$\frac{1}{2}$
75%	
80%	
100%	
150%	
500%	

Taking the Percent of a Number

Recall that " **of**" means "**multiply**." When you take the percent of a number, you *multiply*.

For example, 25% of 100 means 25% × 100, or $\frac{25}{100}$ × 100, which is just $\frac{1}{4}$ × 100, or 25.

"I Will Save" versus "I Will Pay"

If you are buying an item on sale, you may see, for instance, a sign that says "40% off." Let's say the item was initially $50. You can find out the new price by thinking "I will take 40% off of the price of this item."

$$40\% \text{ of } \$50$$
$$.40 \times 50$$
$$= \$20 \text{ off}$$

Then you would subtract the $20 from the original price:

$$\$50 - \$20 \text{ discount} = \$30 \text{ sale price.}$$

Or, you can use a shortcut. If you are saving 40% off of the original price then you are spending 60% of the original price. When you see the item for 40% off, you can think "I will pay 60% of the original price." Notice that this calculation is quicker:

$$60\% \text{ of } \$50$$
$$.60 \times \$50$$
$$= \$30$$

Here we were discussing sales, so we were thinking in terms of "**I will save**" versus "**I will pay**." You can use this line of thinking in other situations as well. For example, if a container is 25% (or $\frac{1}{4}$ full), then it is 75% (or $\frac{3}{4}$ empty).

Example: Of the 14 million species on Earth, at least 50% live in tropical rainforests. Which of the following statements is true?
    a. 70,000,000 species or more live in the tropical rainforests.
    b. 7,000,000 species or more live in the tropical rainforests.
    c. 70,000 species or more live in the tropical rainforests.
    d. 7,000 species or more live in the tropical rainforests.
    Because 50% = $\frac{1}{2}$, just take $\frac{1}{2}$ of the 14 million. $\frac{1}{2}$ × 14 million = 7 million. You can express 7 million as 7,000,000. Thus, choice **b** is correct.

Percent of a Percent

When you take the percent of a percent, you just multiply. For example if you wanted to know what 20% of 50% of 500 was equal to, you multiply:

$$20\% \text{ of } 50\% \text{ of } 500$$
$$.20 \text{ of } .50 \text{ of } 500$$
$$.20 \times .50 \times 500$$
$$= 50$$

Percent Proportion

You can set up a simple proportion when calculating percents. Let's say Noah scored an $\frac{18}{25}$ on a quiz. What would that be out of 100? Just set up a proportion:

His score out of 25 → $\frac{18}{25} = \frac{?}{100}$ ← His score out of 100

Cross multiply to get 18 × 100 = 25 × ?, or 1800 = 25 × ?. Dividing both sides by 25, we get 72. Thus, your score is equivalent to $\frac{72}{100}$, or 72%.

Example: If you wash the dishes with the tap water running, you will use about 30 gallons of water. Alternatively, if you wash and rinse the dishes in standing water, you will use about 5 gallons of water. What percent of the amount of water required if the tap was running does this alternate method represent?

    a. $83\frac{1}{3}\%$

    b. 70%

    c. 50%

    d. $16\frac{2}{3}\%$

amount used out of 30 → $\frac{5}{30} = \frac{?}{100}$ ← Amount out of 100

First, we cross multiply to get 5 × 100 = 30 × ?, or 500 = 30 × ?. Dividing both sides by 30, we get $16\frac{2}{3}$. Thus, the answer is $16\frac{2}{3}\%$, choice **d**.

Integrate

Math and Economics
Take a field trip to the local shopping mall and do some comparison pricing with percents. Look for the same item at two or more stores, and determine which store has the better buy. Calculate what it means if a store is having a "50% off sale, plus an extra 10%." What percent of the original cost are you paying?

Unknown Percent

When you see the phrase "four percent," how do you express this mathematically? That's right, you write $\frac{4}{100}$.

When you see the phrase "twenty-three percent," how do you express this mathematically? $\frac{23}{100}$.

When you see the phrase "what percent," how do you express this mathematically? You just put a "?" over 100.

"What percent" means: $\frac{?}{100}$

So, just as 4% was $\frac{4}{100}$, "what percent" means $\frac{?}{100}$.

For example, what percent of 250 is 30?

- "What percent" means $\frac{?}{100}$
- "of 250" means $\times\ 250$
- "is 30" means $= 30$

Thus:

$$\frac{?}{100} \times 250 = 30$$

Percent Change, Percent Increase, and Percent Decrease

Any situation involving **percent change, percent increase**, or **percent decrease** can be solved with the formula below.

Your change out of initial → $\frac{change}{initial} = \frac{?}{100}$ ← Your change out of 100

What we put into this formula:

- The "**change**" is just the **change in value**. If something was $17 and now it is $10, the change is $7.
- The "**initial**" is the **initial value**. If something was $17 and now it is $10, the initial value is $17.

Placing the **change** over the **initial** creates a ratio of the *change in value* to the *initial value*. (The ratio is $\frac{change}{initial}$.) This is the premise of any percent change, percent increase, or percent decrease question. Once you know the ratio of the change to the initial, you can figure out how much of a change out of 100 this is equivalent to.

Example: In 1973, the average house was 1600 ft^2. In 2000, the average house was 2000 ft^2. What is the percent increase in square feet from 1973 to 2000?
  a. 15%
  b. 20%
  c. 25%
  d. 50%

$$\frac{change}{initial} = \frac{?}{100}$$

$$\frac{400}{1600} = \frac{?}{100}$$

$$\frac{4}{16} = \frac{?}{100}$$

Cross multiplying, you get $4 \times 100 = 16 \times ?$, or $400 = 16 \times ?$. Dividing both sides by 16, you get $? = 25$. If $? = 25$, then $\frac{?}{100}$ equals $\frac{25}{100}$, or a 25% increase. Thus, choice **c** is correct.

Successive Percent Changes

When you have a situation where there is a percent increase, followed by a percent decrease, followed by another percent decrease, be forewarned:

There Are No Shortcuts When Dealing with Successive Percent Changes!

What you think may be a shortcut will ultimately result in a wrong answer.

Resources Around You

Calculate the percent decrease when making ShrinkyDinks™. First, measure your drawing and write down the calculation. Next, measure the ShrinkyDink™ after it has cooled. Finally, calculate the percent decrease.

To experiment with taking successive percent increase or decrease draw a 10 cm by 10 cm square on a piece of paper. Photocopy the square while the machine is set to a 50% reduction. Next, make a photocopy of the new square with enlargement set to 80%.

square → smaller square → final square

–50% +80%

Some would see a 50% decrease followed by an 80% increase and would take a 30% increase. Is this true? Photocopy the original 10 cm × 10 cm square with a 30% enlargement on. Did you get the same result?

▶ SIMPLE INTEREST

You calculate simple interest with a simple formula:

Interest = Principal × Rate × Time

What we put into the $I = PRT$ formula:

- The **interest** is the money you make on top of your initial investment.
- The **principal** is your initial investment. In other words, it is the amount of money you started with.
- The **rate** at which you earn money is expressed as a percent. You may earn money at a rate of 3%. This means you would put $R = 3\%$, or better yet, $R = .03$ into the $I = PRT$ formula.
- The amount of **time** that your investment earns money is always expressed in years. Make sure you convert the time into years if it isn't given in years.

For example, If the rate of interest is 20% a year, what will the interest be on a $6,000 investment for 2 years?

1. Express the percent as a decimal (or fraction). Thus, $R = 20\% = .20$.
2. Make sure that time is in years.
3. Use the formula: $I = PRT$

$$I = \$6000 \times .20 \times 2$$
$$= \$2400$$

Dive into the Web

Want more practice with interest and percentages? The Mint (www. themint.org) teaches middle and high schoolers about the mathematics of money through a collection of games, puzzles, and online activities. Kids can learn practical skills like making a budget and get information on saving and paying for college; a glossary helps them become familiar with financial terms. Other topics include starting a small business, government spending, and building credit. Most activities are interactive and don't require parental assistance, but the site does also provide four detailed lesson plans for use at home.

▶ COMPOUND INTEREST

Sometimes you earn interest on your interest! For example, if you put money into an account that pays 5% interest compounded annually, 5% of your principal is added to your account after the first year. You would then have a new (and larger) principal that earns interest for the second year.

Terms to know:

- **compounded annually** means interest is paid each year
- **compounded semiannually** means interest is paid 2 times a year
- **compounded quarterly** means interest is paid 4 times a year
- **compounded monthly** means interest is paid every month
- **compounded daily** means interest is paid every day

Example: You open a savings account that pays 3% interest semiannually. If you put in $1,000 initially, how much do you have after two years?

   a. $1,610.36

   b. $1,061.36

   c. $1,060.00

   d. $1,006.00

After half a year, the $1,000 principal above would earn $I = PRT$, or $I = 1,000 \times .03 \times \frac{1}{2} = \$15$. Now the account has $1,015.

In another half year you earn $I = PRT = 1,015 \times .03 \times \frac{1}{2} = 15.225$, and you would have $1,030.225. Notice that one year is up.

In another half year you earn $I = PRT = 1,030.225 \times .03 \times \frac{1}{2} = 15.453375$, and you would have $1,045.6784.

In another half year you earn $I = PRT = 1,045.6784 \times .03 \times \frac{1}{2} = 15.685176$, and you would have $1,061.36. The two years are up. We always round to the nearest cent, so you would have $1,061.36, choice **b**.

Advanced Technique

Here is the compound interest formula:

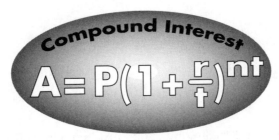

What we put into the $A = P(1 + \frac{r}{n})^{nt}$ formula:

- A is the total amount
- P is the original principal
- r is the rate
- n is the number of yearly compounds
- t is time (in years)

So, let's look at the above example again—this time using the formula. You open a savings account that pays 3% interest semiannually. If you put in $1,000 initially, how much do you have after 2 years?

We use $A = P(1 + \frac{r}{n})^{nt}$, and we substitute in the following values:

$P = 1,000$

$r = 3\%$, or .03

$n = 2$ (compounded semiannually means twice a year)

$t = 2$

$A = P(1 + \frac{r}{n})^{nt} = 1,000(1 + \frac{.03}{2})^{2 \cdot 2}$

$= 1,000(1 + .015)^4$

$= 1,000(1.015)^4$

$= 1,000(1.06)$

$= 1,061.3\overline{6}$

$= 1,061.37$

Always round money to the nearest cent. Thus, you would have $1,061.37.

Resources Around You

Use your middle schooler's savings bank statement to find out how the interest in the account is being compounded. Compare the interest earned on the balance if it is compounded daily, as opposed to annually or semiannually.

Algebraic Percents

Let's say that Margaret buys a printer for D dollars and gets a 20% discount. How do you represent her cost mathematically?

Well, if Margaret is getting a 20% discount, she must be paying 80% of the original price. What is the original price? D. So she is paying 80% of D. This is just $.8 \times D$, or $.8D$.

What if she was buying three items that cost D, E, and F dollars each, and she was getting the same 20% discount on her entire order?

Well, without the discount, her cost would be $(D + E + F)$.

non-discounted $= (D + E + F)$

▶ PRACTICE

The questions in this section have been divided into three categories: Basic, Intermediate, and Advanced. Questions 1–16 are Basic, questions 17–32 are Intermediate, and questions 33–49 are Advance. An answer key with explanations can be found in Appendix C.

BASIC

1. 0.97 is equal to
   a. 97 percent
   b. 9.7 percent
   c. 0.97 percent
   d. 0.097 percent

2. 62.5 percent is equal to
   a. $\frac{1}{16}$
   b. $\frac{5}{8}$
   c. $6\frac{1}{4}$
   d. $6\frac{2}{5}$

3. Which of the following is 14% of 232?
   a. 3.248
   b. 32.48
   c. 16.57
   d. 165.7

4. What is 44% of 5?
   a. 0.22
   b. 2.2
   c. 2.02
   d. 2.002

5. Firefighter Annunziata earns $26,000 a year. If he receives a 4.5% salary increase, how much will he earn?
   a. $26,450
   b. $27,170
   c. $27,260
   d. $29,200

It's A Fact

Multiplying by 1.045, instead of just 0.045, will calculate the total money earned in one step instead of having to do two steps.

6. Change 35% into a decimal.
   a. 3.5
   b. .35
   c. 35.0
   d. .035

7. Change 42% to a fraction.
   a. $\frac{1}{42}$
   b. $\frac{1}{4.2}$
   c. $\frac{21}{50}$
   d. $\frac{4.2}{100}$

8. Change 0.525 to a percent.
   a. 525%
   b. 5.25%
   c. 0.525%
   d. 52.5%

9. A merchant buys a product for $12.20 and then marks it up 35% to sell it. What is the selling price of the item?
   a. $4.27
   b. $7.93
   c. $16.47
   d. $20.13

10. At the city park, 32% of the trees are oaks. If there are 400 trees in the park, how many trees are NOT oaks?
    a. 128
    b. 272
    c. 278
    d. 312

11. Which symbol belongs in the box below?

12.5% $\boxed{}$ $\frac{3}{8}$

   a. <

   b. >

   c. =

   d. ≥

12. 400% of 30 is

   a. 1.2

   b. 12

   c. 120

   d. 1200

13. Using the chart below, which salespeople, when combined, sold 85% of the total?

SALES FOR 2001

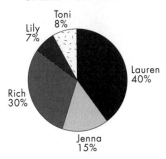

   a. Toni, Rich, and Jenna

   b. Rich, Lily, and Lauren

   c. Lauren, Jenna, and Rich

   d. Lily, Toni, and Rich

14. Which expression below can be used to solve the following statement:

20% of $325.

   a. 2 × 325

   b. .02 × 325

   c. 2 × .10(325)

   d. 325 − .2(325)

15. Taking 150% of a number is the same as

   a. multiplying the number by 15.

   b. increasing the number by 50%.

   c. adding 1.5 times the number to itself.

   d. decreasing the number by .5 times that number.

16. The pie chart below shows Siobhan's monthly expenses.

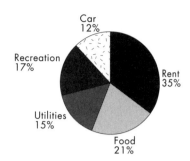

Which of these expenses combined represent half of her total expenses?
- **a.** Rent and Car
- **b.** Car, Utilities, and Recreation
- **c.** Car, Food, and Recreation
- **d.** Food and Rent

INTERMEDIATE

17. What percentage of 50 is 12?
- **a.** 4 percent
- **b.** 14 percent
- **c.** 24 percent
- **d.** 34 percent

18. What is $7\frac{1}{5}\%$ of 465 rounded to the nearest tenth?
- **a.** 32.5
- **b.** 33
- **c.** 33.5
- **d.** 34

19. 33 is 12% of which of the following?
- **a.** 3,960
- **b.** 396
- **c.** 275
- **d.** 2,750

20. 75 people were invited to the Farthings' wedding. All but 9 were able to attend. What percent couldn't come?
- **a.** 8.33%
- **b.** 7.5%
- **c.** 12%
- **d.** 9%

21. Which of the following expressions can be used to calculate 14% of 232?

    a. 14×232

    b. $.14 \times 232$

    c. $\frac{14}{100} \times 232$

    d. **b** and **c**

22. Swimming Pool World pledged 3.2% of their sales for the second week of May. Below is their sales chart for May.

May Sales	
Week 1	$5,895
Week 2	$73,021
Week 3	$54,702
Week 4	$67,891

How much did Swimming Pool World donate to the children's hospital?

    a. $2,336.67

    b. $3,651.05

    c. $23,366.72

    d. $36,510.50

23. At a President's Day sale, Lisa chose a sweater that was on sale for $16.20. The original price of the sweater was $36.00. What percent did Lisa save?

    a. 40%

    b. 45%

    c. 55%

    d. 60%

24. For her summer job, Karima operates a drink stand at the zoo. The graph below shows the types of drinks she sells on a typical day.

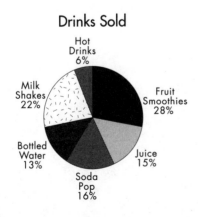

If Karima sells 325 drinks one day, how many fruit smoothies does she sell?
- **a.** 11
- **b.** 91
- **c.** 253
- **d.** 8,624

25. Given that 7% of men and 1% of women are born colorblind, use the information in the chart below to predict how many people in Mastic are colorblind.

Population of Mastic

Men	Women
4,700	4,900

- **a.** 329
- **b.** 378
- **c.** 567
- **d.** 768

26. If 30% of a given number is 600, what is 50% of that number?
- **a.** 1,500
- **b.** 1,000
- **c.** 800
- **d.** 300

27. Which proportion can be used to solve for the percent of a year that 180 days is equivalent to?
- **a.** $\frac{180}{365} = \frac{X}{100}$
- **b.** $\frac{180}{365} = \frac{X}{365}$
- **c.** $\frac{180}{100} = \frac{X}{365}$
- **d.** $\frac{365}{180} = \frac{X}{100}$

28. Change $12\frac{1}{2}\%$ to a fraction.
- **a.** $\frac{1}{8}$
- **b.** $\frac{1}{12.5}$
- **c.** $\frac{12}{100}$
- **d.** $\frac{25}{1}$

29. A school purchases four televisions. If they receive a discount of 15% of the list price of $300 per television, how much money do they save?

    a. $45

    b. $60

    c. $90

    d. $180

30. A dealer buys a car from the manufacturer for $13,000. If the dealer wants to earn a profit of 20% based on the cost, at what price should he sell the car?

    a. $16,250

    b. $15,600

    c. $15,200

    d. $10,833

    e. none of the above

31. 20% of Ms. Nakata's class is left-handed. If there are 5 left-handed students in Ms. Nakata's class, how many students are there in the class?

    a. 1

    b. 20

    c. 25

    d. 40

32. 20% of what number is equal to 50% of 200?

    a. 20

    b. 50

    c. 200

    d. 500

ADVANCED

33. If Harry deposits $8,000 in an account with a yearly interest rate of 5%, and leaves the money in the account for 6 years, how much interest will his money earn? (Use $I = PRT$).

    a. $2,400

    b. $2,800

    c. $3,200

    d. $4,800

34. Use the chart below to calculate the percent increase in profits made on "Charge Card Interest" from 1999 to 2001.

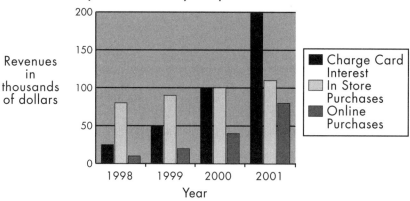

Yearly Profits for Perry's Department Stores

a. 3%

b. 50%

c. 150%

d. 300%

35. Of 9,125 patients treated in a certain emergency room in one year, 72% were male. Among the males, 3 out of 5 were under age 25. How many of the emergency room patients were males age 25 or older?

a. 2,628

b. 3,942

c. 5,475

d. 6,570

36. Yesterday, 220 people dined at Jimmy's Italian Restaurant. Of those, 60% ordered the pasta special. How many people did NOT order the pasta special?

a. 36

b. 55

c. 88

d. 132

37. A certain number when added to 50% of itself is 27. What is the number?

a. 7

b. 9

c. 11

d. 18

38. If 400 compact discs were sold altogether, which expression can be used to calculate the number of country music compact discs sold?

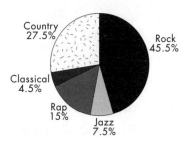

Country 27.5%
Rock 45.5%
Classical 4.5%
Rap 15%
Jazz 7.5%

a. $45.5 \times \frac{400}{100}$

b. $.275 \times \frac{400}{100}$

c. $\frac{400}{45.5} \times 100$

d. $\frac{27.5}{100} \times 400$

39. A small business is looking to set up a network of computers in its office. Four companies gave the original price quotes indicated in the chart below, followed by a second price quote at a later date. Based on the second price quote, which company is offering the lowest price?

	Original Quote	Second Quote
K Tech	$12,000	decrease original quote by $\frac{1}{4}$
L Tech	$13,400	75% of original quote
M Tech	$11,500	less 15% from original quote
N Tech	$15,000	$\frac{7}{8}$ of original offer

a. K Tech
b. L Tech
c. M Tech
d. N Tech

40. There are 92 women in Professor Halpern's *Intro to Anthropology* class. This is 40% of all the students. What is the total number of students?

a. 300
b. 192
c. 230
d. 92

41. If the volume in a water tank, V, is increased by 25%, which of the following expressions represents the new volume of water?

a. $V + \frac{1}{4}V$

b. $1.25V$

c. $V + .25V$

d. all of the above

42. A navy blue jacket costs $200 and a gray jacket costs $400. If the cost of the navy blue jacket increases by 10%, and the cost of the gray jacket decreases by 5%, what will be the sum of their costs?

a. $600

b. $610

c. $620

d. $630

43. Amelia has $12.50 to spend on spiral notebooks. Each notebook costs $0.80, and sales tax is 8%. What is the maximum amount of notebooks she can purchase?

a. 12

b. 14

c. 14.46

d. 15

44. A five-gallon tank is completely filled with a solution of 50% water and 50% alcohol. Half of the tank is drained and 2 gallons of water are added. How much water is in the resulting mixture?

a. 2.5 gallons

b. 3.25 gallons

c. 3.5 gallons

d. 4.5 gallons

45. How much does $500 grow to if it is compounded semiannually for one year at 8% interest?

a. $540.80

b. $583.70

c. $586.93

d. $680.24

46. Natasha bought a set of golf clubs for $340. If she sold them for $255, what was her percent loss?

a. 75%

b. 65%

c. 35%

d. 25%

47. Sheila has a hard time waking up to an alarm. In one month, she only woke up to her alarm 12 of the 27 mornings that it went off. Which expression could be used to find the percent of mornings that Sheila woke up to her alarm?

a. $\frac{(12)(100)}{(12 + 27)}$

b. $\frac{(27)(100)}{12}$

c. $\frac{(27 - 12)(100)}{27}$

d. $\frac{(12)(100)}{27}$

48. Use the chart below to calculate the percent increase in oil cost from 1997 to 1998.

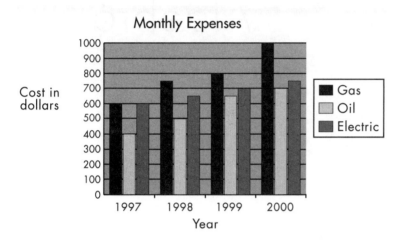

a. 25%

b. 50%

c. 75%

d. 100%

49. If a school buys three computers at a, b, and c dollars each, and the school gets a discount of 10%, which expression would determine the average price paid by the school?

a. $0.9 \times \frac{a + b + c}{3}$

b. $\frac{(a + b + c)}{0.9}$

c. $(a + b + c) \times 0.9$

d. $\frac{a + b + c}{3}$

14

Algebra

There are many faces of algebra. You can interpret a sentence and translate it into algebra. You can take an algebraic expression and turn it into words. You may get a test question that says to "Solve for *x*," or a "simplify the equation" question. More advanced questions require simultaneous equations. Read on to find out about algebra for the middle school years.

▶ VARIABLES

Variables are used to denote the unknown numbers in mathematic equations and expressions. For example, it is common for *x* to represent a number as in $x + 3 = 5$. You can think of this expression as *"Some number plus three equals five."* You should always keep in mind that variables must obey the same rules as numbers, because they are in fact numbers.

▶ ENGLISH TO EQUATION

In English, "Felice is 3 years older than Samantha." This can be written mathematically as:

- ◆ Felice is $F =$
- ◆ 3 years older than $+ 3$
- ◆ Samantha S

We can put this all together: $F = S + 3$.

Let's say Felice is 3 years younger than Eva. How can this be expressed mathematically?

- ◆ Felice is $F =$
- ◆ 3 years less than -3
- ◆ Eva E

Put this all together: $F = E - 3$. This means, take Eva's age and subtract 3 years, to get Felice's age.

Let's say that there is 1 more girl. Gabrielle is twice as old as Samantha. How can this be expressed?

- ◆ Gabrielle is $G =$
- ◆ twice as old as $S \times 2$

Put this all together to get $G = S \times 2$, or $G = 2S$.

Example: How can you represent the following phrase mathematically?

   Patrick has 3 fewer CDs than Danny.

   a. $D = P - 3$
   b. $D = 3 - P$
   c. $P = 3 + D$
   d. $P = D - 3$

3 fewer CDs than Danny would be $D - 3$. If Patrick has 3 fewer CDS than Danny, Patrick has $P = D - 3$, choice **d**.

It's A Fact!

The word *algebra* dates from about 825 A.D. It comes from the Arabic word *al-jebr*, meaning "the reunion of broken parts."

▶ SUBSTITUTION

Sometimes algebra is just a matter of sticking, or "substituting," numbers in for the right variables. For example, you are told that $a = b + c$. If $b = 5$ and $c = 7$, what is the value of a? You simply substitute a 5 for b and a 7 for c to get:

$$a = 5 + 7$$
$$= 12$$

Example: What is the value of $\frac{b^2 + b}{a}$ when $b = 1$ and $a = 2$?

   a. $\frac{1}{2}$

   b. 1

   c. $1\frac{1}{2}$

   d. 2

Here we put 1 in for each b we see in the equation. We put 2 in for the a in the denominator:

$$\frac{b^2 + b}{a} = \frac{1^2 + 1}{2} = \frac{1 + 1}{2} = \frac{2}{2} = 1$$

Thus, the answer is **b**.

Simplifying Equations

One way to simplify equations is to combine like terms. What does this mean? $3x$, $4x$, and $5x$ are considered like terms because they all involve x. Here, the 3, 4, and 5 are called **coefficients** of the x term. If you are trying to simplify $3x + 4x + 5x$, just add the coefficients to get $12x$.

Sometimes you may see a mixture of different types of terms. Suppose you have $2x + 4x^2 + 3x$. Here you can combine the x terms together: $(2x + 3x) + 4x^2 = 5x + 4x^2$.

Example: Simplify the expression $x + 3x + 5 - 2$.

   a. $4x - 3$

   b. $4x + 3$

   c. $2x - 3$

   d. $2x + 3$

Here you can combine the x and the $3x$. You can also combine the 5 and the −2. You get $4x + 3$, which is choice **b**.

Sometimes you can simplify an equation by multiplying the entire equation by a certain number. This is mathematically acceptable because we are just generating an equivalent multiple of the equation. Suppose you had $2x = 2$. (Here, it is easy to see that $x = 1$.) But let's take a multiple of

$2x = 2$. You could write $4x = 4$, $8x = 8$, $16x = 16$, and so forth. Our x would still be 1. Let's look at a situation where multiplying the entire equation by a certain number would come in handy.

For example, let's look at:

$$\tfrac{1}{4}x + \tfrac{1}{6} = \tfrac{2}{3}$$

To get rid of the fractions, you can multiply the *entire equation* by 12:

$$12(\tfrac{1}{4}x + \tfrac{1}{6} = \tfrac{2}{3})$$

Distribute the 12 to get:

$$12 \times \tfrac{1}{4}x + 12 \times \tfrac{1}{6} = 12 \times \tfrac{2}{3}$$
$$3x + 2 = 8$$

This equation is much simpler than the one you started with.

Solve For x

When you want to solve for x, you want to get your x all by itself. This is called "**isolating the variable**." In order to preserve the equality of any equation at hand, you need to be sure that you are doing the same thing to both sides of the equation. This means that you should perform corresponding operations on both sides of the equal sign. If you subtract 2 from the left side, you need to subtract 2 from the right side. If you divide the left side by 3, you must divide the right side by 3.

Given: $2x + 7 = 15$, solve for x.

Here is $2x + 7 = 15$. In order to get x by itself you will first get rid of the 7. This means you will subtract 7 from both sides.

$$\begin{array}{rcl} 2x + 7 &=& 15 \\ -7 & & -7 \\ \hline 2x &=& 8 \end{array}$$

Next, you divide both sides by 2 in order to get x by itself:

$$\tfrac{2x}{2} = \tfrac{8}{2}$$
$$x = 4$$

Carschooling® Tricks

Use these new algebra skills to work out practical problems while driving. For example, have your child figure out the gas mileage you've been getting by writing a simple equation with a variable. If you have traveled 66.75 miles on 2.5 gallons of gas, your child's equation would look like this:

$$m \text{ (mileage)} = \frac{distance}{gas} \text{ or } m = \frac{66.75}{2.5} = 26.7 \text{ miles per gallon.}$$

He can also create algebraic equations to
- **figure out the price of gasoline.**
- **find the distance to your destination.**
- **calculate how long it will take you to get there.**

Example: Solve for x.

Given $7x + 2 = 5x + 14$, what is the value of x?

   a.   4
   b.   6
   c.   8
   d.   10

The first thing you want to do is isolate your variable. This means you want to combine your x terms on one side of the equation, and your numbers on the other side of the equation. Next you will subtract $5x$ from both sides in order to combine x terms:

$$
\begin{array}{rcl}
7x + 2 & = & 5x + 14 \\
-5x & & -5x \\
\hline
2x + 2 & = & 14
\end{array}
$$

Now you will subtract 2 from both sides in order to isolate the x term.

$$
\begin{array}{rcl}
2x + 2 & = & 14 \\
-2 & & -2 \\
\hline
2x & = & 12
\end{array}
$$

Finally, divide both sides by 2 to get $x = 6$, or choice **b**.

Integrate

Math and History

Born in the 4th century, Hypatia of Alexandria was the daughter of Theon, considered to be one of the most educated men in Alexandria, Egypt. Theon raised Hypatia in a world of education, and she is recognized as a mathematician, scientist, and philosopher.

Taught by her scholarly father, Hypatia began to develop an enthusiasm for mathematics and the sciences of astronomy and astrology. Soon, she became expert in these and other areas. Today, she is renowned for her work on the ideas of conic sections, first introduced by Apollonius. She was also a great teacher and orator.

Hypatia's accomplishments are extraordinary, especially for a woman of her era. Philosophers such as Descartes, Newton, and Leibniz considered her a woman of great knowledge and expanded on her groundbreaking work.

To read more about Hypatia and other great female mathematicians, go to Biographies of Women Mathematicians Website: www.scottlan.edu/lriddle/women/hypatia.htm.

Source: Ginny Adair, Biographies of Women Mathematicians Website, Agnes Scott College, 1995

▶ INEQUALITIES

Inequalities contain the greater than, less than, greater than or equal to, or less than or equal to symbols. When you solve the inequalities for *x*, you are figuring out a range of numbers that your unknown is "allowed" to be.

This symbol . . .	Means . . .
>	"Greater than"
≥	"Greater than or equal to"
<	"Less than"
≤	"Less than or equal to"

There is one rule that you need to remember when dealing with inequalities:

When you multiply or divide by a negative number, you need to reverse the sign.

Example: $-5x + 3 > 28$ can also be expressed as

   a. $x < -3\frac{1}{5}$

   b. $x > -3\frac{1}{5}$

   c. $x > -5$

   d. $x < -5$

This type of question is a lot like the "Solve for x" questions that we did above. The goal here is to isolate your x. First we will subtract 3 from both sides.

$$
\begin{array}{r}
-5x + 3 > 28 \\
-3 \quad -3 \\
\hline
-5x \quad\;\; > 25
\end{array}
$$

Now there is one rule that you need to remember when dealing with inequalities: When you multiply or divide by a negative number you need to reverse the sign. So when you divide by -5, you get

$$\frac{-5x}{-5} > \frac{25}{-5}$$

$x < -5$, which is choice **d**.

Dive into the Web

For more activities involving algebra and other math skills, visit SuccessLink (www.successlink.org), sponsored by the Missouri Department of Education. This site features a huge database of lessons and activities submitted by K–12 teachers. The index is searchable by keyword, subject, and grade level, and includes math and many other subjects. Many of the activities connect math with real-life activities like basketball, baking chocolate chip cookies, and balancing a checkbook. While the lessons are designed for traditional classrooms, most should be easy to adapt for use by home-schooling families.

▶ FUNCTION TABLES

Function tables usually portray an x and a y. Usually you are told that there is a relationship between x and y, and that you must figure out exactly what that relationship is.

x	y
0	—
1	3
2	4
3	—
4	6

In the function table above, some of the data was left out. Don't worry about that. You can still figure out what you need to do to our x in order to make it our y. You see that $x = 1$ corresponds to $y = 3$, $x = 2$ corresponds to $y = 4$, and $x = 4$ corresponds to $y = 6$. Did you spot the pattern? The y value is just our x value plus 2.

Example: The table below shows the relationship between 2 variables: x and y. Which answer choice best represents this relationship?

x	y
0	0
1	—
2	6
3	—
4	12

a. $x = 3y$
b. $y = 3x$
c. $y = x^2$
d. $x = y^2$

When x is 0, y is 0. When $x = 2$, $y = 6$. And when $x = 4$, $y = 12$. What is the pattern? y is 3 times x. Thus, **b**, $y = 3x$ is correct.

▶ ALGEBRAIC FORMULAS

Two algebraic formulas that you should be familiar with are:

- $D = R \times T$
- $w \times d = W \times D$

The **Constant Rate Equation,** or $D = R \times T$ means:

$$\text{Distance} = \text{Rate} \times \text{Time}$$

Example: Darcy and Kira are 14 miles apart and they start walking toward each other. If Darcy walks at a constant rate of 3 mph and Kira walks at a constant rate of 4 mph, how long will it take them to meet?

   a. 2 hours

   b. 3 hours

   c. 4 hours

   d. It cannot be determined by the information given.

It is easy to solve this kind of question if you draw a diagram:

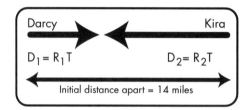

You know that the total distance (14 miles) is equal to $D_1 + D_2$.

$$14 = D_1 + D_2$$

You know $D_1 = R_1 \times T$ and $D_2 = R_2 \times T$, so we can rewrite the above equation as:

$$14 = (R_1 \times T) + (R_2 \times T)$$

We know Darcy walks at 3 mph (this is R_1) and Kira walks at 4 mph (this is R_2), so we put these two rates into the equation:

$$14 = 3T + 4T$$
$$14 = 7T$$

Dividing both sides by 2 yields $T = 2$ hours, choice **a.**

For a **Balanced Fulcrum,** $w \times d = W \times D,$ which means:

$$\text{Weight}_1 \times \text{Distance}_1 = \text{Weight}_2 \times \text{Distance}_2$$

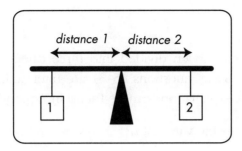

Example: In the figure below, Block A weighs 6 g and Block B weighs 12 g. If the fulcrum is perfectly balanced, how far away from the center is B?

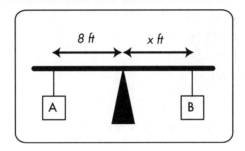

    a. 10 ft

    b. 8 ft

    c. 6 ft

    d. 4 ft

Here we use the formula $wd = WD$. Substituting in the given values, we have $6 \times 8 = 12 \times x$, or $48 = 12x$. We divide both sides by 12 to yield $x = 4$ ft, choice **d**.

Factoring

Sometimes expressions are easier to deal with when you pull out common factors from the terms. For example, if you had $6xy^2 + 3xy$, you could notice that each term is divisible by 3. Each term is also divisible by x. And each term is divisible by y as well. You can "pull out" a $3xy$ from each term to yield $3xy(2y + 1)$. You can check your work by distributing the $3xy$:

$$3xy(2y + 1)$$

$$= 3xy \times 2y + 3xy \times 1$$

$$= 6xy^2 + 3xy$$

► PRACTICE

The questions in this section have been divided into three categories: Basic, Intermediate, and Advanced. Questions 1–14 are Basic, questions 15–31 are Intermediate, and questions 32–57 are Advanced. An answer key with explanations can be found in Appendix C.

1. If $2a + a + 3a = 36$, what is the value of a?
   a. 4
   b. 6
   c. 7.2
   d. 12

2. Which of the following means $5n + 7 = 17$?
   a. 7 more than 5 times a number is 17
   b. 5 more than 7 times a number is 17
   c. 7 less than 5 times a number is 17
   d. 12 times a number is 17

3. What is the value of y when $x = 3$ and $y = 5 + 4x$?
   a. 6
   b. 9
   c. 12
   d. 17

4. Twelve less than four times a number is 20. What is the number?
   a. 2
   b. 4
   c. 6
   d. 8
   e. 28

5. If $8n + 25 = 65$, then n is
   a. 5
   b. 10
   c. 40
   d. 90
   e. 720

6. $(7x^3y^2)^2$
   a. $49x^3y^2$
   b. $49x^5y^4$
   c. $49x^6y^4$
   d. $7x^5y^4$
   e. $14x^6y^4$

7. Solve for x in the following equation: $\frac{1}{3}x + 3 = 8$.

   a. 33
   b. 15
   c. 11
   d. 3
   e. 1

8. The sum of a number and its double is 69. What is the number?

   a. 46.6
   b. 34.5
   c. 23
   d. 20
   e. 13

9. $\frac{x}{4} + \frac{3x}{4} =$

   a. $\frac{1}{2}x$
   b. $\frac{x^3}{4}$
   c. 1
   d. x
   e. $\frac{x}{2}$

10. Solve for x: $3x = 21$

   a. 4
   b. 6
   c. 7
   d. 18
   e. 63

11. Which inequality below is equivalent to $8x - 3 > 29$?

   a. $-4 < x > 4$
   b. $x < 4$
   c. $x > 4$
   d. $-4 < x$

12. Alan is 5 years less than twice Helena's age. If Alan is 27, which equation can be used to solve for Helena's age?

   a. $22 = 2H$
   b. $27 = H - 5$
   c. $22 = 2H + 5$
   d. $27 = 2H - 5$

13. Three more than three times a number is eighteen. What is the number?

    a. 3

    b. 4

    c. 5

    d. 6

14. If $16j + 4 = 28$, what is the value of j?

    a. 1.5

    b. 2

    c. 2.5

    d. 8

15. Which value of x will make this number sentence true? $x + 25 \leq 13$.

    a. −13

    b. −11

    c. 12

    d. 38

16. What is the solution for $6x > 16$?

    a. $x > 22$

    b. $x < 10$

    c. $x > \frac{8}{3}$

    d. $x < \frac{3}{8}$

17. Third grade student Stephanie Wink goes to the school nurse's office, where her temperature is found to be 98 degrees Fahrenheit. What is her temperature in degrees Celsius?
$C = \frac{5}{9}(F - 32)$

    a. 35.8

    b. 36.7

    c. 37.6

    d. 31.1

    e. 22.4

18. The sum of $x^2 - 3x + 6$ and $2x^2 - 4$ is

    a. $3x^2 + 3x - 2$

    b. $3x^2 - 3x + 10$

    c. $-x^2 - 3x + 10$

    d. $3x^4 - 3x + 2$

    e. $3x^2 - 3x + 2$

19. Find the sum of $2x - 5y + 5$ and $6x + 3y - 2$

    a. $8x + 2y - 3$

    b. $8x + 8y + 7$

    c. $8x + 8y + 3$

    d. $8x - 2y + 3$

    e. $8x - 2y + 7$

20. If $\frac{2x}{16} = \frac{12}{48}$, what is x?

    a. 2

    b. 3

    c. 4

    d. 5

    e. 6

21. Solve the following equation for x: $2x - 7 = 4$.

    a. $-\frac{3}{2}$

    b. $\frac{3}{2}$

    c. $\frac{11}{2}$

    d. $\frac{22}{11}$

    e. 22

22. Solve for x in the following equation: $1.5x - 7 = 12.5$.

    a. 29.25

    b. 19.5

    c. 13

    d. 5.5

    e. 6

23. Solve for x: $4x + 9 + 2x = 27$

    a. 0

    b. 1

    c. 2

    d. 3

    e. 4

24. The sum of $3x^2 - 2$ and $x^2 + 4x - 5$ is

    a. $2x^2 + 4x + 3$

    b. $4x^2 + 4x - 7$

    c. $4x^2 + 2x - 5$

    d. $3x^4 + 4x + 10$

    e. $4x^2 + 4x + 7$

25. Six less than three times a number is four more than twice the number. Find the number.

    a. 44

    b. 2

    c. 1

    d. 10

    e. 12

26. Susan is buying oranges and she sees that the price of oranges has increased by 30% since the last time she went shopping. If the price of oranges is now $1.95, how much were the oranges originally?

    a. $1.50

    b. $2.54

    c. $2.60

    d. It cannot be determined from the information given

27. $x(3x^2 + y) =$

    a. $4x^2 + xy$

    b. $4x^2 + x + y$

    c. $3x^3 + 2xy$

    d. $3x^3 + xy$

    e. None of these

28. Which of these is equivalent to 35° C? $(F = \frac{9}{5}C + 32)$

    a. 105° F

    b. 95° F

    c. 63° F

    d. 19° F

29. White stones cost $3.59 for 25 pounds. Which proportion can be used to solve for the cost, c, of 100 pounds?

    a. $\frac{25}{100} = \frac{c}{3.59}$

    b. $\frac{3.59}{100} = \frac{25}{c}$

    c. $\frac{3.59}{25} = \frac{c}{100}$

    d. $\frac{c}{3.59} = \frac{25}{100}$

30. $(3x^4y^2)(5xy^3)$ is equivalent to

    a. $15x^4y^5$

    b. $15x^5y^4$

    c. $15x^5y^5$

    d. $15x^4y^4$

31. A train travels at a constant rate of 30 miles per hour. How long will it take the train to travel 100 miles?

    a. 3 hours and 15 minutes

    b. 3 hours and 20 minutes

    c. 3 hours and 30 minutes

    d. 3 hours and $33\frac{1}{3}$ minutes

    e. 3 hours and 40 minutes

32. Most infants gain 1.2 pounds per month, so that their weight can be found using the expression $1.2m + b$, where m is the infant's age in months and b is the infant's weight at birth. If Ian weighed 9.4 pounds at birth and is 3 months old, how much does he probably weigh now?

    a. 10.6 lbs

    b. 11.8 lbs

    c. 12.4 lbs

    d. 13.0 lbs

33. $3b(b + 5)$ is equivalent to

    a. $3b + 15$

    b. $3b^2 + 15b$

    c. $18b$

    d. $15b^2$

34. If $\frac{x}{3} + \frac{x}{4} = 3$, what is x?

    a. $\frac{1}{12}$

    b. $\frac{7}{36}$

    c. $\frac{1}{4}$

    d. $5\frac{1}{7}$

35. If $\frac{1}{16} = \frac{x}{54}$, what is x?

    a. 3.375

    b. 3.5

    c. 4

    d. 4.5

36. Solve for x in the following equation: $\frac{1}{3}x + 3 = 8$.

    a. 33

    b. 15

    c. 11

    d. 3

37. If $x = 6$, $y = -2$, and $z = 3$, what is the value of the expression $\frac{xz - xy}{z^2}$?

    a. $-\frac{2}{3}$

    b. $\frac{2}{3}$

    c. $3\frac{1}{3}$

    d. 5

38. Jason is six times as old as Kate. In two years, Jason will be twice as old as Kate is then. How old is Jason now?

    a. 3 years old

    b. 6 years old

    c. 9 years old

    d. 12 years old

39. Ms. Carrillo wants to take the students in her band class to the City Pops concert. To get the group rate of $6 per ticket, a $7 service charge must be paid. Which equation should Ms. Carrillo use to find the total cost c for taking her students to the concert? Let n represent the number of people.

    a. $C = 7n + 6$

    b. $C = 6n - 7$

    c. $C = 6n + 7$

    d. $C = 13n$

40. If a pebble is dropped off of a 144-foot vertical cliff, its height (in feet) h after t seconds is given by the equation $h = -16t^2 + 144$. How long will it be before the pebble hits the ground?

    a. −3 seconds

    b. 16 seconds

    c. 9 seconds

    d. 3 seconds

41. Jerry is $\frac{1}{3}$ as old as his grandfather was 15 years ago. If the sum of their ages now is 95, how old is Jerry's grandfather?

    a. 80

    b. 75

    c. 65

    d. 60

    e. 50

42. What is the value of y when $x = 8$ and $y = \frac{x^2}{4} - 2$?
   a. 8
   b. 14
   c. 16
   d. 18
   e. 20

43. Which of the following ordered pairs is *not* a solution to the equation $y = 5x - 3$?
   a. $(-2, -13)$
   b. $(3, 12)$
   c. $(5, 21)$
   d. $(6, 27)$

44. Find the value of a when $b = 6$.
   $12a + \frac{b^2}{4} = 93$
   a. 5
   b. 6
   c. 7
   d. 8

45. If $V = \pi r^2 h$, what is h equal to?
   a. $\frac{\pi V}{r^2}$
   b. $V\pi r^2$
   c. $\frac{V}{\pi r^2}$
   d. $\frac{Vh}{r^2}$

46. What is the value of $3x^2 - 2xy^3$ when $x = 1$ and $y = -2$?
   a. -19
   b. -5
   c. 13
   d. 19

47. Use the chart below to determine which answer choice contains an expression that can be used to solve for the percent increase, I, in the speed of sound through air at 100°C as compared with the speed of sound through air at 0° C.

Medium	Speed of Sound (m\s)
Air 0°C	331
Air 20°C	343
Air 100° C	366

a. $\frac{12}{331} = \frac{I}{100}$

b. $\frac{35}{331} - \frac{I}{100}$

c. $\frac{35}{366} = \frac{I}{100}$

d. $\frac{12}{343} = \frac{I}{100}$

48. If 175 bolts weigh $28x$ ounces, how many ounces do 75 bolts weigh?

a. $\frac{7}{3x}$

b. $\frac{75}{28}x$

c. $3x$

d. $12x$

e. $14x$

49. The Tigers and the Cobras were playing each other in a basketball game. After the Tigers scored 8 points and the Cobras scored 13 points, the Tigers were still ahead. Which inequality describes the relationship between T, the number of points the Tigers scored, and C, the number of points the Cobras scored in the basketball game?

a. $T + C < 8 + 13$

b. $T - 8 > C + 13$

c. $T + 8 > C + 13$

d. $T \times 8 < C \times 13$

e. $T + 8 > 13C$

50. If a fire truck travels at the speed of 62 mph for 15 minutes, how far will it travel?
(Distance = Rate × Time)

a. 9.3 miles

b. 15.5 miles

c. 16 miles

d. 24.8 miles

51. A bicyclist passes a farmhouse at 3:14 P.M. At 3:56 P.M. the bicyclist passes a second farmhouse. If the bicyclist is traveling at a uniform rate of 12 mph, how far apart are the farmhouses?

    a. 1.2 miles

    b. 3.6 miles

    c. 8.4 miles

    d. 17.1 miles

52. Hilga and Jerome leave from different points walking toward each other. Hilga walks $2\frac{1}{2}$ miles per hour and Jerome walks 4 miles per hour. If they meet in $2\frac{1}{2}$ hours, how far apart were they?

    a. 9 miles

    b. 13 miles

    c. $16\frac{1}{4}$ miles

    d. 17 miles

    e. $18\frac{1}{2}$ miles

53. Factoring $2pq^2 - 4p^2q^3$ yields which of the following expressions?

    a. $2pq^2(1 - 2pq)$

    b. $2pq(q - 2pq)$

    c. $2p^2q(q - 2pq^2)$

    d. $2pq(q - 4pq^2)$

54. Factor $16a^3b - 4ab^2$.

    a. $16ab(4a^2 - b)$

    b. $ab(16a^2 - 4b)$

    c. $4ab(4a^2 - b)$

    d. $16ab(4a^2 - 4b)$

    e. $4(4a^3b - ab^2)$

55. Which input–output equation was used to create this table?

Input	Output
3	11
4	15
5	19

    a. Output = Input + 8

    b. Output = 3 × Input + 2

    c. Output = 3 × Input + 4

    d. Output = 4 × Input − 1

56. What is the value of x in the diagram below?

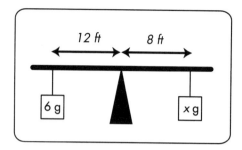

   a. 8 grams

   b. 9 grams

   c. 10 grams

   d. It cannot be determined by the information given.

15

Geometry and Measurement

*G*eometry and measurement are closely related, so both subjects are covered here. Where measurement differs, such as in conversions, is the last item covered.

▶ GEOMETRY

This chapter covers the basic building blocks of geometry: rays, angles, line segments, and planes. Also, you will learn the basic properties you need to know in order to apply these terms.

Rays and Angles

Terminology
- ◆ A **ray** is part of a line that has one endpoint. (It extends indefinitely in one direction.)
- ◆ An **acute angle** is less than 90°.
- ◆ A **right angle** equals 90°.
- ◆ A **straight line** is 180°.
- ◆ An **obtuse angle** is greater than 90°.

- Two angles are **supplementary** if they add to 180°.
- Two angles are **complementary** if they add to 90°.
- If you **bisect** an angle, you cut it exactly in half.
- **Vertical Angles** are formed when 2 lines intersect; the opposite angles are equal.

Example: Refer to the figure below when completing the following chart.

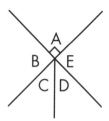

An example of . . .	Would be . . .
Vertical angles	
An acute angle	
A right angle	
Complementary angles	
Supplementary angles	

∠B and ∠E are vertical angles. ∠C and ∠D are acute angles. ∠A is a right angle (so are angles B and E). ∠C and ∠D are complementary angles. ∠A and ∠E are supplementary angles, as are the threesome of ∠E, ∠D, and ∠C. Angles B, C, and D are also supplementary, as are angles B and A.

It's A Fact!

The measure of an angle greater than 180° is called a reflex angle.

Parallel Lines

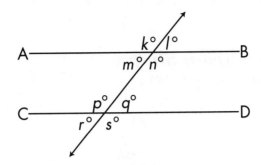

Facts

- A line that crosses the pair of parallel lines will generate **corresponding angles** that are equal. (For example, angles *p* and *k* are in corresponding positions, so they are equal.)
- **Alternate interior angles** are equal. (*m* and *q* are alternate interior angles, so they are equal. This is also true for *p* and *n*.)
- **Alternate exterior angles** are equal. (This means *k* = *s*, and *r* = *l*.)

Example: If line segments $\overline{AB}$ and $\overline{CD}$ are parallel, what is the value of *y*?

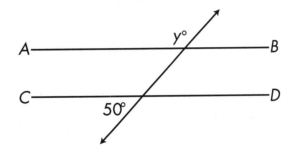

Here, the 50° beneath $\overline{CD}$ corresponds to the angle beneath $\overline{AB}$. You can then add in a new 50° angle:

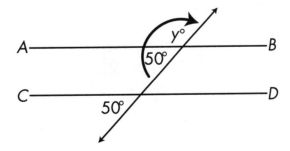

You will see that the "new" 50° angle and *y* are **supplementary**; that is, they form a straight line. Straight lines are 180°, so you know that $50 + y = 180$. Subtracting 50 from both sides yields $y = 130°$.

Interior Angles of Common Shapes

The interior angles of a **triangle** add up to 180°.

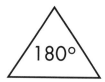

The interior angles of **any** four-sided figure, or **quadrilateral**, add up to 360°.

- square
- rectangle
- parallelogram
- rhombus
- trapezoid

The interior angles of a **circle** add up to 360°.

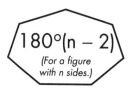

For a **polygon with *n* sides**, the interior angles will add up to 180° (*n* – 2).

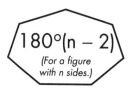

Congruence

When two figures are congruent, they are exactly the same.

Similarity

Similar figures must have

- ◆ matching angles that are congruent
- ◆ matching sides that are proportional

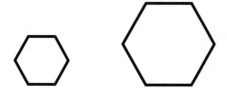

Similar triangles are the most common similar figures that you will see:

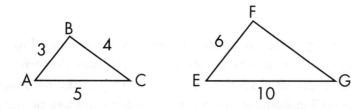

You can set up a proportion to solve for the missing side, $\overline{FG}$.

$$\frac{3}{6} = \frac{4}{\overline{FG}}$$

Cross multiplying, you get:

$$3(\overline{FG}) = 6 \times 4$$
$$3(\overline{FG}) = 24$$

Next, divide both sides by 3 to get:

$$\overline{FG} = 8$$

Symmetry

Shapes are said to be symmetrical if you can make a line through that shape, forming 2 halves that are mirror images of each other.

This hexagon has a line of symmetry:

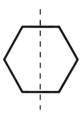

This quadrilateral does not have a line of symmetry. Notice that no matter how we draw the dashed line, we will not make 2 mirror-image halves:

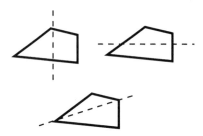

Dive into the Web

For an interesting twist on math lessons, try experimenting with teaching (and learning) mathematics through origami. Paperfolding. com includes a specific section on the mathematics of origami (www.paperfolding.com/math), with ideas for activities at various skill levels and links to a multitude of other resources. The pages of Tom Hull (chasm.merrimack.edu/~thull/OrigamiMath.html), a math professor, provide more advanced information on the links between geometry and origami, as well an excellent bibliography and some amazing photographs of mathematical origami models.

Perimeter and Circumference

Measuring the distance around a noncircular shape is called the **perimeter**. When measuring the distance around a circle, it is called a **circumference**.

The perimeter of a **square** is equal to *4s*, where *s* is the length of a side. Since all 4 sides are equal, if you measure the distance around a square, you get *s* + *s* + *s* + *s*, or *4s*.

4s

The perimeter of a **rectangle** is *2l* + *2w*, where *l* equals the length and the *w* equals the width. Always remember that the length is longer.

2*l* + 2*w*

The circumference of a **circle**, *C,* equals π*d*, or 2π*r*

$C = \pi d$

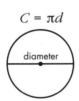

diameter

$C = 2\pi r$

radius

Notice that both of these formulas make sense because *2r = d*.

To find the perimeter of a **triangle**, you just add up the lengths of all three sides:

Add up sides

To find the perimeter of a **regular polygon**, you just need to know one side. This is because regular polygons have all sides equal. For example, a regular hexagon has 6 equal sides:

Add up sides

If a figure is not regular, sometimes markings will denote congruent sides:

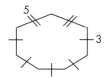

The sides with the same markings are equal:

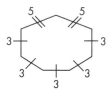

The perimeter is then 3 × 5 + 5 × 2 = 15 + 10 = 25 units.

Area

When measuring lengths, you can use different units, such as feet, meters, inches, and so on. When finding the area, you use square units. The area measures the amount of square units inside of a figure. Here are the area formulas that you should know:

Square $A = s^2$

$$s^2$$

Triangle $A = \frac{1}{2}bh$

Rectangle $A = lw$

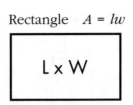

Trapezoid $A = \frac{1}{2}h(b_1 + b_2)$

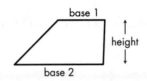

Parallelogram $A = bh$

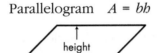

Circle $A = \pi r^2$

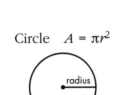

Surface Area

The surface area is just the area on the surface of a solid figure. Surface area is also measured in units^2 (square units). If you have a cube, in order to find the surface area, you would find the area of each face and then find the total of all of the faces. Since the area of a square is s^2, you will have six faces with an area of s^2, so in all you will have $6s^2$.

Cube   S.A. $= 6(s^2)$

Right Circular Cylinder   S.A. $= 2\pi rh + 2\pi r^2$

Rectangular Solid   S.A. = 2(lw) + 2(hw) + 2(lh)

Volume

The volume measures the amount of cubic units needed to fill a 3-D solid. As you might have guessed, volumes are measured in units[3] (cubic units).

Cube $V = s^3$

Right Circular Cylinder $V = \pi r^2 h$

Rectangular Solid $V = lwh$

A Closer Look at Triangles

Triangle Terminology

- ◆ **Acute triangles** have all angles less than 90°.
- ◆ **Equilateral triangles** have all angles equal to 60°. All sides of equilateral triangles are congruent (equal).
- ◆ **Obtuse triangles** have one angle that is greater than 90°.
- ◆ **Right triangles** have one right (90°) angle.
- ◆ **Isosceles triangles** have 2 congruent sides (and the angles opposite these equal sides are equal as well).
- ◆ **Scalene triangles** have no sides that are congruent.

Triangle Facts

- ◆ **Triangle Inequality Theorem**: A side of a triangle is always less than the sum of the other 2 sides (and greater than their difference).
- ◆ Given a triangle, congruent sides are opposite congruent angles. In other words, equal sides are opposite equal angles.
- ◆ Given a triangle, larger sides are opposite larger angles, and smaller sides are opposite smaller angles.

Resources Around You

Take a piece of uncooked spaghetti and break it into 3 pieces. Measure each piece to the nearest centimeter. Will the three pieces form a triangle if you connect the ends of each piece? Try the activity again by breaking up the spaghetti in different sized pieces than the first time, and measure each piece. In each case, add up the two smaller pieces and compare the sum with the larger piece. Which lengths will form triangles and which will not?

Right Triangles:

Right triangles are special because you can use the Pythagorean theorem to find the length of a side. The Pythagorean theorem is:

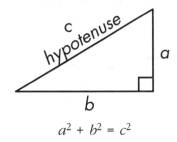

$$a^2 + b^2 = c^2$$

where *a* and *b* are the legs, and *c* is the hypotenuse.

A Closer Look at Quadrilaterals

Quadrilateral Terminology and Facts

- ◆ **Trapezoids** have exactly 1 pair of parallel sides.
- ◆ **Parallelograms** have 2 pairs of parallel sides. The opposite sides are congruent. The opposite angles are congruent. The diagonals of parallelograms bisect each other.

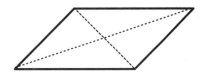

- ◆ **Rectangles** are parallelograms with 4 right angles. This means that the diagonals of a rectangle bisect each other.

◆ A **rhombus** is a parallelogram with 4 congruent sides. The diagonals of a rhombus not only bisect each other, they bisect the angles that they connect as well. Also, the diagonals are perpendicular.

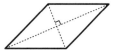

◆ A **square** is a rhombus with 4 right angles.

Example: In the Venn Diagram below, fill in the terms Rhombus, Rectangle, and Square in the appropriate positions.

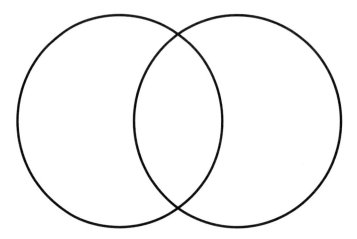

A Closer Look at Circles

Circle Terminology

◆ A **chord** is a line segment which joins 2 points on a circle.
◆ A **radius** is a line segment from the center of the circle to a point on the circle.
◆ A **diameter** is a chord which passes through the center of the circle and has endpoints on the circle.
◆ A **minor arc** is the smaller curve between 2 points.
◆ A **major arc** is the larger curve between 2 points.

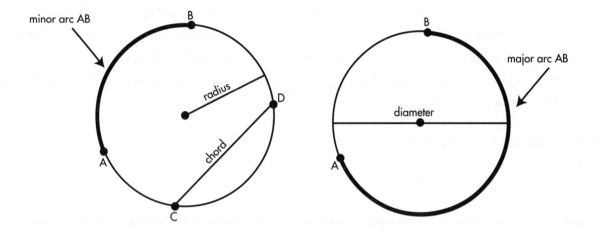

It's A Fact!

The ratio of the circumference of any circle as compared to its diameter is π.

Tips on Dealing with Circles

◆ Questions that involve *rolling* a wheel are usually circumference questions in disguise. As the wheel rolls, the distance around (circumference of) the wheel is in contact with the ground. Questions that ask "How many times will the wheel rotate?" are really based on circumference.

◆ You can use the angle measure of a shaded "slice" of a circle to determine its area. If the shaded slice has a measure of 90°, you know that this is $\frac{1}{4}$ of the circle. The area of the slice would then be $\frac{1}{4}$ of the area of the whole circle. A shaded "slice" that has an angle of 60° would be $\frac{1}{6}$ of the total area, and so forth.

Example: Which distance below represents the number of feet traveled by the wheel pictured below as it revolves 20 times along its path?

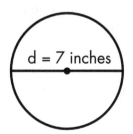

   a. $36\frac{2}{3}$

   b. 40

   c. $42\frac{1}{3}$

   d. 45

In the diagram, the 7″ represents the *diameter*. The rolling wheel will have the distance around its outer edge in contact with the ground as it revolves. This question boils down to a *circumference* question. Using $C = \pi d$, with $\frac{22}{7}$ substituted in for π this equation becomes: $C = \frac{22}{7}(7) = 22$ inches. If the wheel revolves 20 times, multiply 22×20 to get the number of inches traveled. This value, 440″, can be then converted into feet: $\frac{440'' \times 1 \text{ ft}}{12''} = 36\frac{2}{3}$ ft, choice **a**.

Coordinate Geometry

A coordinate grid is used to plot or locate points in a plane. The horizontal axis is called the *x*-axis, and the vertical axis is called the *y*-axis. There are 4 quadrants created by the intersection of the *x* and *y*-axis.

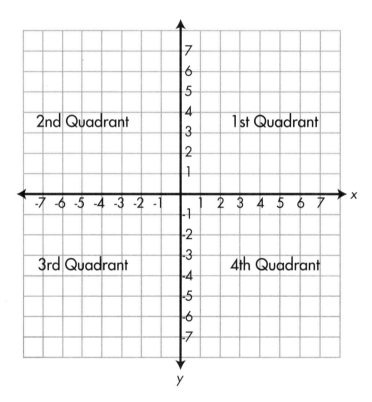

It is easy to plot points on the coordinate grid. Points are given as **ordered pairs**, which are just *x/y* pairs. An ordered pair is always written (x, y). You simply go left or right along the *x*-axis to find your *x*, and then you go up or down to the appropriate *y*-coordinate.

Transformations

A given figure can be moved and altered in a number of ways. The way in which the old points of the figure are moved to "new" spots is called a **transformation**.

Common Transformations

- ◆ **Translations** are a slide.
- ◆ **Rotations** are turns.

◆ A **reflection** is a flip (mirror-image)

◆ A **dilation** is a proportional change in size.

Tessellations

A shape is said to **tessellate** if it can tile and cover a surface without any gaps. For example, the parallelogram below tessellates, because each "tile" locks into the next, leaving no gaps:

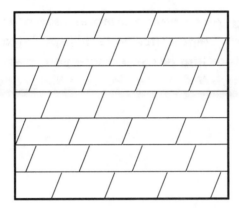

What shapes tessellate? Sometimes irregular shapes can tessellate too:

Resources Around You

Try to find examples of tessellating patterns in the real world, especially in nature. You may find them in places such as tiled floors, quilts, and honeycombs. What is the shape that bees choose to use to create their honeycombs, and what might be some of the reasons nature would choose that shape?

You can create **semi-regular tessellations** by combining different types of shapes, like rectangles and triangles or octagons and squares. Think of some combinations that will work.

Dive Into the Web

Using your favorite Internet search engine, type in "Escher Web Sketch." Many sites have this special (and free) online "sketching" interface that lets you create your own tessellations! While online, research M.C. Escher, Penrose tiling, and the Golden Mean.

▶ METRIC SYSTEM

The metric system is an alternative way to measure distances, volumes, and masses. Once you understand what the prefixes mean and what the basic terms used for measurement are, you will have no problem dealing with these units. For example, meters (m) are used to measure length.

$$1m = 1000 \text{ millimeters} = 1000 \text{ mm}$$
$$1m = 100 \text{ centimeters} = 100 \text{ cm}$$
$$1m = 10 \text{ decimeters} = 10 \text{ dm}$$

Here are the other prefixes you will see:

The prefix . . .	Means . . .	Example . . .
milli	$\frac{1}{1000}$ of	1 milliliter is $\frac{1}{1000}$ of a liter
centi	$\frac{1}{100}$ of	1 centimeter is $\frac{1}{100}$ of a meter
deci	$\frac{1}{10}$ of	1 decigram is $\frac{1}{10}$ of a gram
deca	10 times	1 decameter is 10 meters
hecto	100 times	1 hectoliter is 100 liters
kilo	1000 times	1 kilometer is 1000 meters

So what is a liter, a meter, and a gram? A liter is used to measure volume. A gram is used to measure mass. And a meter is used to measure length.

Term	Used to measure
Liter	Volume
Gram	Mass
Meter	Length

Advanced Conversions

1 acre = 43,560 square feet

1 liter = 1000 cubic centimeters

You may already be used to the customary system. Here are some units that you should know:

Customary Units

1 foot = 12 inches	1 cup = 8 fluid ounces
3 feet = 1 yard	1 pint = 2 cups
1 mile = 5280 feet	1 quart = 2 pints
1 pound = 16 ounces	1 gallon = 4 quarts
1 ton = 2000 pounds	

Operations with Mixed Measures

A mixed measure is part one unit and part another unit. For example, "12 feet 5 inches" is part *feet* and part *inches*. When adding or subtracting mixed measures, you just need to align the units and perform the operation at hand. You can then **rename** units as necessary.

Example: Ryan's band played for 1 hour and 35 minutes. Ray's band played for 1 hour and 40 minutes. When combined, the two performances lasted how long?

$$
\begin{array}{r}
1 \text{ hr} + 35 \text{ min} \\
+\ 1 \text{ hr} + 40 \text{ min} \\
\hline
2 \text{ hr} + 75 \text{ min}
\end{array}
$$

Rewrite 75 minutes as 60 min + 15 minutes.

2 hr + (60 min + 15 min)

Rename 60 minutes as 1 hour.

$$2 \text{ hr} + 1 \text{ hr} + 15 \text{ min}$$
$$3 \text{ hr} + 15 \text{ min}$$

Using Proportions to Convert Units

Proportions can be used to convert units. Look at the equivalents below:

1 cup = 8 ounces	1 hour = 60 minute
1 meter = 100 cm	1 min = 60 seconds

If you know that 1 cup equals 8 ounces, you can easily figure out how many cups are in 64 ounces by setting up a proportion:

$$\frac{1 \text{ cup}}{8 \text{ oz}} = \frac{? \text{ cup}}{64 \text{ oz}}$$

Cross-multiplying, you get 64 × 1 = 8 × ?, or 64 = 8 × ?. Dividing both sides by 8 you get ? = 8.

Advanced Technique: Using Conversion Factors to Convert Units

A snail slides along at a rate of 2 cm per minute. How many meters does it move in an hour?

Here we have to convert centimeters to meters and minutes to hours. We can do this easily with conversion factors:

Unwanted units on top...

$$\frac{2 \text{ cm}}{\text{min}} \times \frac{1 \text{ m}}{100 \text{ cm}} \times \frac{60 \text{ min}}{1 \text{ hr}}$$

...so put unwanted units on bottom

Notice that we strategically placed the centimeters in the bottom of the conversion factor so that it would cancel out the unwanted units on top.

To get rid of the "unwanted" minutes on the bottom, make a conversion factor that has minutes on top:

Unwanted units on bottom...

$$\frac{2\ cm}{min} \times \frac{1\ m}{100\ cm} \times \frac{60\ min}{1\ hr}$$

...so put unwanted units on top

Multiply to get $\frac{120\ m}{100\ hr} = \frac{1.2\ m}{hr}$.

▶ PRACTICE

The questions in this section have been divided into three categories: Basic, Intermediate, and Advanced. Questions 1–15 are Basic, questions 16–32 are Intermediate, and questions 33–52 are Advanced. An answer key with explanations can be found in Appendix C.

BASIC

1. In a triangle, angle A is 70 degrees and angle B is 30 degrees. What is the measure of angle C?
   a. 90 degrees
   b. 70 degrees
   c. 80 degrees
   d. 100 degrees

2. In the diagram, lines a, b, and c intersect at point O. Which of the following are NOT adjacent angles?

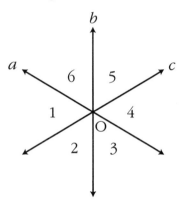

   a. Angle 1 and Angle 6.
   b. Angle 1 and Angle 4.
   c. Angle 4 and Angle 5.
   d. Angle 2 and Angle 3.
   e. All of the angles are adjacent.

3. A triangle has angles of 71 degrees and 62 degrees. Which of the following best describes the triangle?
   a. acute scalene
   b. obtuse scalene
   c. acute isosceles
   d. obtuse isosceles

4. What is the perimeter of the parallelogram shown below?

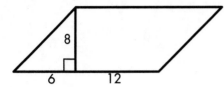

    a. 26
    b. 32
    c. 48
    d. 56

5. What is the perimeter of the figure?

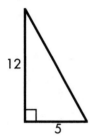

    a. 17
    b. 20
    c. 30
    d. 60

6. What is the measure of angle F in the following diagram?

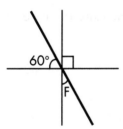

    a. 15 degrees
    b. 45 degrees
    c. 30 degrees
    d. 90 degrees

7. Which side of the triangle shown below is the shortest, if angles BAC and ABC are 60 degrees?

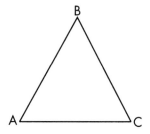

    a. AB

    b. AC

    c. BC

    d. All sides are equal

8. Circle O has a diameter of 8 cm. What is the area of Circle O?

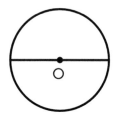

    a. 64π cm^2

    b. 32π cm^2

    c. 16π cm^2

    d. 8π cm^2

9. In the figure below, angle POS measures 90 degrees. What is the measure of angle ROQ?

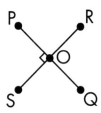

    a. 45 degrees

    b. 90 degrees

    c. 180 degrees

    d. 270 degrees

10. Which polygon *must* have two equal angles?

    a. An isosceles triangle

    b. A right triangle

    c. A trapezoid

    d. A pentagon

11. A line intersects two parallel lines in the figure below. If angle P measures 40 degrees, what is the measure of angle Q?

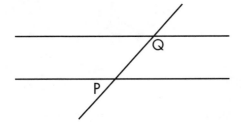

    a. 50
    b. 60
    c. 80
    d. 140

12. Which of these angle measures form a right triangle?
    a. 45 degrees, 50 degrees, 85 degrees
    b. 40 degrees, 40 degrees, 100 degrees
    c. 20 degrees, 30 degrees, 130 degrees
    d. 40 degrees, 40 degrees, 40 degrees
    e. 40 degrees, 50 degrees, 90 degrees

13. How much greater is the area of Circle B than the area of Circle A?

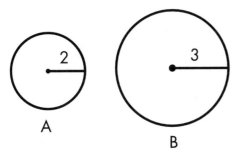

    a. 5π cm^2
    b. 12π cm^2
    c. 20π cm^2
    d. 36π cm^2

14. How many of the figures below are regular polygons?

    a. 0
    b. 1
    c. 2
    d. 3

15. A square is a special case of all of the following geometric figures EXCEPT a

   a. parallelogram.

   b. rectangle.

   c. rhombus.

   d. trapezoid.

INTERMEDIATE

16. If pentagon ABCDE is similar to pentagon FGHIJ, and AB = 10, CD = 5, and FG = 30, what is HI?

   a. $\frac{5}{3}$

   b. 5

   c. 15

   d. 30

17. What is the area, in square inches, of an isosceles trapezoid with side lengths 5, 5, 10, and 18 inches?

   a. 21 in²

   b. 38 in²

   c. 42 in²

   d. 56 in²

   e. 70 in²

18. The coordinates for a rectangle are shown on the graph below. What are the coordinates of point *H*?

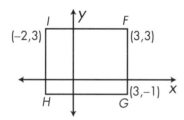

   a. (−2, −3)

   b. (−3, −1)

   c. (−2, −1)

   d. (3, 3)

   e. (−1, 2)

19. If the area of a circle is 16π square inches, what is the circumference?

   a. 2π inches

   b. 4π inches

   c. 8π inches

   d. 12π inches

20. If the two triangles in the diagram are similar, with angle A equal to angle D, what is the perimeter of triangle DEF?

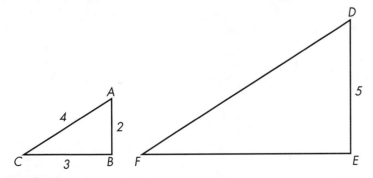

    a. 12

    b. 21

    c. 22.5

    d. 24.75

21. What is the value of X in the figure below?

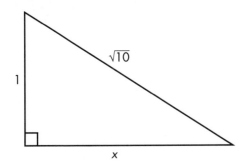

    a. 2

    b. 3

    c. 5

    d. 9

22. Find the length of the missing side in the right triangle.

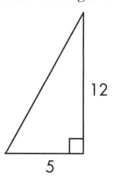

12

5

   a. 17
   b. $\sqrt{34}$
   c. 8.5
   d. 169
   e. 13

23. What are the coordinates for the end points of line segment *AB*?

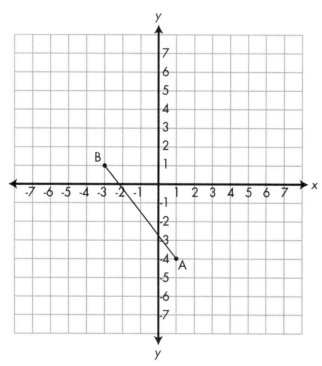

   a. (−3, 1) and (1, −4)
   b. (1, −3) and (−4, −1)
   c. (−1, −3) and (4, 1)
   d. (−3, −1) and (1, 4)

24. A group of volunteers is searching for a lost camper within a 45-mile radius of the forest ranger's station. Which formula below can be used to calculate the total search area, *T*, in square miles?

a. $T = 902\pi$

b. $T = 2025\pi$

c. $T = 90\pi$

d. $T = 45\pi$

25. If a 10 ft ladder is leaning against a building as shown in the diagram below, how many feet above the ground, *h*, is the top of the ladder?

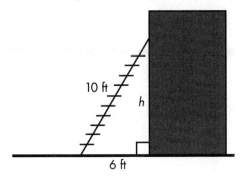

a. 8

b. 10

c. $\sqrt{8}$

d. $\sqrt{10}$

26. Zelda cuts a pizza in half in a straight line. She then cuts a line from the center to the edge, creating a 35-degree angle. What is the supplement of that angle?

a. 55 degrees

b. 145 degrees

c. 35 degrees

d. 70 degrees

27. Line *A* is parallel to line *B* in the figure below. What is the value of *x*?

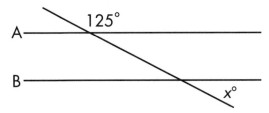

a. 45

b. 55

c. 65

d. 76

e. Cannot be determined from the given information

28. What is the area in square units of the shaded region of the diagram?

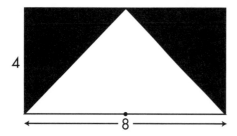

   a. 2π

   b. 4

   c. 4π + 2

   d. 12π

   e. 16

29. What is the measure of angle C in the following triangle?

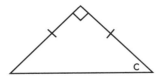

   a. 90 degrees

   b. 60 degrees

   c. 45 degrees

   d. 25 degrees

   e. Cannot be determined from the information given

30. Simon needed some cardboard boxes for storage. A moving company sold boxes in several sizes. Two of the boxes are shown below. Each dimension of the larger box is 2 inches greater than the same dimension of the smaller box. How much *more* storage does the larger box have?

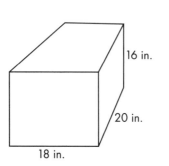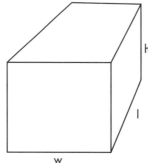

   a. 1440 cubic inches

   b. 1800 cubic inches

   c. 2160 cubic inches

   d. 2680 cubic inches

31. If the side of the cube below is doubled, what happens to its volume?

2

   a. it is doubled
   b. it is tripled
   c. it is quadrupled
   d. it is multiplied by eight

32. In which diagram is the polygon a reflection of polygon A across the *y*-axis?

   a.

   b.

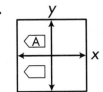

   c.

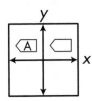

   d.

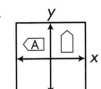

33. In the figure shown below in the standard (x, y) coordinate plane, what is the area, in square feet, of square *ABCD*?

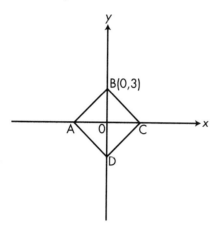

   a. 9 ft²
   b. 12 ft²
   c. 8√3 ft²
   d. 18 ft²
   e. 12√2 ft²

34. If the figure below is a regular decagon with a center at Q, what is the measure of the indicated angle?

   a. 36 degrees
   b. 45 degrees
   c. 90 degrees
   d. 108 degrees

35. The figure below contains both a circle and a square. What is the area of the entire shaded diagram?

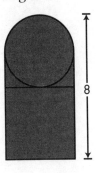

- **a.** 16 + 4π
- **b.** 16 + 16π
- **c.** 24 + 2π
- **d.** 8 + 2π

36. If angle 1 is 30 degrees and angle 2 is a right angle, what is the measure of angle 5?

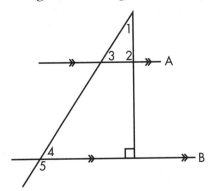

- **a.** 30 degrees
- **b.** 60 degrees
- **c.** 120 degrees
- **d.** 140 degrees

37. In the diagram below, a half-circle is laid adjacent to a triangle. What is the total area of the shape, if the radius of the half-circle is 3 and the height of the triangle is 4?

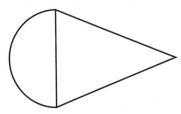

- **a.** 6(π + 4)
- **b.** 6π + 12
- **c.** $\frac{3\pi}{2}$ + 12
- **d.** $\frac{9\pi}{2}$ + 12

38. If the triangle below is reflected over the *y*-axis, what will be the new *x* coordinate of point R?

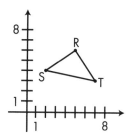

   a. (−5, 6)
   b. (−6, 5)
   c. (−2, 4)
   d. (−7, 3)

39. During a trip to Yosemite National Park, Jason observed a climber high on a rock wall. Jason was standing 125 meters from the vertical rock face. Use the diagram below to find how high the climber was above the ground.

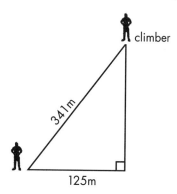

   a. 317.3 m
   b. 329.2 m
   c. 363.2 m
   d. 466.1 m

40. If BC is parallel to DE, and DB = 6, what is the value of AE?

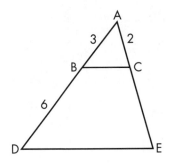

    a. 4
    b. 6
    c. 8
    d. 10

41. What is the perimeter of the rectangle shown below?

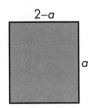

    a. $(2 - a)^2$
    b. $(2 - a)(a)^2$
    c. $4 + 8a$
    d. 4

42. If line segment $\overline{AB}$ is parallel to line segment $\overline{CD}$, what is the value of x?

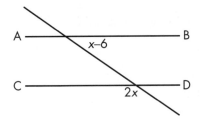

    a. 58°
    b. 62°
    c. 56°
    d. 60°

43. A circular pool with a 30-foot diameter is surrounded by a 4-foot-wide walk, as shown in the figure below. What is the area, in square feet, of the walk?

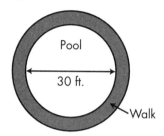

    a. 16π
    b. 136π
    c. 169π
    d. 676π
    e. $1,444\pi$

44. Find the area of the shaded portion in the figure below.

    a. π
    b. $\pi - 1$
    c. $2 - \pi$
    d. $2 - \pi^2$
    e. $4 - \pi$

45. In which figure is triangle ABC a reflection of triangle XYZ over the *x*-axis?

    a.

    b.

c.

d.

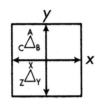

46. Which point on the graph is on the line $x = 4$?

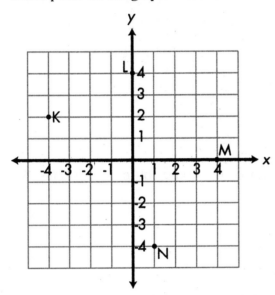

   a. K
   b. L
   c. M
   d. N

47. Which is an equation of line q?

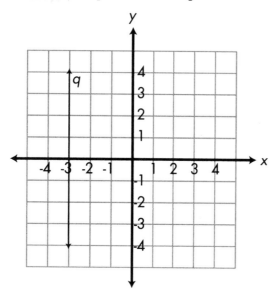

   a. $y = 3$
   b. $y = -3$
   c. $x = 3$
   d. $x = -3$

48. In the drawing below, the figure has been moved by a series of transformations. Which list below correctly lists the transformations?

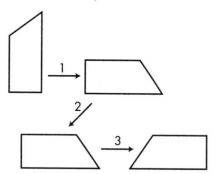

   a. 1-translation; 2-reflection; 3-rotation
   b. 1-rotation; 2-reflection; 3-translation
   c. 1-reflection; 2-translation; 3-rotation
   d. 1-rotation; 2-translation; 3-reflection

49. Mr. Tape was giving his grandson a bath one evening. Because his grandson was very young, he did not fill the bathtub up all the way. The bathtub, which was in the shape of a rectangular prism, is shown in the diagram.

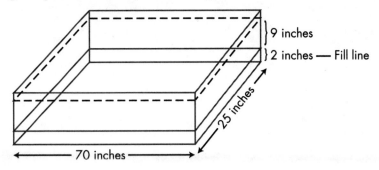

How much water was in the bathtub?

    a. 1,750 in.^{3}

    b. 3,500 in.^{3}

    c. 15,750 in.^{3}

    d. 19,250 in.^{3}

50. Pedro wanted to find the volume of his dog's house. He measured the dimensions of the house and got a volume of 31.32 cubic feet. Which group could be the dimensions of the dog house?

    a. 2.7 ft × 2.9 ft × 4 ft

    b. 2.4 ft × 2.8 ft × 3.9 ft

    c. 3 ft × 4 ft × 2.5 ft

    d. 2 ft × 2 ft × 8 ft

51. Which of the following figures will tessellate?

a.

b.

c.

d.

52. Plattville is 80 miles west and 60 miles north of Quincy. How long is a direct route from Plattville to Quincy?

    a. 100 miles

    b. 110 miles

    c. 120 miles

    d. 140 miles

CHAPTER

16

Probability and Statistics

***P*robabilities** or predictions are made all the time. Listening to the weather report, you may hear that there is a 60% chance of rain tomorrow. At karate lessons, you may hear that 19 out of 20 advanced students will attain a brown belt. On television, you might hear that four out of five dentists recommend a certain toothbrush. These are all ways to express probability. In this chapter, you will learn what probability is and how to calculate it.

Similarly, statistics are everywhere—in news reports, sports, and on your favorite websites. Mean, median, and mode are three common statistics that give information on a group of numbers. They are called *measures of central tendency* because they are different ways of finding the central trend in a group of numbers. In the first section, you will learn all about mean, median, and mode.

Dive Into the Web

Over 50 free lessons, designed for students in grades 5–8, are available from Mrs. Glosser's Math Goodies (www.mathgoodies.com). Topics range from integers to statistics, and lessons are illustrated and written in accessible language, with supplemental materials like crosswords and word search puzzles for each section. The site also features message boards where parents and teachers can exchange ideas on favorite math activities, integrating math into other disciplines, math news, and "real world connections." There's even a forum specifically for homeschooling families!

▶ MEAN

Mean is another way of saying **average**. Averages are used to *typify* a group of numbers. To find the average, you total up all the values and then divide by the number of values.

$$\text{Average (mean)} = \frac{\text{total of all values}}{\text{\# of values}}$$

▶ MEDIAN

When considering a list of values in order (from smallest to largest), the **median** is the middle value. If there are 2 "middle" values, then you just take their average.

Example: Find the median of 2 3 4 4 6 6 7 8.

    a. 4
    b. 5
    c. 6
    d. 7

The answer is **b.** The numbers are already listed in order so we do not have to worry about arranging them. Notice that this list of numbers has 2 middle terms:

$$2\ 3\ 4\ \mathbf{4}\ \mathbf{6}\ 6\ 7\ 8$$

We take the average of these 2 numbers to find the median. $\frac{4+6}{2} = \frac{10}{2} = 5$.

▶ MODE

In a list of values, the **mode** is the number that occurs the most. On the rare chance that more than one number occurs the most, then you have 2 modes (bimodal).

Example: Find the mode of 2 3 4 4 6 6 7 8.

    a. 4

    b. 5

    c. 6

    d. Both **a** and **c** are true.

        The answer is **d.** When we look at: 2 3 4 4 6 6 7 8, we notice that both 4 and 6 occur the most. Therefore the mode equals 4 and 6.

▶ PROBABILITY

Probability is the mathematics of chance. It is a way of calculating how likely it is that something will happen. Probabilities help us predict the likelihood of events. For example, probability helps us predict the weather. Doctors look at the outcomes of procedure they have performed in the past in order to tell you something like "Don't worry, this operation has a 99% success rate."

        In order to calculate the likelihood of a certain event you just place the number of favorable outcomes over the number of total possible outcomes:

$$\text{Probability} = \frac{\text{\# favorable outcomes}}{\text{\# total outcomes}}$$

Example: Barry has 3 blue socks, 5 purple socks, and 2 green socks in his dresser drawer. If he reaches in and grabs a sock, what is the probability that it will be green?

    a. $\frac{3}{10}$

    b. $\frac{1}{5}$

    c. $\frac{1}{3}$

    d. $\frac{1}{2}$

        The total number of outcomes is 3 + 5 + 2, or 10. Of these 10 possible outcomes, only 2 are favorable because there are only 2 green socks in the drawer. $\frac{2}{10} = \frac{1}{5}$, choice **b**.

▶ EXPERIMENTAL PROBABILITY

In theory, if we toss a die, we know that there is a 1 in 6 chance of getting a 2. But sometimes when we conduct dice-tossing experiments, we get statistics that do not reflect the theoretical probability.

When analyzing results of such experiments, you should consider that maybe the die wasn't tossed enough times.

Experiment with Dice: Toss a die 24 times. Did you get the expected amount of ones, twos, threes, and so on? Or does it seem like the odds of tossing one number are better than the odds of tossing another? Toss the die another 48 times and see how the odds even out.

▶ COUNTING PRINCIPLE

If there are 2 events and there are a ways that the first event can occur and b ways that the second event can occur, then there are $a \times b$ ways that these events can occur together. This is called the **counting principle**.

Let's say that you can buy white chocolate or dark chocolate hearts and they come in small, medium, or large. Our total choices will equal color of chocolate × size = 2 × 3 = 6.

List the 6 different choices of chocolate hearts below:

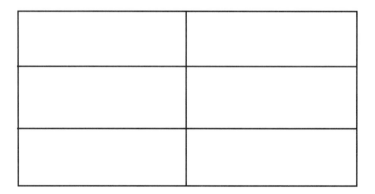

▶ PERMUTATIONS

The term **permutation** is just a fancy way of saying **arrangements**. When calculating a permutation, you are figuring out the number of possible arrangements. Just remember to use a **p**ermutation when **p**recise order matters.

*Permutations are for **P**recise Order!*

What do we mean by "precise order"? Well, suppose you took the letters A, B, C, and D and wanted to see how many different arrangements you could make. Here, the precise order of the letters matters. Thus, ABCD ≠ BCAD ≠ CABD, and so forth.

To calculate a permutation for taking a things in all and into groups of c things chosen, we use this formula:

$$_{ALL}P_{CHOSEN} = {_aP_c}$$

Which means: Start taking the factorial of **a**, and stop after **c** spots.

mnemonic: A Piece of Cheese

It's A Fact!

0! = 1

In our example we have ALL, or $a = 4$ (the four letters) and we are choosing all four, so $c = 4$ as well.

$$_aP_c = {_4}P_4$$

So we will take the factorial of 4 and stop after 4 spots:

$$\overline{\qquad}_{\text{spot 1}} \times \overline{\qquad}_{\text{spot 2}} \times \overline{\qquad}_{\text{spot 3}} \times \overline{\qquad}_{\text{spot 4}}$$

This is simply:

$$\frac{4}{\text{spot 1}} \times \frac{3}{\text{spot 2}} \times \frac{2}{\text{spot 3}} \times \frac{1}{\text{spot 4}}$$

$$= 24$$

How many different "word" arrangements would be possible if we were only choosing 2 letters from the 4 letters A, B, C, and D? In this example, a is still 4 (the four letters). But now we are choosing 2, so CHOSEN, or $c = 2$ this time.

$$_aP_c = {_4}P_2$$

So we will take the factorial of 4 and stop after 2 spots:

$$\overline{\qquad}_{\text{spot 1}} \times \overline{\qquad}_{\text{spot 2}}$$

This is simply:

$$\frac{4}{\text{spot 1}} \times \frac{3}{\text{spot 2}}$$

$$= 12$$

Can you confirm this by writing all 12 two-letter arrangements that are possible when choosing from the letters A,B, C, and D?

Arrangements

▶ COMBINATIONS

When you are choosing a group (or cluster) of items and the order does not matter, you are calculating a combination.

Combinations are for Clusters where order does not matter!

Consider this scenario:

Geri has 3 different types of stickers: stars, hearts, and clovers. She will put 2 stickers in each party bag. How many different combinations are possible?

The possible arrangements (permutation) would be $_3P_2 = 3 \times 2 = 6$, but notice that because the stickers are just going in a bag, the order does not matter. This means that some of the sets listed are equivalent.

♥ ✳ = ✳ ♥

♣ ✳ = ✳ ♣

♣ ♥ = ♥ ♣

Thus, there are only 3 combinations. In this case, it was easy to just count them for ourselves, but what if you had 100 stickers to choose from and you were putting 2 in each envelope? That's where using the combination formula comes in handy. First, let's look at the formula when we have 3 stickers and we are picking 2:

$$\text{ALL}C_{\text{CHOSEN}} = \frac{_aP_c}{c!}$$

mnemonic: A Piece of Cheese over Crackers!

$$_aP_c \qquad \div \qquad c!$$

$$\text{ALL}C_{\text{CHOSEN}} = \frac{_aP_c}{c!}$$

becomes

$$_3C_2 = \frac{_3P_2}{2!}$$

$$= \frac{(3 \times 2)}{(2 \times 1)}$$

$$= \frac{6}{2}$$

$$= 3$$

Resources Around You

Use permutations to determine the total possible number of area codes we could have. Also consider some of the numbers we may not want to use for an area code. Is it possible to actually "run out" of these codes? What are some things that could be done if this were to happen? Explore the same idea with other important numbers such as zip codes and license plates.

Questions 1–14 are Basic, questions 15–30 are Intermediate, and questions 31–42 are Advanced. An answer key with explanations can be found in Appendix C.

BASIC

1. What is the mean of the following numbers?

49, 54, 67, 75, 75

a. 64
b. 67
c. 75
d. 80

2. What is the mode of the following series of numbers?

$\sqrt{3}$ $\sqrt{3}$ $\sqrt{3}$ $\sqrt{3}$ 4 6 $\sqrt{8}$ 9

a. 9
b. 4
c. $\sqrt{3}$
d. $\sqrt{8}$

3. If you drove 22 miles on Monday, 25 miles on Tuesday, and 19 miles on Wednesday, what was the average number of miles driven each day?

a. 19 miles
b. 21 miles
c. 22 miles
d. 23 miles

4. What is the median of the following group of numbers?

5 10 15 20 25 30 36

a. 36
b. 22.5
c. 20
d. 5

5. Calculate the mean of the following test scores: 92, 89, 96, 93, 93, and 83.

a. 93
b. 91
c. 92.5
d. 91.5

6. What is the median of the following group of numbers?

10 20 30 40 50 60

   a. 30

   b. 35

   c. 60

   d. 40

7. Find the mode of the following series of numbers:

2 3 7 7 9 9 9 9 14

   a. 2

   b. 7

   c. 9

   d. 14

8. Lefty keeps track of the each length of the fish that he catches. These are the lengths in inches of the fish that he caught one day: 12, 13, 8, 10, 8, 9, 17. What is the median fish length that Lefty caught that day?

   a. 8 inches

   b. 10 inches

   c. 11 inches

   d. 12 inches

   e. none of the above

9. The chart below lists the number of students present at the monthly meetings for the Environment Protection Club. What was the average monthly attendance over the course of all the months listed?

Month	# of Students
September	54
October	61
November	70
December	75

   a. 71

   b. 65

   c. 61

   d. 56

10. In Derrick's sock drawer, there were 5 blue socks, 12 white socks, and 7 black socks. He reached into the drawer without looking and pulled out the first sock he touched. What were the odds he pulled out a blue sock?

 a. 5:19
 b. 19:5
 c. 5:24
 d. 24:5

11. A bag contains 4 red tokens, 5 yellow tokens, and 3 blue tokens. What is the probability that the first token drawn at random from the bag will be red?

 a. $\frac{1}{4}$
 b. $\frac{1}{3}$
 c. $\frac{5}{12}$
 d. $\frac{1}{2}$
 e. $\frac{3}{4}$

12. The quiz scores for 7 students are listed below:

 12 10 14 8 7 3 13

 What is the median score?

 a. 12
 b. 10
 c. 8
 d. 7

13. What is the mode of the following numbers?

 35 52 17 23 51 52 18 32

 a. 52
 b. 35
 c. 33.5
 d. 18

14. Use the chart below to determine the mean score of the people listed.

Name	Score
Alec	75
George	81
Felicia	93
Maria	77
Ashley	84

  a. 82
  b. 102
  c. 76
  d. 89

INTERMEDIATE

15. Which statement is true regarding the following numbers?
12 14 15 19 20 22
  a. The average is greater than the median.
  b. The median is greater than the mean.
  c. The mean equals the median.
  d. The mean is greater than the average.

16. As a promotion, a record company will hand out random CDs to a crowd. If the company brought along 300 rap CDs, 500 rock CDs, 200 easy listening CDs, and 400 country CDs, what is the probability that a given person will get an easy listening CD?
  a. $\frac{1}{8}$
  b. $\frac{1}{7}$
  c. $\frac{1}{6}$
  d. $\frac{1}{5}$

17. Julia is wrapping presents to give to her friends. She has 6 different kinds of boxes, 9 different types of wrapping paper, and 11 different colors of ribbon. How many different combinations of packaging and decorations can Julia use?
  a. 26
  b. 75
  c. 594
  d. 693

18. The Burnsville Neighborhood Association has been growing for the past 3 years. Its membership was 486 in 1997, 563 in 1998, and 591 in 1999. Which is a reasonable average membership for these 3 years?

    a. 30
    b. 100
    c. 510
    d. 5501

19. Rita made a list of all of her relatives and then counted up the number of people in each category. She counted 7 aunts, 8 uncles, 4 grandparents, 22 cousins, 3 siblings, and 4 nieces. What is the mode of these numbers?

    a. 3
    b. 4
    c. 8
    d. 11

20. Stephen recorded the number of butterflies that he saw in his backyard for 4 months and put the information in the table below.

Month	Number of Butterflies
May	28
June	44
July	64
August	56

    What was the mean number of butterflies in Stephen's backyard during these 4 months?

    a. 60
    b. 54
    c. 48
    d. 43

21. There are 36 blue marbles, 16 white marbles, and 28 green marbles in a bag. If one marble is drawn from the bag, what is the probability it is a white marble?

    a. $\frac{1}{3}$
    b. $\frac{1}{4}$
    c. $\frac{1}{5}$
    d. $\frac{1}{16}$

22. Joe worked 3 months during the summer, earning $522.75 during the first month, $498.25 in the second month and $530 in the third month. Calculate the mean of his paychecks.
   a. $517
   b. $522.75
   c. $1,551
   d. $530

23. A bag of jellybeans contains 8 black beans, 10 green beans, 3 yellow beans, and 9 orange beans. What is the probability of selecting either a yellow or an orange bean?
   a. $\frac{1}{10}$
   b. $\frac{2}{5}$
   c. $\frac{4}{15}$
   d. $\frac{3}{10}$

24. At the Knott Block Party, two drawings were held for a new rose bush and a pair of gardening gloves. A jar held the names of 26 people, and without looking, Mrs. Fikstad, the oldest woman on the block, drew a name. After picking Benjamin's name for the rose bush, Mrs. Fikstad replaced it in the jar and mixed up the names. What is the probability that Mrs. Fikstad then selected Benjamin's name to win the pair of gardening gloves?
   a. 1 in 13
   b. 1 in 26
   c. 1 in 52
   d. 1 in 676

25. Carmen is selecting an outfit to wear, including a top, bottoms, and shoes. She can wear a T-shirt, blouse, or sweater, shorts or slacks, and sandals, loafers, or tennis shoes. How many different outfits could she create?
   a. 8
   b. 14
   c. 16
   d. 18
   e. 23

26. On the cardiac ward, there are 7 nursing assistants. Basil has 8 patients; Hobbes has 5 patients; McGuire has 9 patients; Mattie has 10 patients; Garcia has 10 patients; James has 14 patients; and Lydia has 7 patients. What is the average number of patients per nursing assistant?
   a. 7
   b. 8
   c. 9
   d. 10

27. At the diner, a kid's meal comes with a burger or veggie burger, fries or onion rings, and ice cream, pudding, or shake. How many different kids' meals can be made?
   a. 8
   b. 10
   c. 12
   d. 18

28. Jack bought a figurine at the gift shop and would like to have it gift-wrapped. He has the choice of 6 different styles of wrapping paper, 5 different gift cards, and 3 different bows. How many different choices does he have if he will have the gift wrapped, including a card and a bow?
   a. 15
   b. 30
   c. 45
   d. 90

29. Athena tosses a six-sided die. What is the probability that the number she rolls is greater than 4?
   a. $\frac{1}{3}$
   b. $\frac{2}{3}$
   c. $\frac{1}{2}$
   d. $\frac{3}{4}$

30. Eight software developers will have an opportunity to speak briefly at a computer show. Evan needs to list the developers in the order in which they will speak. How many different arrangements are possible?
   a. 56
   b. 336
   c. 1,680
   d. 40,320

31. All of the tickets for a raffle were purchased by the 4 people listed in the chart below. What is the probability that J.T. will win?

Name	# Tickets purchased
Jane	5
J.T.	3
Brian	7
Zoey	9

    a. $\frac{3}{4}$

    b. $\frac{1}{2}$

    c. $\frac{1}{8}$

    d. $\frac{3}{8}$

32. During the last week of training on an obstacle course, an athlete achieves the following times in seconds: 66, 57, 54, 54, 64, 59, and 59. The athlete's three best times this week are averaged for his final score on the course. What is his final score?

    a. 57 seconds

    b. 55 seconds

    c. 59 seconds

    d. 61 seconds

33. Five dancers are performing in a recital. Sammy will stand in the middle because she is the smallest. If the other 4 dancers will be arranged on either side of her, how many arrangements are possible?

    a. 120

    b. 24

    c. 12

    d. 6

34. Jade has enough space on her shelf to display 3 trophies; however, she owns 6 different trophies. How many different arrangements of trophies are possible?

    a. 120

    b. 60

    c. 40

    d. 203

35. The average purchase price (arithmetic mean) of 4 shirts must be $9. If one shirt was priced at $15, and another at $7, which could be the prices of the other 2 shirts?

   a. $4 and $3

   b. $7 and $15

   c. $9 and $9

   d. $10 and $4

   e. $11 and $7

36. Jen's median bowling score is greater than her mean bowling score for 5 tournament games. If the scores of the first four games were 140, 192, 163, and 208, which could have been the score of her fifth game?

   a. 130

   b. 145

   c. 168

   d. 177

   e. 270

37. If a drawer contains 7 navy socks, 4 white socks, and 9 black socks, what is the probability that the first sock randomly drawn out of the drawer will *not* be white?

   a. $\frac{1}{5}$

   b. $\frac{1}{4}$

   c. $\frac{7}{20}$

   d. $\frac{4}{5}$

   e. 16

38. Cassie bought 5 CDs. The average price per CD came out to $13. If she knows that three CDs cost $12, and the fourth cost $15, what was the price of the fifth CD?

   a. $12

   b. $13

   c. $14

   d. $15

39. A six-sided die with sides numbered 1 through 6 is rolled. What is the probability that the number rolled is a multiple of 3?

   a. $\frac{1}{3}$

   b. $\frac{1}{6}$

   c. $\frac{2}{3}$

   d. $\frac{3}{6}$

40. Reanna went to the bookstore and bought four books at an average price of $18.95. If three of the books sold for $25.25, $14.95, and $19.95, what is the cost of the fourth book?

    a. $20.05
    b. $18.95
    c. $15.65
    d. $14.25

41. Erika wrote 5 names on a piece of paper, put them in a bag, and will choose 3 names from the bag. How many different combinations are possible?

    a. 60
    b. 30
    c. 20
    d. 10

42. Ten dancers are auditioning for a role in the Nutcracker Ballet, but only 2 will get a part. How many different combinations are possible?

    a. 90
    b. 75
    c. 45
    d. 30

A

*Language
Arts
Answer
Key*

Note: Some of the questions, exemplars, and comments in this Appendix are adapted from the Nation's Report Card and the New York, California, and Illinois archives of actual language arts standardized test questions.

Chapter 4

pp. 56–57 Sample Standardized Test Problem Set: "Treating Burns"

   1. d.; 2. a.; 3. d.; 4. b.

p. 61 Narrative Writing "The Castle"

   Remember, a rubric is just a guide for subjective evaluation of writing. Use it for your student to grow as a writer, while learning techniques to:

- ◆ Establish focus by asserting a main or controlling idea
- ◆ Develop content using sufficient and appropriate supporting details
- ◆ Provide a logical pattern of organization
- ◆ Convey a sense of style with the use of varied vocabulary and sentences
- ◆ Demonstrate control of the conventions of standard written English

   Chapter 4 displays one type of rubric and another rubric is included here. You may prefer one version over the other, or your family may devise its own.

   For example, the following is a rubric for evaluating your learner's narrative writing.

SCORE & DESCRIPTION FOR NARRATIVE WRITING

Excellent

- Tells a well-developed story with relevant descriptive details across the response.
- Events are well connected and tie the story together with transitions across the response; narration is interesting.
- Sustains varied sentence structure and exhibits specific word choices.
- Exhibits control over sentence boundaries; errors in grammar, spelling, and mechanics do not interfere with understanding.

Skillful

- Tells a clear story with some development, including some relevant descriptive details; narration is interesting.
- Events are connected in much of the response; may lack some transitions.
- Exhibits some variety in sentence structure and exhibits some specific word choices.
- Generally exhibits control over sentence boundaries; errors in grammar, spelling, and mechanics do not interfere with understanding.

Sufficient

- Tells a clear story with little development; has few details.
- Events are generally related; may contain brief digressions or inconsistencies.
- Generally has simple sentences and simple word choice; may exhibit uneven control over sentence boundaries.
- Has sentences that consist mostly of complete, clear, distinct thoughts; errors in grammar, spelling, and mechanics generally do not interfere with understanding.

Uneven

May be characterized by one or more of the following:

- Attempts to tell a story, but tells only part of a story, gives a plan for a story, or is list-like.
- Lacks a clear progression of events; elements may not fit together or be in sequence.
- Exhibits uneven control over sentence boundaries and may have some inaccurate word choices.
- Errors in grammar, spelling, and mechanics sometimes interfere with understanding.

Unsatisfactory

May be characterized by one or more of the following:

- Attempts a response but may only paraphrase the prompt or be extremely brief.
- Exhibits no control over organization.
- Exhibits no control over sentence formation; word choice is inaccurate across the response.
- Characterized by misspellings, missing words, incorrect word order; errors in grammar, spelling, and mechanics severely impede understanding across the response.

p. 61 Sample Standardized Test Problem: Narrative Completion, "The Castle."

The following is an excellent basic-level response to the prompt. It had a few spelling and grammar errors which we are correcting for this exemplar.

> "Wow! A castle!" said John. He had no clue of how it got there or where it came from. He walked inside and found that it was rather damp. He wandered around until finally he found someone. This person didn't look normal—he was dressed as royalty, with a purple cape and a crown of jewels.
>
> Then the person spoke out, "There you are! You are supposed to be training right now." John had no clue what the person was talking about. Suddenly he thought of something—was this the king of the castle? Then the king told him to get on his armor.
>
> John thought and thought. Then he knew what was happening. He was to become a knight! If he was to be a knight, then he would never see his family again. Then he thought of his older sister, Jennifer, and he decided to stay. After about two months, he was finally knighted. John fought many dragons and men. He finally died but is still a legend today.

Comments: *This beginning writer uses dialogue effectively, develops characters, and provides a coherent plot. For a basic writer, he provides some vivid details: "He was dressed in royalty with a purple cape and a crown of jewels." He uses humor to please his audience.*

p. 61 Persuasive Writing "Write a Letter to a TV Producer"

These answers will vary considerably, depending on the topic chosen. You are looking for a clear statement at the beginning and then examples and\or reasons to support the production of this suggested TV show. A compelling opening and closing shows exemplary writing. To help you evaluate and discuss the writing, be guided by this rubric for persuasive writing.

SCORE & DESCRIPTION FOR PERSUASIVE WRITING

Excellent

- Takes a clear position, is persuasive, and develops support with well-chosen details, reasons, or examples across the response.
- Is well organized; maintains focus.
- Sustains varied sentence structure and exhibits specific word choices.
- Exhibits control over sentence boundaries; errors in grammar, spelling, and mechanics do not interfere with understanding.

Skillful

- Takes a clear position, is persuasive, and develops support with some specific details, reasons, or examples.
- Provides some organization of ideas by, for example, using contrast or building to a point.
- Exhibits some variety in sentence structure and exhibits some specific word choices.
- Generally exhibits control over sentence boundaries; errors in grammar, spelling, and mechanics do not interfere with understanding.

Sufficient

- Takes a clear position, is somewhat persuasive, with support that is clear and generally related to the issue.
- Is generally organized.
- Generally has simple sentences and simple word choice; may exhibit uneven control over sentence boundaries.
- Has sentences that consist mostly of complete, clear, distinct thoughts; errors in grammar, spelling, and mechanics generally do not interfere with understanding.

Uneven

May be characterized by one or more of the following:

- Takes a position and offers limited or incomplete support; some reasons may not be clear or related to the issue; not very persuasive.
- Is disorganized OR provides a disjointed sequence of information.
- Exhibits uneven control over sentence boundaries and may have some inaccurate word choices.
- Errors in grammar, spelling, and mechanics sometimes interfere with understanding.

Unsatisfactory

May be characterized by one or more of the following:

- Takes a position but provides no support, OR attempts to take a position (is on topic) but the position is very unclear; not persuasive; may only paraphrase the prompt.

- Exhibits no control over organization.
- Exhibits no control over sentence formation; word choice is inaccurate across the response.
- Characterized by misspellings, missing words, incorrect word order; errors in grammar, spelling, and mechanics severely impede understanding across the response.

Chapter 5

p. 77 "An Invisible Friend"

This letter is an example of an excellent basic response.

Dear Invisible Friend,

I got your letter. So now you know how to make yourself visible—congratulations! But you're afraid to do it? If you like living in my imagination, you'll love living in the real world. When you're invisible, you miss out on a lot of things normal people enjoy: sports, games, pets, amusement parks, ice cream, and a whole lot more. There are probably lots of people who would like to take care of you. Also, there are probably lots of people who would like to be your friend.

I do think that you should become visible. One thing that you could do for fun is use computers. Please decide to become visible!

From your (visible) friend

Comments: *The varied sentences in this "Excellent" response represent an understanding of interesting persuasive writing. The writer shows social interaction skills by being able to understand the friend's point of view and show empathy. The writer uses rhetorical questions, colons, and transitions with skill. Statements such as "If you like living in my imagination, you'd love living in the real world" demonstrate the writer's persuasiveness, clarity, and logic. The writer makes smooth transitions from addressing the fears of the imaginary friend through providing a list of activities available to visible people to mentioning the final enticement of using computers. This is a persuasive, impressive, and ultimately convincing response.*

pp. 77–78 "The Object"

This response is an exemplar of an intermediate to advanced response.

"And there's a long fly ball—it must be, it could be, it's a home run!" The announcer shouted this out of his small press box above home plate. I was six and I remember everyone in my section standing up and yelling. My hero, Omar Gonzalez, had just hit a home run and it was coming my way. As the ball approached, beer and nachos were flying left and right and everyone was getting all excited. The ball landed onto a pillow held by Cubs fans about three rows below me and almost miraculously bounced off of them and landed perfectly in my tanned Wilson glove.

For weeks I dragged the details of the story on and on, and just when my parents thought they could recite it from memory, I would change it so, for example, I would become a heroic figure instead of just a lucky kid. But that ball, it too changed, just as the story did. I would play catch with the neighborhood kids, and it seemed like the ball would come right to my glove. It almost became a part of me, or at least a good luck charm. Once I realized how important that ball was to me, I placed it on my bookcase shelf and dreamed about it and my dream to play for the Cubs.

As I grew up, I continued to play baseball and was remarkably good, but I began to forget where I'd got that old baseball on the shelf. Slowly I began to dream about other things and my desire was lost somewhere in the past. As playing ball in college became more of a reality, I kept practicing and practicing and eventually made the practice team. I can still remember packing up my gear to go to college, and my mother asked why I didn't take the ball.

"You mean that old thing? Why would I need that?"

"Don't you remember, don't you know where this came from?"

So she retold the story, the actual story. She convinced me to take the ball off with me to school, where I put it in a drawer. I played the worst baseball I had ever played. So I took my mom's advice, and I started playing catch with the ball I had caught at Wrigley Field. Out of nowhere, my skills and talent, but especially my desire, returned. I made the starting line-up and eventually progressed my way into the major leagues.

Now I am an overweight designated hitter on some AA farm team in Iowa. My days in the bigs are over. But on my last at bat as a major league ball player, I hit a home run, and I only pray that the little guy who caught it will never put it up on his shelf.

Comments: *This response, rated Excellent, is one where the elements of good writing come together. It is both clear and consistently developed with details, as in the opening description of how the narrator caught the ball. It is well organized; the student moves easily from past to present to describe how the baseball has affected his life and aspirations. The story is so vivid that it seems autobiographical; it seems as if we are having a social conversation with the first-person storyteller; it is surprising to realize at the end that the student has in fact created an older character.*

Chapter 6

p. 96 "Treating Burns"

More multiple-choice questions for information and understanding.

1. **b.** A question that asks you to choose a title for a passage is a main idea question. This main idea is expressed in the second sentence, which is the topic sentence. Answers **a**, **c**, and **d** are too limited.

2. **d.** The informational answer to this fact question is clearly expressed in the sentence "These burns should be immersed in warm water and then wrapped in a sterile dressing or bandage." The hard part may be keeping track of which kind of burns "these burns" refers to. It is easy to choose the wrong answer because all of the answer choices are mentioned in the passage. You need to match the right burn to the right treatment.

3. **a.** This is another fact or detail question. The passage says that first-degree burns turn the skin red. Answer **b** can be eliminated right away, but the other two choices are mentioned in the text.

4. **c.** Another main idea question answered with "It is important for firefighters to be able to recognize each of these types of burns so that they can be sure burn victims are given proper treatment."

1. **c.** This is a vocabulary question. *Irate* means *ill-tempered, angry.* It should be clear that **b**, *happy, cheerful,* is not the answer; dealing with happy people is not a "challenge." Answers **a** and **d** aren't appropriate. In addition, the passage explains that irate customers are not "*angry* at you," and *irate* is used as a synonym for *irritable* in the first sentence.

2. **d.** This is an inference question, as the phrase "the passage *suggests*" might have told you. The idea that angry customer service representatives might give bad service is implied in the passage as a whole, which is an attempt to prevent angry reactions to irate customers. Further, the last sentence in particular makes this inference possible: "If you react to their anger . . . the results will be unproductive for both of you." While **c** may be true, there is no mention of suits in the passage. Likewise, answer **b** is wrong; the passage does not recommend not talking to the customer. In answer choice **a**, watch out for words such as "easily," which may distort the meaning of the passage.

3. **a.** The writer seems to believe that some customers just want attention. It should be clear that **b** cannot be the answer, because it includes an absolute: "Irate customers are *always* miserable." Perhaps *some* of the customers are *often* miserable, but an absolute like *always* is almost always wrong! Answer **c** is not a logical answer, considering that the passage is about how to help customers. Finally, **d** may be true, but career is not mentioned in this passage.

4. **b.** If you don't know what an *imprecation* is, the context should reveal that it's something you can ignore. Neither **a**, an object, nor **d**, a software box, is a likely answer. Further, **c** is not possible, since an irate customer is not likely to be making jokes.

5. **b.** Answer **d** is too general for this passage and **c** is irrelevant. Answer **a** is the second best possibility—and some might argue for it—but the *best* choice is probably **b**, "Handling Angry Customers," which covers both the customer service rep and the customer.

p. 97 Researched Informational Essay on the Iroquois, Intermediate Mastery

The Iroquois

Iroquois were people of strong beliefs. They respected the world of nature and knew its importance.

Hunting was very important to the Iroquois. Bullheads, sunfish, and perch were main parts of their diet. They ate other food such as corn, squash, and beans. These were called the three sisters because of their importance to the Iroquois. They also ate meat and a variety of nuts. They grew and hunted only what they needed and wasted nothing. They used fish for fertilizer and rotated their crops. Today we use chemicals, and often we do not let the soil rest.

Building shelter took about a week, seven suns. They sent the men to get bark while the others built a frame, which was made from young saplings. Trees were not clear cut for money, as we do today. They used every part of the tree, too. The bark used, if laid out, would be seventy-seven feet long.

Ceremonies usually started in the evening. The Iroquois first gave thanks and then danced and feasted. They sometimes threw tobacco in the fire as an offering. They gave thanks to the

Spirits for their good fortune, harvests, good weather, and plentiful crops. They worshipped the natural world; they didn't hurt it.

The Iroquois used bones, rocks, and wood to make tools and weapons from. They also used parts of the animals when making these tools and weapons. Today our tools use electric power and are not as good for the environment.

Comments: *This essay:*

♦ *reflects a range of resources*
♦ *demonstrates a clear understanding of what was studied and learned*
♦ *shows skillful use of language, but needs more variety and sophistication in vocabulary choices*
♦ *makes appropriate connections by developing a paragraph for each subtopic*
♦ *weaves in details of hunting, building, ceremonies, and tools to support main ideas*

p. 95 Instructional essay on how to do a complex task in an engaging way
This essay is a great opportunity for your learner to be very inventive. What to evaluate?

♦ point of view
♦ opening/closing
♦ originality
♦ humor
♦ enthusiasm
♦ examples and supporting details
♦ vocabulary appropriate to the task being taught and the method used to teach it
♦ graphics, maps, cartoons, or sketches appropriate to the task being taught

Chapter 7

pp. 109–112 "A Day at the Nature Center" problem set and short essay answers

1. **c.**
2. **b.**
3. **d.**
4. **a.**
5. **c.**
6. **a.**
7. **a.**
8. **c.**
9. possible answers: "stared sadly," "She thought about the farm all the time," "overwhelmingly shy," "With a sigh," "looked around apprehensively," "She didn't have any friends yet," "hesitated," "tentatively."
10. possible facts: "The farm was only fifty miles outside of town." "Emma sat next to Julia." possible opinions: "Good job, Emma!" " I thought you were shy and scared of everything, . . . "

This question leads to differentiating fact from opinion, which can be practiced in oral readings, and when viewing commercials and print ads.

11. Opinions will vary—they must, however, be supported with detail to show critical analysis and evaluation.

p. 112 Cross-Cultural Research and Evaluation

For this advanced critical analysis and informational assignment, the performance indicators you will be looking for include

- interpreting complex resources
- synthesizing information from several sources
- making perceptive connections to previous knowledge and experience
- weaving personal reactions and insights into the analysis
- making effective use of poetic language and challenging vocabulary
- presenting a controlled idea and supporting it with detail and example
- making connections in a cross-cultural way

Note: Reports may be read aloud or shared in a group discussion, with positive critiques following readings. Reports may include visual aids, art, audio taping, or video taping.

Here is one example of a middle schooler's well-written opening to an essay on Chinese Art:

> Broad, sweeping landscapes; benevolent figures meditating; snow-capped peaks thrusting out from misty clouds; a few brush strokes suggesting so much. What do all of these artistic elements have in common? They are all prevalent in Chinese painting.

Chapter 8

pp. 126–127 Standardized Problem Set for The Things They Carried

Notice that this is a deceptively simple, yet highly powerful, passage. The passage may be best absorbed when read aloud, in a slightly marching, monotonous tone. You and your learner might discuss how close to poetry the passage is and why (use of rhythm, alliteration, assonance, repetition of words, sounds, phrases, metaphor, and so on).

Note: Your homeschooler may make a case for other answers than the ones listed here. That's okay as long as your child makes a good, supported case for his or her choice.

1. a.
2. d.
3. a.
4. c.
5. a.

p. 127 A Third-Person Narrative About Homeschooling

Narratives will vary, but your learner might combine personal response with research from the library or the Internet or a homeschooling resource center. Or your learner might artistically create a story, a poem, a scene, a tale, or a song that incorporates what he or she has experienced and learned about being a homeschooler.

What you are looking for in this form of literary expression includes:

- knowledge of the narrative, third-person form
- a good opening understanding chronology of a narrative
- an ending that connects with the beginning
- appropriate use of language and story conventions

p. 127 The Spaceship Story

A "Sufficient" Exemplar

The space ship it was about as big as a school. When the door opened an alien stepped out. He had an egg shaped head with black misty eyes, short white body with long arms and three long fingers. He took his helmet off and started talking in some language. Then he pressed a button and started speaking in English. Greetings, earthling, my name is Racabae. what is yours? My name is frank nice to meet you. he asked me if I wanted to go on a journey with him and I said sure. We got in his spaceship and shot up through the clouds at 2,000 knots plus. He asked what I would like to do. I said let's go exploring other galaxies. We wnet where no man has gone before. We went to the Condegua galaxie. It had seven suns 12 moons and 54 planets in its system. That's when he said It's time to go home and he dropped me off. And then all of a sudden I awoke from my great dream.

Comments: *This "Sufficient" response has a clear beginning, middle, and end, and does apply the general conventions of storytelling. Though the conventions of dialogue are not followed precisely, this writer attempts to add speaking parts to the story to heighten interest. Some nice detail ("We went to the Condegua galaxie. It had seven suns 12 moons and 54 planets in its system.") is hampered by many errors in punctuation and spelling and thin development of plot. The sentences, for the most part, are simple and unvaried. This response is a good example of a "Sufficient" paper that, though hampered by lack of development and some writing flaws, still tells a story that is clear and relatively detailed.*

An "Uneven" Exemplar:

I was just staring out my window at the creature I was so frightened. Its eyes were pitch black and huge, it was just barely 3 feet tall, it was wearing a purple velvet spacesuit and had off white yellowish skin. All of a sudden it started walking towards me. I froze. The it shattered my window with its fist and grabbed my hand as if to shake it. I said "Welcome to Earth."

Comments: *This "Uneven" response has some vivid description of the space creature: "it was wearing a purple velvet spacesuit." It does not provide much beyond description and a couple of plot events. The lack of development, as well as problems with sentence structure, earned this paper an "Uneven" rating.*

p. 127 The English/Biology "Through An Organism's Eyes" Research and Story

Note: This highly creative literary expression assignment can include from a small amount to a large amount of research. Your learner can also write a formal science research paper on the same organism and then discuss and compare both writing experiences. Your learner can write and perform a play or a dialogue or some other oral convention.

As perhaps more pre-writing planning and post-writing review will enhance an assignment of this scope, here are some graphically presented tips on planning and reviewing writing, adapted from the Nation's Report Card website.

IDEAS FOR PLANNING YOUR WRITING

To plan your writing, you could do one or more of the following:

Brainstorm
List lots of ideas; choose which ones to use.

Imagine
Imagine talking about your topic with someone.

Draw
Draw a picture or a diagram of your topic.

Web
Draw lines between ideas to connect them.

Outline
Organize ideas into main points and subpoints.

IDEAS FOR REVIEWING YOUR WRITING

After writing, think about the following:

Purpose
Have I said what I want to say?

Development
Do I need to add more details? Do I need to take out some details?

Organization
Are the parts in the right order? Do the parts fit together?

Clarity
Will my audience understand? Is my writing easy to read?

Correctness
Grammar? Punctuation? Spelling? Capitalization?

B

Glossary of Language Arts Terms

Alliteration? Diphthong? Find these words and more in this helpful collection of language arts terms.

Abstract   A summary of the essential points in writing.

Aesthetic   Appreciative of beauty, especially in writing and art.

Affixes   One or more sounds or letters attached to the beginning or end of a word or base; also known as prefixes or suffixes.

Alliteration   Repetition of the same letter or sound at the beginning of two or more consecutive words near one another; as in *fly o'er waste fens and windy fields*.

Allusions   An implied or indirect reference to another person or thing found in another piece of literature or in history; in Western literature, quite often a reference to a figure or event in the Bible or mythology.

Analogy   A comparison based upon a resemblance between two things; probably the two most common are the simile and the metaphor.

Antecedent   Pronouns are words that take the place of nouns; the antecedent for the pronoun is the noun it takes the place of. For example, "John fell down, but he didn't hurt himself." Here, the pronouns *he* and *himself* take the place of *John*; therefore, John is the antecedent for *he* and *himself*.

Antonyms   Words with opposite meanings; for example, *hot* and *cold*.

Appositives   A word or phrase that renames the noun or pronoun before it; for example, "John, *an experienced teacher*, serves on several curriculum committees.

Blends   Two or more consecutive consonants that begin a syllable, such as *bl*end.

Brainstorming   Collecting ideas in groups by freely sharing a large number of possibilities.

Comparative   The form of an adjective or adverb used when comparing two things, such as *warmer, more beautiful*, or *better*.

Connotation   The suggested or emotional meaning of a word; the following words have the same *denotation* (dictionary definition) but their connotations are different: *thin, skinny, slender*.

Conventions   The usual rules of grammar, punctuation, and spelling.

CVC   A simple spelling pattern—a *c*onsonant, a *v*owel, and a *c*onsonant: *cat*.

Declarative Sentences   Sentences that make statements; for example, "Becky is a student."

Decode   To recognize and interpret; in this case, in reading words.

Dialects   Regional or social varieties of language with vocabulary, grammar, or pronunciation different from other regional or social varieties.

Diphthongs   A vowel sound produced when the tongue glides from one vowel to another such as in *bee, bay, toy, buy*.

Environmental   Print and other graphic symbols, other than books, found in the physical print environment, such as street signs, billboards, and so on.

Exclamatory Sentence   Sentence that expresses emotion; for example "I just qualified for the Olympics!"

Expository   The form of nonfiction writing which informs or explains.

Extemporaneous   Prepared, but spoken without notes or text.

External Punctuation   Punctuation found at the end of a sentence such as a period, question mark, or exclamation point.

Figurative Language   Comparing or identifying one thing with another that has a meaning or connotation familiar to the reader; see *metaphor* or *simile* as examples.

Graphic Organizer   A teacher- or student-related tool used to record and organize information when reading, such as a schematic drawing; see *webbing*.

Homographs   Words that are spelled the same but have different pronunciations or meanings; for example, the *bow* of a ship and a *bow* and arrow.

Hyperbole   A figure of speech that uses intentional exaggeration: She cried *buckets of tears.*

Hypothesis   An assumption made to test its logical consequences.

Idioms   An expression used in a language that has a meaning that cannot be derived from the words themselves; an example would be "I ran into Joe the other day." (Here, the meaning is not that you physically "ran into" the other person but that you met him.)

Imperative Sentence   Sentences that give commands; for example, "Open your books to page 322."

Impromptu   Composed or performed on the spur of the moment.

Inferences   Conclusions arrived at by reasoning from evidence.

Informative Paper   Any paper that offers information, such as a report or a how-to essay.

Internal Punctuation   Punctuation within a sentence, such as commas, semicolons, or apostrophes.

Interrogative Sentence   Sentences which ask questions; for example, "Who is that?"

Intonation   The rise and fall in pitch of the voice in speech.

Inversion   A change in normal word order, such as from "I see the cat" to "The cat I see."

Irony   Twisting the meaning of words in ways that create the opposite impression. There are three major types:

Verbal irony: when someone says the opposite of what is meant; for example, "Having the flu is so much fun, isn't it?"

Irony of situation: when there is a discrepancy between what may reasonably be expected to happen in a situation and what actually occurs; for example when Character #1 sets a trap for Character #2 but Character #1 falls into the trap himself.

Dramatic irony: when the reader/audience knows something that the character does not know.

Jargon   The technical terminology or characteristic idiom of a special activity or group; for example, people who do not use computers might not know the special computer meaning of such words as *mouse* or *icon* or *megabyte.*

Metaphor   An implied comparison between two objects or actions, such as "The ship knifed through the water" or "The moon was tossed upon cloudy seas" (the action of the ship being compared to the slicing of a knife and the cloudy sky being compared to an ocean with waves); see *simile*.

Modifiers   Adjectival and adverbial words, phrases, or clauses.

Multimedia   Using different means of communication such as overhead transparencies, flip charts, or audiotapes.

Onomatopoeia   The use of a word whose sound suggests the sense of the word, such as *sizzle*, *clang*, or *snap*, *crackle*, and *pop*.

Parallelism   Ideas in a series are arranged in words, phrases, sentences, or paragraphs that are similar in grammatical structure: Words: "he was left *alone, lonely*, and *heartbroken*" (adjectives). Phrases: " . . . government *of the people, by the people*, and *for the people* . . . " (prepositional phrases).

Paraphrase   To read text and then put it in your own words.

Personification   Figure of speech in which something that is not human is given human characteristics, such as "The tree lifts its arms to the sky."

Phonics   The system by which symbols represent sounds in an alphabetic writing system.

Point of View   The perspective from which a story is presented to a reader; the most common are first person, third person singular (or limited), and third person omniscient.

Prose   Anything not written in poetry form.

R-Controlled Vowel   In English, when an *r* colors the way the preceding vowel is pronounced, such as *bad* and *bar* or *can* and *car*.

Reading Rate   The speed at which a selection is read and the manner in which it is read, depending on the purpose; skimming, scanning, studying, or reading for pleasure.

Reflective Texts   Writing based on a writer's prior knowledge or experience.

Rhetorical   Relating to the art of writing as a means of communication or persuasion.

Rubric   Scoring guide; written criteria used to judge a particular kind of performance.

"Showing" Not "Telling"   Writing that allows the reader to see, hear, touch, taste, or smell what is written. Rather than saying "He was angry," saying "He trembled and pounded his fist on the table, frightening us all."

Simile   An explicit comparison between two objects or actions using *like* or *as*, such as "Soft as a feather" or "The cat's tongue feels like sandpaper." See *metaphor*.

Stylistic Devices   Techniques of writing used by an author to achieve a purpose, such as diction, detail, or point of view.

Subject/Verb Agreement   Using a singular verb with a singular subject or a plural verb with a plural subject.

Subordination   The act of putting an idea of lesser importance in a clause that cannot stand alone; for example, "*Because he was late*, he missed the bus."

Superlative Modifier   The form of an adjective or adverb used when comparing three or more things, such as *warmest, most beautiful*, or *best*.

Synonyms   Words with similar meanings; for example, *pretty* and *beautiful*.

Syntax   The way in which words are put together or related to one another in a sentence; "I ate the sandwich." "The sandwich I ate." "Ate I the sandwich?"

Synthesize   To combine several sources of ideas in order to produce a coherent whole; a high-level critical-thinking skill.

Theme   The dominant idea of a work of literature.

Thesis   A proposition to be proved.

Thesis Statement   A sentence containing the main idea of a piece of writing.

Topic   The subject being written about.

Usage   The way words are used correctly in a sentence, such as subject/verb agreement, pronoun/antecedent agreement, or consistency of tense.

Voice   The presence of the writer on the page; writing with strong voice leaves the reader feeling a strong connection to the writing and/or the writer.

Webbing   A prewriting technique that often makes use of circles or squares to organize ideas regarding a topic for writing.

C

Mathematics Answer Key

Chapter 9

1. To find the number of phone books left in Marcy's truck, subtract the number she delivered from the number she started out with. 470 − 378 = 92 (choice **a**).
   b. This answer is incorrect because it incorrectly subtracts 378 from 470.
   c. This answer is incorrect because it incorrectly subtracts 378 from 470.
   d. This answer is incorrect because it adds the number of phone books Marcy started with and the number she delivered.

2. To find the total of the 4 games, add the 4 scores together, giving a sum of 2542 points (choice **d**).
   a. This answer is incorrect because it incorrectly carries during addition.
   b. This answer is incorrect because it incorrectly carries during addition.
   c. This answer is incorrect because it incorrectly carries during addition.

3. The number marked is −3, choice **c**.

4. 237 divided by 3 equals 79 (choice **c**). The other numbers are not evenly divisible by 3.

5. First add 47 + 84 = 131. Then multiply by four: 131 × 4 = 524. Last, subtract the amount he already has from the total that he needs to buy to get the answer: 524 − 131 = 393, so choice **c** is correct.

6. The correct answer choice is **d**. This expression shows 2,037,804 in expanded notation.

7. Choice **d** is correct. Answer **a** equals 276; **b** equals 2,706; **c** equals 20,076.

8. When you are looking for the absolute value of a number, you are looking to see how many places away from zero it is. For example, 4 is 4 places away from zero. But also see that −4 is 4 places from zero. So the easiest way to remember absolute value is to find the positive number. Since 47 − 64 = −17, the absolute value (or positive) of −17 is 17, answer **a**.

9. First you add up what she made: 153 + 167 + 103 = 423. Then you add up what she spent: 94 + 19 = 113. Lastly, you subtract the second number from the first to see how much is left: 423 − 113 = 310, choice **d**.

10. The correct answer is choice **d**. Don't let the fraction throw you off; you are still simply trying to find the positive value of that number, which is $\frac{2}{3}$.

11. $|-423|$ = 423, $|423|$ = 423, so add the two numbers together to get 846, choice **c**.

12. Perform the operations in the parentheses first: (12 × 79) − 162 = 786, so choice **d** is correct.

13. 4! means 4 *factorial*, which is equivalent to 4 × 3 × 2 × 1, choice **b**.

14. **c.** First you should list all factors of each of the given numbers. Factors are the numbers that "go into" your number evenly. Next, list the factors of 56 and 64 respectively:

Factors of 56	Factors of 64
1, 56	1, 64
2, 28	2, 32
4, 14	4, 16
7, 8	8

Notice how these factors are listed in a methodical fashion. For example, 1 × 56 = 56 so 1 and 56 are listed. 2 × 28 = 56, so 2 and 28 are listed. If you keep your scratch work orderly, it is easy to spot your answer. What is the largest *factor* that these two numbers have in common? The answer is 8.

15. Choice **a** is correct. The *quotient* is the solution to a division problem, and in this case the division problem is "*nine divided by three,*" or 9 ÷ 3. The given statement says: "*The quotient of nine divided by three is decreased by one,*" so now you must decrease the quotient by 1. The answer is: 9 ÷ 3 − 1.

16. The first box is one greater than −5; the second is one greater than 0, so choice **a** is correct.

17. To find the total number of batches of jam they can make, divide the number of crates they receive by the number of crates that go into each batch of jam. $\frac{2052}{12}$ = 171, choice **d.** The other answers divide incorrectly.

18. Choice **d** is correct. To simplify (−5)(−3)(2) − |-20|, let's find the absolute value of −20. |−20| = 20 because the *absolute value* is just the *positive* distance from zero on the number line. Rewriting the questions as (−5)(−3)(2) − 20 makes it appear less intimidating. Now you can multiply out the first part of this expression: (−5)(−3)(2) = 30. Note that multiplying a negative by a negative produced a positive. The whole expression becomes 30 − 20, which equals 10, choice **d.**

19. You need 4 consecutive even numbers whose sum is 44. Consecutive means that that numbers will be in order, and because you are told that you need consecutive *even* numbers, you are looking for even numbers that are in order and add to 44. Choice **a** contains odd numbers and is therefore wrong. Looking at choice **b**, you see that these are, in fact, consecutive even numbers. Do they add to 44? 4 + 6 + 8 + 10 = 28. No. Try **c**: 8 + 10 + 12 + 14 = 44. Thus, **c** is correct.

20. Choice **b** is correct. If you look closely at the sequence 31 23 17 13 __, you should first note that the numbers are decreasing. How much are they decreasing by? Well from 31 to 23 you **decreased by 8**. From 23 to 17 you **decreased by 6**. From 17 to 13 you **decreased by 4**. From 13 to the blank space you should **decrease by 2**. 13 − 2 = 11.

21. This problem has multiple steps. First, figure out what Deanna spent: $7 for popcorn, 2 hot dogs × 2 girls × $3 each equals $12, 2 sodas × $4 = $8. Then add them up: $7 + $12 + $8 = $27. Next, figure out what Jamie spent: $13 × 2 = $26. Last, subtract the two numbers: $27 − $26 = $1. Deanna spent $1 more, so **a** is the correct choice.

22. The total on the right is 35. On the left, you need an operation you can do on 5 to get 35. Multiplying by 7, or 5 + 2, does the trick, so the correct answer is **a**.

23. Choice **b** is correct. First, notice that the numbers in the sequence are increasing.

$$4 \quad 28 \quad \underline{} \quad 62 \quad 79$$

To go from 4 to 28, it **increased by 17**. To go from 62 to 79, it **increased by 17**. Let's increase 28 by 17. 28 + 17 = 45. Does 45 make the sequence work? 45 + 17 = 62. Yes. This works:

$$4 \quad 28 \quad 45 \quad 62 \quad 79$$

The missing number is 45, choice **b**.

24. Multiply the average pledge amount ($796) times the number of callers (182). 796 × 182 = 144,872, choice **c**.

25. First, for Brian, divide to determine the number of 20-minute segments there are in an hour: 60 ÷ 20 = 3. Now multiply that number by the number of times Brian can circle the block: 3 × 4 = 12. Brian can make it around 12 times in one hour. Now do the same thing for Jaclyn: 60 ÷ 12 = 5, and 5 × 3 = 15. Lastly, subtract 15 − 12 = 3. Jaclyn can go around three more times in one hour, choice **c**.

26. 157 is rounded to 200; 817 is rounded to 800. (200)(800) = 160,000, choice **a**.

27. Choice **b** is correct. First, multiply: 253 × 631 = 159,643. Next, round to nearest hundred to get 159,600. Choice **c** represents the product *before* rounding. Choice **a** represents the result of rounding *before* finding the product.

28. To find how many people, total, can be seated at Megan and Nathan's wedding, multiply the number of tables by the number of seats at each table. 23 × 9 = 207. This answer is not listed as a choice, so the answer is not here, choice **d**.
   a. This answer is incorrect because it adds 23 and 9 instead of multiplying them.
   b. This answer is incorrect because it incorrectly carries during multiplication.
   c. This answer is incorrect because it incorrectly multiplies 23 and 9.

29. 84 (choice **c**) is divisible by 6 and 7.

30. $24,355 + $23,000 = $47,355. When this is rounded to the nearest $100, the answer is $47,400, choice **b**.

31. $|5 - 9| - |7 - 1| = |-4| - |6| = 4 - 6 = -2$, choice **b**.

32. This is a problem with several steps. First, figure out how many *dozen* bracelets Janice makes each day. To do this you would divide 36 by one dozen, or 12, and $36 \div 12 = 3$. So she makes 3 dozen bracelets per day. Now, figure out how much she makes on bracelets per day: $18 × 3 = $54. Finally, figure out how much Janice makes per week. To do this, you must multiply how much she makes per day ($54) by how many days per week (5) she works: $54 × 5 = $270. Choice **b** is correct.

33. It takes Eric 9 minutes to bake 1 dozen cookies, so to bake 4 dozen cookies, multiply 4 and 9. Then it takes him 16 minutes to clean up after he is done baking, so add 16. The total time it takes him to bake and clean up is given by the equation $t = (9 × 4) + 16$, choice **a**.
  b. This answer is incorrect because it multiplies the number of dozens of cookies by the time it takes to clean up and then adds the time it takes to bake one dozen.
  c. This answer is incorrect because it multiplies all the increments of time together.
  d. This answer is incorrect because it sets the number of dozens of cookies equal to the total time plus the clean up time, all multiplied by the time it takes to bake 1 dozen cookies.

34. On average, it takes Carla about 6 minutes to do each math problem. Multiplying 6 minutes by 20 problems gives an answer of about 120 minutes to do her math homework, so choice **c** is correct.

35. Choice **d**, 28, is divisible by 2 and 4 but is not divisible by 8.

36. Choice **d** is correct. Following the order of operations: $|6^2 - (-3)^3| = |6^2 - (-27)| = |36 + 27| = |63| = 63$.

37. Choice **d** is correct. 8BA × 1000 = 9BA000, which you know is 932000. Thus, B = 3 and A = 2. BA ÷ 4 becomes 32 ÷ 4, which is 8. Thus, **c** = 8.

38. The number is $8 × 10 + U = 80 + U$. Since the number is divisible by U, 80 must be divisible by U. The only number among the answer choices that 80 is not divisible by is 3, choice **b**. Alternatively, you can test out the answer choices to see which one works.

39. If there were 123 cars in the lot after 37 drove away, then there were 123 + 37, or 160 cars in the lot at 3:00 P.M. This amount was $\frac{2}{3}$ greater than the number at 1:00 P.M. You can use an equation with x representing the number of cars at 1:00 P.M.

$$1\tfrac{2}{3} = \tfrac{5}{3}, \text{ so } \left(\tfrac{5}{3}\right)x = 160$$
$$5x = 3 \times 160 = 480 \longrightarrow x = 480 \div 5 = 96$$

If there were 96 cars at 1:00 P.M. and this value is double the number of cars in the lot at noon, then the number of cars at noon was half of 96, or 48 cars, choice **b.**

40. To find the temperature when Mitchell got up, make the necessary additions (temperature rise) and subtractions (temperature drop) to the original temperature of 68 degrees: 68 – 9 + 5 + 2 = 66 degrees, choice **b.**

41. Divide the amount of money raised ($242) by the cost per chance to toss a pie ($2.75): 242 ÷ 2.75 = 88, choice **a.**

42. Choice **b** is correct. You know that the concentration of carbon monoxide did not remain constant, so **d** must be wrong. Let's see which answer choice makes sense. We'll make a chart for all of the possibilities:

Concentration of carbon monoxide:

Time	if quadrupled every hour . . .	if tripled every hour . . .	if doubled every hour . . .
9 A.M.	50 ppm	50 ppm	50 ppm
10 A.M.	200 ppm	150 ppm	100 ppm
11 A.M.	800 ppm	450 ppm	200 ppm
12 NOON	3200 ppm	1350 ppm	400 ppm
	Too high! Choice **a** is wrong.	**Exactly right!** Pick choice **b**.	**Too low!** Choice **c** is wrong.

43. **b.** To find $\sqrt{35}$, you need to find out what number, when squared, will yield 35. If you notice that $6^2 = 36$ and $5^2 = 25$, you know that the number you need must be between 5 and 6.

44. If 3 out of 20 words are misspelled, you can set up a ratio and cross multiply to find the unknown amount of misspelled words.

$$\frac{3 \text{ misspelled}}{20 \text{ total}} \times \frac{x \text{ misspelled words}}{160 \text{ words}}, \frac{20x}{20} = \frac{480}{20}, x = 24.$$ Choice **c** is correct.

  a. This answer is incorrect because it is the number of times that 20 goes into 160, but it does not multiply by 3.
  b. This answer is incorrect because it is the number of words that would be misspelled if 2 out of every 20 were misspelled instead of 3 out of every 20.
  d. This answer is incorrect because it is the rounded number of times that 3 goes into 160, not the number of misspelled words.
  e. This answer is incorrect because it multiplies 20 and 3 together instead of finding the number of misspelled words out of 160.

45. It would cost $7 to get three sandwiches and a piece of fruit, so choice **a** is correct.

46. The pies were cut into eighths, so there were 66 pieces of pie to begin with. Multiply the number of pies (8) by the number of pieces in each pie (8) and add the pieces in the one-fourth pie: $8 \times 8 = 64$; $64 + 2 = 66$. Then subtract the number of pieces that were left: $66 - 5 = 61$, choice **b**.

47. The correct choice is **b**. Fill in the missing line, based on your judgment:

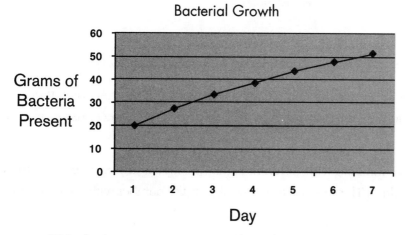

38 is the best approximation. The other answers would be too far above or below the line drawn.

Chapter 10

1. To change a mixed number to a fraction, you take the whole number potion of it, multiply it by the denominator, and add it to the numerator. The result goes on top of the denominator. Thus, $4\frac{1}{3}$ becomes $\frac{4 \times 3 + 1}{3} = \frac{13}{3}$. $3\frac{3}{10}$ becomes $\frac{3 \times 10 + 3}{10} = \frac{33}{10}$. The least common denominator (LCD) of these two fractions is 30. $\frac{13}{3} = \frac{130}{30}$, and $\frac{33}{10} = \frac{99}{30}$. You add $\frac{130}{30}$ to $\frac{99}{30}$ to yield $\frac{229}{30}$. Last, you divide: $229 \div 30 = 7\frac{19}{30}$, choice **d.**

2. Only 0.0043, choice **d**, is less than 0.043. Remember that $0.0043 = \frac{43}{10,000}$ and $0.043 = \frac{43}{1,000}$. 43 ten thousandths is less than 43 hundredths.

3. First, convert the mixed numbers to improper fractions, then multiply. $\frac{23}{6} \times \frac{14}{3} = \frac{322}{18}$. Reduce this fraction to $\frac{161}{9}$. Change to a mixed number by dividing 161 by 9. The correct answer is $17\frac{8}{9}$, choice **a.**

4. Point T (choice **c**) is $\frac{1}{3}$ of the way between 0 and –1, and would thus equal $-\frac{1}{3}$. If you picked choice **d**, you accidentally picked $\frac{1}{3}$ instead of $-\frac{1}{3}$.

5. To work this kind of division problem, you have to move each decimal point to the right (4 places) and then bring the point straight up into the answer:

$$8758\overline{)29000.}$$

   $29,000 \div 8758 = 3.31$, so choice **a** is correct.

   If you got answer **c**, you divided 0.8758 by 2.9 instead of the reverse.

6. First, change $2\frac{4}{7}$ to an improper fraction $\frac{18}{7}$. In order to divide the fractions, the divisor $\frac{18}{7}$ must be inverted $\frac{7}{18}$ and then multiplied by the first fraction. The correct answer is $\frac{7}{72}$, choice **b.**

7. To find the sum of two numbers with different signs (positive and negative), find the difference of their absolute values. The sum has the same sign as the number with the greater absolute value.

$$\begin{array}{r} {\scriptstyle 2\ 10}^{12} \\ 3.\cancel{1}\cancel{2}5 \\ -\ 0.590 \\ \hline 2.535 \end{array}$$

   Since you use the sign of the number with the larger absolute value, the answer is –2.535, choice **b.**

8. 6.005 (choice **d**), because it has zeroes in both the tenths and the hundredths places, is the smallest.

9. Because the value in the hundredths place (1) is less than 5, you leave the tenths place as it is (7). Thus, when rounded to the nearest tenth, the number 0.716 becomes 0.7, so choice **a** is correct. Choice **c** is rounded to the thousandths place. Choice **d** is rounded to the nearest whole number. Choice **b** is rounded up rather than down.

10. To the right of the decimal point, the places are: tenths, hundredths, thousandths. Thus, choice **a** has a 9 in the thousandths place: 3.00**9**5. In **b**, the 9 is in the hundredths place. In **c**, it is in the tenths place; in **d**, the ten-thousandths place.

11. First calculate $\frac{3}{4} \times \frac{1}{5}$. You multiply the first fraction by the reciprocal of the second: $\frac{3}{4} \times \frac{5}{1} = \frac{15}{4}$. Then you convert the improper fraction into a mixed number: $\frac{15}{4} = 3\frac{3}{4}$. The absolute value of $3\frac{3}{4}$ is the positive value, which is still $3\frac{3}{4}$, choice **b.**

12. By multiplying the numerator and denominator be 4, it is easy to see that the fraction $\frac{13}{25}$ is equal to $\frac{52}{100}$. "52 hundredths" can also be written as .52, choice **d.**

13. To solve this problem, you must first convert all the fractions to the lowest common denominator, which is 24. $\frac{7}{8} = \frac{21}{24}$; $\frac{3}{4} = \frac{18}{24}$; $\frac{2}{3} = \frac{16}{24}$; $\frac{5}{6} = \frac{20}{24}$. Thus, choice **a**, $\frac{7}{8}$ is correct.

14. When multiplying 2 negative values, the result will be a positive number. Therefore, choices **b** and **c** are WRONG. $-2.9 \times -6.03 = +17.487$, choice **a.**

$$\begin{array}{rl} -2.9 & \text{decimal is 1 place to the left} \\ \times\ -6.03 & \text{decimal is 2 places to the left} \\ \hline 17.487 & \text{decimal is 3 places to the left} \end{array}$$

15. -0.15, choice **a**, is less than -0.02, the smallest number in the range.

16. You know the ratio of Drake's charge to Jean's charge is 3 to 4, or $\frac{3}{4}$. To find what Jean charges, you use the equation $\frac{3}{4} = \frac{36}{x}$, or $3x = 4(36)$. $(4)(36) = 144$, which is then divided by 3 to arrive at $x = 48$, choice **a.**

17. To order these fractions, it is easiest to find the decimal equivalents. In choice **d** you have: 2.5, 2.41666 . . . ., 2.3333 . . . ., 2.25.

18. Write out the equation. Remember "is" means *equals* and "of" means *times*. To find the answer, you first write one-eighth and one-sixth as fractions, and then you multiply straight across: $\frac{1}{8} \times \frac{1}{6} = \frac{1}{48}$, so choice **a** is correct.

19. To find the estimate of the price they can pay for each snow cone, round 14 up to 15 and $31.00 down to $30.00. Then divide $30.00 by 15, giving a price of $2.00, choice **c.**

20. To find the number of houses cleaned, divide the total donation ($1,291.50) by the donation per house ($5.25): $1,291.5 \div 5.25 = 246$, choice **c.**

21. Dennis ate $\frac{1}{4}$ of $\frac{1}{2}$. Remember that "of" means multiply: $\frac{1}{4} \times \frac{1}{2} = \frac{1}{8}$. Dennis ate $\frac{1}{8}$ of the pizza pie, so choice **c** is correct.

22. Properly converting the mixed numbers into improper fractions is the first step in finding the answer. Thus $\frac{7}{3} \times \frac{15}{14} \times \frac{9}{5} = \frac{945}{210} = 4\frac{1}{2}$, choice **d.**

23. $37.27 multiplied by six equals $223.62 choice **b.**

24. The recipe is for 16 brownies. Half of that, 8, would reduce the ingredients by half. Half of $1\frac{1}{2}$ cups of sugar is $\frac{3}{4}$ cup. This is easy to see by converting to decimals. $1\frac{1}{2}$ cups = 1.5 cups. Dividing by 2 yields .75 cups, which is $\frac{3}{4}$ of a cup, choice **a.**

25. Let's first convert all of the denominators to tenths: $4\frac{2}{10} + 1\frac{4}{10} + 3\frac{3}{10} = 8\frac{9}{10}$. Converting to decimals is also an easy way to handle this problem: 4.2 + 1.4 + 3.3 = 8.9 = 8 and nine tenths = $8\frac{9}{10}$, so choice **b** is correct.

26. Make sure you line up your decimals properly when you add 373.5 + 481.6 + 392.8 + 502 + 53.7 to get 1803.6 miles.

$$
\begin{array}{r}
373.5 \\
481.6 \\
392.8 \\
502. \\
+\ 53.7 \\
\hline
1803.6
\end{array}
$$

Choice **b** is the correct answer.

27. No other combination will be greater than or equal to 3, so choice **d** is correct.

28. To find how much the soccer team spent on uniforms, multiply the number of uniforms by the cost of each one. 18 × $21.79 = $392.22. This answer is not given so the answer is *none of the above*, choice **e.**

29. The halfway point between –3 (point M) and $2\frac{1}{2}$ (point N) is $-\frac{1}{4}$. The total distance can be found by adding the absolute values of these numbers: $3 + 2\frac{1}{2} = 5\frac{1}{2}$. Next, you divide this value by 2 to yield $2\frac{1}{4}$. Thus, the halfway point is $2\frac{1}{4}$ units away from both M and N, namely at $-\frac{1}{4}$, so the correct choice is **a.**

30. Choice **d** is correct. When comparing and ordering decimals, it may help to imagine these numbers with additional zeros: 513.260, 513.514, 513.590, 513.700.

31. First, convert $38\frac{1}{5}$ into a decimal. $\frac{1}{5}$ = .20, so $38\frac{1}{5}$ = 38.20. Then multiply 7.75 times 38.20 to get 296.05, choice **b.** This problem could also be solved by converting both numbers to improper fractions and then multiplying them.

32. Arrange the numbers in order from least to greatest. Changing the mixed numbers to decimal numbers will make the comparison easier. The correct order for the numbers is as follows: $5\frac{1}{6}$ (5.17), 5.2, 5.25, 5.4, $5\frac{1}{2}$ (5.5), $5\frac{3}{4}$ (5.75), 5.8, $5\frac{7}{8}$ (5.875). The third number is 5.25, choice **b.**

33. Marina ate $\frac{1}{12}$ of 360: $\frac{1}{12} \times \frac{360}{1} = \frac{360}{12}$, which is equal to 30. Christina ate $\frac{1}{4}$ of 360: $\frac{1}{4} \times \frac{360}{1} = \frac{360}{4}$, which is equal to 90. Athena ate $\frac{1}{5}$ of 360: $\frac{1}{5} \times \frac{360}{1} = \frac{360}{5}$, which is equal to 72. Finally, Jade ate $\frac{1}{8}$ of 360: $\frac{1}{8} \times \frac{360}{1} = \frac{360}{8}$ which is equal to 45. Add them all up: 30 + 90 + 72 + 45 = 237. Then subtract that from the original amount: 360 – 237 = 123, choice **d.**

34. First find out how long the entire hike can be, based on the rate at which the hikers are using their supplies. If 1 = all supplies and x = entire hike, then $\frac{\frac{2}{5}}{3} = \frac{1}{x}$. Cross multiply to get $\frac{2x}{5} = 3$, so that $x = \frac{(3)(5)}{2}$, or $7\frac{1}{2}$ days for the length of the entire hike. This means that the hikers could go forward for 3.75 days altogether before they would have to turn around. They have already hiked for 3 days, which leaves 0.75 for the amount of time they can now go forward before having to turn around, so choice **a** is correct.

35. To find the weight of each jar, divide the total weight of the case by the number of jars in the case. $\frac{8.64}{24}$ = 0.36 pounds, so choice **c** is correct.

36. Remember that "minus a negative" is the same as "plus a positive." Thus you know that

$$-12\frac{2}{7} - (-3\frac{4}{7}) = -12\frac{2}{7} + 3\frac{4}{7}$$

Since the signs are different, subtract the number with the smaller absolute value from the number with the larger absolute value. You may find it easier to convert the mixed numbers to improper fractions. Keep the sign of the number that has the larger absolute value.

$$-\frac{86}{7} + \frac{25}{7} = -\frac{61}{7} = -8\frac{5}{7}, \text{ choice } \mathbf{d.}$$

37. This is a two-step problem. First, add all of the money the girls have, as well as the money from their dad. It is very important to make sure the decimals are lined up properly.

$$
\begin{array}{r}
5.00 \\
13.00 \\
2.50 \\
7.19 \\
2.00 \\
+10.00 \\
\hline
40.42 \\
\end{array}
$$

The total is $40.42. Then, you have to subtract this number from the cost of the bracelet, which is $50.00. Again, remember to line up your decimal points.

$$
\begin{array}{r}
50.00 \\
-40.42 \\
\hline
9.58
\end{array}
$$

The answer is $9.58, choice **d.**

38. The recipe for 16 cookies calls for $\frac{2}{3}$ cup butter. An additional $\frac{1}{3}$ cup would make 8 more cookies, for a total of 24 cookies, so choice **c** is correct.

39. The formula for the sequence is $\frac{1}{2^n}$, where n is the number of the term in the sequence. So the tenth term is $\frac{1}{2^{10}}$, whose denominator is 1,024, choice **d.**

40. $2\frac{1}{2}$ is equal to 2.5. $1\frac{1}{4}$ is equal to 1.25. 2.5 × 1.25 is equal to 3.12 or $3\frac{1}{8}$, so choice **b** is correct. You could also solve this problem by converting the mixed numbers into improper fractions and multiplying.

41. Choice **b** is correct. Since $\frac{1}{3}$ of the "half that aren't 2″ long" are 3″ long, and you know there are 300 3″ nails, you can ask "$\frac{1}{3}$ of what number is 300?" Mathematically, you write: $\frac{1}{3}$ × ? = 300. Multiplying both sides by 3 you get ? = 900. Thus the nails that represent the "half that aren't 2″ long" = 900. So there are also 900 2″ long nails, and 900 + 900 = 1,800 nails in all.

42. Each number in the pattern is one-half of the previous number. Thus, the blank spot will contain a number that is half of 15. $\frac{1}{2}$ × 15 = 7.5, or $7\frac{1}{2}$, choice **a.**

43. This problem is done by dividing: 1.5 ÷ 600 = 0.0025 inches, choice **c.**

44. Both **a** and **b** can be ruled out because there is no way to determine how many tickets are for adults or for children. Answer **c** can be ruled out because the price of group tickets is not given. The correct answer is choice **d.**

45. $\frac{1}{3}$ gallon is lost per day over the course of a week, or 7 days. So you multiply: $\frac{1}{3}$ gal per day × 7 days = $\frac{7}{3}$ gal, or $2\frac{1}{3}$ gallons are lost, choice **b.** Notice that it doesn't matter that the tank holds 14 gallons because the amount lost doesn't even come close to 14.

Chapter 11

1. Remember, a negative times a negative equals a positive, so: $-12 \times -12 = 144$, choice **a.**

2. The meaning of 4^3 is 4 times itself 3 times, or $4 \times 4 \times 4$, so choice **c** is correct.

3. 17^2 is equivalent to 17 times 17, which is 289, choice **d.**

4. You must multiply $\frac{2}{3}$ by itself: $\frac{2}{3} \times \frac{2}{3} = \frac{4}{9}$, so choice **d** is correct.

5. $3^4 = (3)(3)(3)(3) = 81$, choice **d.**

6. $8^3 = 8 \times 8 \times 8 = 512$, choice **c.**

7. To find the square root of a number, ask yourself "What number times itself equals the given number?" Eleven times itself, or 11^2, is 121; therefore, the square root of 121 is 11, choice **c.**

8. We know $10^3 = 10 \times 10 \times 10$, or 1000. Next, multiply $7.25 \times 1000 = 7{,}250$—so choice **c** is correct. A shortcut is to simply move the decimal place of 7.25 three places to the right.

9. In a division problem like this, leave the whole number the same and subtract the exponents. $10^5 \div 10^2 = 10^{5-2} = 10^3$, choice **b.**

10. Choice **d** is correct. Given $(-2)^3 + (-3)^2$, first, cube the -2. Remember that a negative number raised to an odd power produces a *negative* value. $-2 \bullet -2 \bullet -2 = -8$. The question simplified to $-8 + (-3)^2$. Square the -3 to get 9. Remember that a negative number raised to an even power produces a *positive* value. Now you have $-8 + 9$, which equals 1.

11. You know $100^2 = (100)(100)$, or 10,000. Next, multiply 2.75 by 10,000: $2.75 \times 10{,}000 = 27{,}500$, choice **c.**

12. The answer is choice **a.** $25^2 = 25 \bullet 25 = 625$. $21^2 = 21 \bullet 21 = 441$. Subtract: $625 - 441 = 184$.

13. Calculate what is in the parentheses first: $4 + 2 = 6$, and then find the value of 6^3, which is 216, choice **c.**

14. $5.133 \times 10^{-6} = 5.133 \times 0.000001 = 0.000005133$, choice **c.** A shortcut is to simply move the decimal point to the left 6 places in the number 5.133.

15. $\sqrt{64} = 8$ because $8 \times 8 = 64$, and $\sqrt{36} = 6$ because $6 \times 6 = 36$, and $8 + 6 = 14$, choice **c.**

16. When any number is squared, that means you are multiplying it by itself. $43 \times 43 = 1{,}849$. Then it is the simple matter of multiplying that answer by 4: $1{,}849 \times 4 = 7{,}396$, choice **c.**

17. $7.359 \times 10^{-6} = 7.359 \times 0.000001 = 0.000007359$, choice **c.** A shortcut is to simply move the decimal point to the left 6 places in the original number (7.359).

18. First, when you are finding the square root of a number, ask yourself "What number times itself equals the given number?" Next, to get the answer to this problem, you can figure out each equation: It's not **a** because $\sqrt{36}$ = 6, $\sqrt{64}$ = 8 and $\sqrt{100}$ = 10, and 6 + 8 = 14, not 10. It's not **b** because $\sqrt{25}$ = 5, $\sqrt{16}$ = 4 and $\sqrt{41}$ is about 6.4, and 5 + 4 = 9, not 6.4. It is **c** because $\sqrt{9}$ = 3, $\sqrt{25}$ = 5 and $\sqrt{64}$ = 8, and 3 + 5 = 8. *Hint:* Regarding answer **a**, you can also remember that square roots can be multiplied or divided, but not added or subtracted.

19. $\sqrt{12}$ is the same as $\sqrt{4} \times \sqrt{3}$. The square root of 4 is 2. So 5 × $\sqrt{12}$ is the same as 5 × 2 × $\sqrt{3}$, which equals $10\sqrt{3}$, choice **b.**

20. Choice **b** is correct. You start with 3,600,000 and then you count over from the current decimal point until you find where you will put your decimal point. In this case you count over 6 places, because your goal is to put a new decimal point after the 3 and before the 6. This is because scientific notation dictates that the answer be in the form 3.6 times a power of 10. Since you counted over 6 places, you will multiply 3.6 by 10^6. This makes sense because 10^6 = 1,000,000, and 3.6 × 1,000,000 = 3,600,000.

21. First, simplify the expression. Remember to use the correct order of operations. The simplified expression is:

$$\frac{9}{3(27)} \longrightarrow \frac{9}{81} \longrightarrow \frac{1}{9}$$

When using exponential notation, you can remove a number from the denominator of a fraction by representing it using a negative exponent: $\frac{1}{9}$ becomes $\frac{1}{3^2}$, which can be represented as 3^{-2}, choice **a.**

22. This is a multi-step problem. First multiply $-\frac{1}{5}$ by $-\frac{1}{5}$. A negative times a negative always equals a positive, so $-\frac{1}{5} \times -\frac{1}{5} = \frac{1}{25}$. Then, since the problem is asking you to find $-\frac{1}{5}$ *cubed*, you multiply that product again by $-\frac{1}{5}$: $\frac{1}{25} \times -\frac{1}{5} = -\frac{1}{125}$, choice **c.** If you chose answer **d**, you only multiplied $-\frac{1}{5}$ by 3, and if you chose answer **a**, you forgot about the signs. These are some common mistakes that you should try to avoid.

23. $(4\sqrt{7})^2 = (4\sqrt{7})(4\sqrt{7}) = 16\sqrt{49} = 16 \times 7 = 112$, so choice **d** is correct.

24. Square roots with **different numbers** under the radical can be multiplied and divided, but they cannot be added or subtracted, so choice a is correct. You can also test the equations: $\sqrt{16}$ = 4, $\sqrt{9}$ = 3, $\sqrt{25}$ = 5, and 4 + 3 = 7, not 5. $\sqrt{4}$ = 2, $\sqrt{36}$ = 6, $\sqrt{144}$ = 12, and 2 × 6 = 12.

25. You have to move the decimal point over twelve places to the right, to get 3,000,000,000,000, which is three trillion, choice **b.**

26. $4.0 \times 10^4 = 40{,}000$ (you move the decimal point four places to the right). Next, $40{,}000 \times 3{,}000 = 120{,}000{,}000$. Now move the decimal point eight places to the left to get 1.2×10^8, choice **d.**

27. $(2\sqrt[3]{9})^3$ is equivalent to $2^3 \times (\sqrt[3]{9})$. Because a cube root and a cube are inverses, $(\sqrt[3]{9})$ simplifies to 9. This results in $2^3 \times 9 = 8 \times 9 = 72$, so choice **d** is correct.

28. To convert numbers into scientific notation, count the number of places the decimal will have to move for the number to be an integer between 1 and 10 (not including 10). The decimal in 0.000013 has to move 5 places to the right, or negative direction, for it to be an integer. 1.3×10^{-5} cm, choice **d**, is the correct answer.

29. Notice that *everything* inside of the parentheses needs to get squared! First square 7 to get 49. Then square each of the variables; this means multiplying each exponent by 2. Thus, you have $49x^6y^4$, choice **c.**

30. The expression y^2 means y times y. So $2y^2 = 2 \times y \times y$. Choice **b** represents this multiplication with parentheses, and is thus correct.

31. **a.** When you solve a log, you are actually figuring out what exponent the base (in this case, 2) was raised to in order to yield the number given (in this case 128). Two to what power is 128? $2^7 = 128$, so $\log_2 128 = 7$.

32. First calculate $\sqrt{(97 - 16)} = \sqrt{81} = 9$. Next, figure out $\sqrt{(48 \div 3)} = \sqrt{16} = 4$. Lastly, you multiply: $9 \times 4 = 36$. Since $6^2 = 36$, the answer is **c.**

33. A number raised to a negative exponent can be represented by writing 1 over that number to the positive exponent. This means you can bring the 4^{-2} in the numerator down to the denominator as 4^2, and you can bring the 2^{-3} in the denominator up to the numerator as 2^3:

$$\frac{4^2 \times (-2)^3}{2^3 \times (-4)^2}$$

Simplify:

$$\frac{8 \times -8}{16 \times 16}$$

$$\frac{-64}{256}$$

$$\frac{-1}{4}$$

choice **c.**

34. To divide two numbers in scientific notation, you must divide the nonexponential terms (6.5 and 3.25) in the usual way, then divide the exponential terms (10^{-6} and 10^3) by subtracting the exponent of the bottom term from the exponent of the top term, so that you get $\frac{(6.5 \times 10^{-6})}{(3.25 \times 10^3)} = \frac{6.5}{3.25} \times \frac{10^{-6}}{10^3} = 2 \times 10^{-6-3} = 2 \times 10^{-9}$, choice **a.**

35. To multiply two numbers expressed in scientific notation, multiply the nonexponential terms (4.1 and 3.8) in the usual way. Then the exponential terms (10^2 and 10^4) are multiplied by adding their exponents. So $(4.1 \times 10^2)(3.8 \times 10^4) = (4.1 \times 3.8)(10^2 \times 10^4) = (15.58)(10^{2+4}) = (15.58)(10^2) = 15.58 \times 10^2$. In order to express this result in scientific notation, you must move the decimal point one place to the left and add one to the exponent, resulting in 1.558×10^3, choice **d.** (A simple way to remember this relationship between moving the decimal in the number and changing the power of 10 is LARS: **L**eft **A**dd **R**ight **S**ubtract. In this question you moved the decimal one to the **L**eft so you **A**dded one to the power of ten.)

36. To divide two numbers in scientific notation, you must divide the nonexponential terms (6.5 and 3.25) in the usual way, and then divide the exponential terms (10^{-6} and 10^{-3}) by subtracting the exponent of the bottom term from the exponent of the top term. You get: $\frac{(6.5 \times 10^{-6})}{(3.25 \times 10^{-3})} = \frac{6.5}{3.25} \times \frac{10^{-6}}{10^{-3}} = 2 \times 10^{-6-(-3)} = 2 \times 10^{-6+3} = 2 \times 10^{-3}$, choice **b.**

37. Choice **d** is correct. $\log_{10}(1 \times 10^5) = \log_{10}(10^5)$. Asking for $\log_{10}(10^5)$ is the same as asking "10 to what power is 10^5"? 10 the 5th power is 10^5, so $\log_{10}(1 \times 10^5) = 5$. Since 5 is not among the choices, calculate $10 \times 10 \times 10 \times 10 \times 10 = 100{,}000$.

38. First multiply the numbers: $7(3) = 21$. Then multiply the variables, adding exponents: $(p^2)(p^4) = p^6$; $(q^5)(q) = q^6$. Putting the terms together, you get: $21p^6q^6$, choice **d.**

39. Choice **c** is correct. If you are familiar with the squares of common numbers, you can recognize that $6^2 = 36$, $7^2 = 49$, and $8^2 = 64$. How would this help you? Well you would know that choices **a** and **b** would be too small because their squares are less than 49. You would also know that choice **d** would be too large because its square would be over 64. Thus **c** is the correct choice.

40. Choice **b** is correct. The square root of 64, or $\sqrt{64}$, is equal to 8 because $8^2 = 64$. Choice **a** represents the *cube root* of 64 and *not* the square root of 64. Choice **b**, $4\sqrt{4} = 4 \bullet 2 = 8$, and is therefore correct. Choice **c**, $4\sqrt{2} \neq 8$, and choice **d**, 8^2, is also not equal to 8.

41. Choice **b** is correct. In this case, it is easiest to use trial and error. You are looking for the answer choice, which, when squared, will result in 1,151. Let's look at choice **a**: $29.7 \times 29.7 = 882.09$. Nope! So let's look at **b**: $33.9 \times 33.9 = 1{,}149.21$. That is awfully close. Since 35×35 is 1,225, you know that choice **c** will be even larger than this, and **d** will be way too large. Thus, the correct choice is **b.**

42. Choice **b** is correct. Asking for $\log_{10}100$ is the same as asking "10 to what power is 100"? Ten squared is 100, so $\log_{10}100 = 2$.

43. Choice **c** is correct. $\log_{10}(10 \times 10^{-6}) = \log_{10}(1 \times 10^{-5}) = \log_{10}(10^{-5})$. Now ask yourself: "10 to what power is 10^{-5}?" 10 to the *minus fifth power* is 10^{-5}, so $\log_{10}(10^{-5}) = -5$.

Chapter 12

1. The first thing you have to do when solving a problem like this is set up a proportion: $\frac{27}{3} = \frac{x}{7}$. In other words, 27 is to 3 as "what" is to 7. Use an "x" to symbolize the number you are solving for. Then it is only a matter of reducing the first fraction:

$$\frac{9}{1} = \frac{x}{7}$$

and then cross multiplying:

$$1(x) = 9(7)$$

$x = 63$, so choice **d** is correct.

2. First set up a proportion: $\frac{\$18}{1 \text{ wk}} = \frac{\$x}{6 \text{ wk}}$. Then solve for x by cross-multiplying: $18 \times 6 = 1 \times x$, or $1x = 108$. Answer choice **c** is correct.

3. You set up the ratio, 1:2, and then you are trying to find x in the ratio 3:x. Three times one equals 3, so three times two equals 6, choice **b**.

4. First set up a proportion: $\frac{5}{3} = \frac{x}{18}$. Then cross multiply: $3x = 18 \times 5$. Finally, solve for your answer: $3x = 90$, so $x = 30$, choice **d.**

5. Choice **d** is correct. Order matters when writing a ratio. This is because you are comparing one kind of a part to another kind of a part. For example if there was a 20 to 50 ratio of boys to girls, you could write this as 20:50. However, it would be wrong to write 50:20 because there are not 50 boys for every 20 girls. Therefore, **a** is wrong. If you take the correct ratio 20:50, you are allowed to divide both sides by 10 to get 2:5. Thus choice **d** is correct.

6. You are told that $\frac{1}{4}''$ represents 2 feet. You can also say that .25" represents 2 feet. To solve to see how many feet 4" represents, set up a proportion: $\frac{.25}{2} = \frac{4}{x}$. Cross multiplying, you get .25 × x = 2 × 4, or $.25x = 8$. Dividing both sides by .25 yields $x = 8 \div .25 = 32$ feet, choice **d.**

7. 26 forms multiplied by 8 hours is 208 forms per day per clerk. 5,600 divided by 208 is approximately 26.9, which means you have to hire 27 clerks for the day, choice **d.**

8. Set up a proportion:

$$\frac{\$5.49}{30 \text{ salads}} = \frac{x \text{ dollars}}{11 \text{ salads}}$$

Cross multiplying, you get: $5.49 \bullet 11 = 30 \bullet x$, which is the same as $60.39 = 30 \bullet x$. Dividing both sides by 30, you get $2.013 = x$, so you round this answer off to 2.00, choice **d.**

9. To find how many total miles Jeanne can drive, you can simply multiply the number of gallons in her tank by the number of miles that can be driven per gallon. 14 gallons × 24.35 mi/gal = 340.90 miles. This answer is not given, so the answer is not here, choice **e.** Also, you can solve by a proportion: 24.35 mi/1 gal = x mi/14 gal. Cross multiplying, you get 14 × 24.35 = 1 × x , or x = 340.90 miles.

10. Set up a proportion: $\frac{12cc}{100 \text{ Pounds}} = \frac{x}{175 \text{ Pounds}}$, where x is the number of cc's per 175 pounds. An alternative to cross-multiplying is to simply multiply both sides by 175 to get $(175)(\frac{12}{100})$ equals x, so x equals 21, choice **c.**

11. Set up a simple proportion: $\frac{80}{100} = \frac{x}{30,000}$. Cross multiplying, you get 30,000 × 80 = 100 × x, or 2,400,000 = 200x. Dividing both sides by 100 yields 24,000. Another way to look at this question is to realize that eighty out of 100 is 80 percent. Eighty percent of 30,000 is 24,000, choice **d.**

12. The ratio of 105,000 to 3 is equal to the ratio of x to 4. This is a simple proportion: $\frac{105,000}{3} = \frac{x}{4}$, and x = 4(105,000 ÷ 3), which is equal to 4(35,000), which is equal to 140,000, choice **c.**

13. Choice **a** is correct. $6\frac{1}{2}$ pounds = 6.5 pounds. Set up a proportion:

$$\frac{1 \text{ lb}}{\$1.50} = \frac{6.5 \text{ lbs}}{\$x}$$

Cross multiply to get 1 × x = 6.5 × 1.50 = $9.75.

14. Choice **c** is correct. The scale is $\frac{1}{4}$ in = 1 mile, or .25 in = 1 mile, so set up a proportion:

$$\frac{.25 \text{ in}}{1 \text{ mile}} = \frac{5.75 \text{ in}}{x \text{ miles}}$$

Cross multiply to get: .25 × ? = 1 × 5.75, or .25 × ? = 5.75. Divide both sides by .25 to get $x = \frac{5.75}{.25}$ = 23 miles.

15. To solve the problem, you can simply take the weight of one gallon of water (8.35) and multiply it by the number of gallons (25): 8.35 × 25 = 208.75. Now round to the nearest unit to get 209 pounds. Otherwise, just set up a proportion: $\frac{1 \text{ gal}}{8.35 \text{ lbs}} = \frac{25 \text{ gal}}{x \text{ lbs}}$. Thus, x = 25 × 8.35 = 208.75, and choice **c** is best.

16. To find the cost of 3 packages of tapioca pudding, first find the cost of a single package. Divide $5.53 by 7 to get the cost of 1 package, $0.79. Then multiply this price by 3, giving a product of $2.37, choice **b.**

17. Choice **c** is correct. Because this question requires an answer in dollars, you must first convert the 95 cents into dollars. 95 cents = $.95. If 1 gallon costs $.95, simply multiply this price by 3 to get the price of 3 gallons: $3 \times .95 = \$2.85$.

18. When you set up a proportion, you need to be careful with units. This question deals with two different units: dollars and pounds. You will set up a proportion with dollars over pounds: $\frac{\text{this many dollars}}{\text{this many pounds}} = \frac{\text{that many dollars}}{\text{that many pounds}}$. Using the numbers in the question, you have $\frac{3.59 \text{ dollars}}{25 \text{ pounds}} = \frac{c \text{ dollars}}{100 \text{ pounds}}$, choice **c.**

19. $1\frac{1}{2}$ cups equals $\frac{3}{2}$ cups. The ratio is 6 people to 4 people, which is equal to the ratio of x to $\frac{3}{2}$. By cross multiplying, you get $6(\frac{3}{2})$ equals $4x$, or 9 equals $4x$. Dividing both sides by 4, you get $\frac{9}{4}$, or $2\frac{1}{4}$ cups, choice **b.**

20. There is a total of 6 people eating (Louisa + 5 guests). If each gets 2 peppers, Louisa will be making a total of 12 peppers. $\frac{1 \text{ cup}}{3 \text{ peppers}} = \frac{x \text{ cups}}{12 \text{ peppers}}$, so $3x = 12$: $x = 4$. Therefore, choice **b** is correct.

21. Choice **d** is correct. Use the proportion: $\frac{.75 \text{ sec}}{1 \text{ word}} = \frac{60 \text{ sec}}{x \text{ words}}$, so $.75x = 60$, and $x = 80$.

22. To find the proportion of students to animals, set up the given ratio: $\frac{5}{3}$. For the second ratio to be correct, it must put the same type of information on the top and bottom of the ratio. The original ratio puts the number of students on top and the number of animals on bottom. So the second ratio has s on top, and the number of animals, 18, on bottom. Set the two ratios equal to each other: $\frac{5}{3} = \frac{s}{18}$, so choice **a** is correct.

23. Set up a proportion:

$$\frac{250 \text{ pieces}}{.5 \text{ in}} = \frac{1 \text{ piece}}{x \text{ in}}$$

Cross multiplying: $250 \times x = .5 \times 1$, which means $250 \times x = .5$. Dividing both sides by 250, to get $x = .5 \div 250 = .002$ in.

24. Choice **b** is correct. First convert the height of the statue to inches. 305 ft. × 12 in. = 3660 in. The statue is 3,660 + 1, or 3,661, inches tall. Next set up a proportion. $\frac{1}{60} = \frac{x}{3661}$. Cross multiply: $60x = 3661$. Divide both sides by 60: $x = \frac{3661}{60}$; x is about 61 inches. Convert to feet by dividing by 12:

$$
\begin{array}{r}
5 \\
12\overline{)61.} \\
\underline{60} \\
1
\end{array}
$$

25. One way to find the smallest ratio is to convert each ratio into a fraction, with the number of males as the numerator. Convert the fractions into decimal numbers, which are easier to compare to determine the smallest number.

Drama $\longrightarrow \frac{11}{13} = 0.846$

Journalism $\longrightarrow \frac{12}{10} = 1.2$

Science Club $\longrightarrow \frac{9}{11} = 0.818$

Debate $\longrightarrow \frac{12}{15} = 0.8$

The smallest decimal number is 0.8, so the lowest ratio of males to females is in Debate, choice **d.**

26. Choice **b** is correct. This is a simple multiplication problem, which is solved by multiplying 35 times 8.2.

27. Choice **b** is the best answer. To solve this question, set up a proportion:

$$\frac{100 \text{ staples}}{2 \text{ in}} = \frac{1 \text{ staple}}{x \text{ in}}$$

Cross multiply to get: $100 \times x = 2$. Divide both sides by 100 to yield $x = 2 \div 100 = .02$ in.

28. To find p, the number of pages Bonnie can read in 50 minutes, set up the original ratio. Bonnie can read 14 pages in 20 minutes, so $\frac{14}{20}$. The number of pages she can read in 50 minutes is $\frac{p}{50}$. Set these two ratios equal to each other, and solve for p. $\frac{14}{20} = \frac{p}{50}$ (so choice **d** is correct); $20p = 700$; $p = \frac{700}{20}$; $p = 35$.

29. The correct choice is **b.** The black piece of the pie represents 300 programming students. The dark gray piece of the pie represents 600 multimedia students. Thus, the ratio of programming students to multimedia students is 300:600. This reduces to 1:2.

30. Heather is cooking for 6 times as many people as the recipe was designed for ($24 \div 4 = 6$). Thus, she will need to add 6 times as much coriander as the recipe lists: $6 \times \frac{1}{2}$ tsp = 3 tsp, choice **a**.

31. Now Heather is cooking for $26 \div 4 = 6\frac{1}{2}$ times as many people as the recipe provides for. Thus, she will need to add $6\frac{1}{2}$ times as much coriander as the recipe lists: $6\frac{1}{2} \times \frac{1}{2}$ tsp = $\frac{13}{2} \times \frac{1}{2}$ tsp = $\frac{13}{4}$ tsp = $3\frac{1}{4}$ tsp, choice **a**.

32. **a.** Because you need an answer in hours, let's convert the 45 minutes into hours. Because 1 hour = 60 minutes, you use the conversion factor $\frac{1 \text{ hr}}{60 \text{ min}}$. Thus, 45 min $\times \frac{1 \text{ hr}}{60 \text{ min}} = \frac{45}{60}$ hr = $\frac{3}{4}$ hr. If he completed $\frac{3}{4}$ of the job in $\frac{3}{4}$ of an hour, it is easy to see that he will complete $\frac{4}{4}$ of the job (the whole job) in $\frac{4}{4}$ of an hour (a whole hour). Thus, the answer is 1 hour.

33. To find the cost of the hat, divide the number of pesetas Michael paid for the hat by the number of pesetas that equal 1 U.S. dollar. $\frac{19,237}{4,750}$ = \$4.04 or about \$4.00, choice **c**.

34. To find the height of the tree, begin by converting the fractions to decimals: $\frac{3}{4}$ = 0.75 and $5\frac{1}{4}$ = 5.25. You can then set up a proportion:

$$\frac{0.75}{68} = \frac{5.25}{x}$$

Cross multiply: $(68)(5.25) = (0.75)(x)$; then, $357 = 0.75x$; $476 = x$, so choice **b** is correct.

35. You have to look at the question and see that the number of boys plus the number of girls equals the total, so with this information you can make an equation:

$$3x + 4x = 28$$
$$7x = 28$$
$$x = 4$$

Then you have to plug the answer back into the equation.

$$3(4) + 4(4) = 28$$
$$12 + 16 = 28$$

or 12 (boys) + 16 (girls) = 28, so there are 16 girls, answer **c**.

36. Choice **d** is correct. Set up a proportion:

$$\frac{\frac{1}{2} \text{ in}}{1 \text{ foot}} = \frac{4\frac{1}{2} \text{ in}}{\textit{height} \text{ in feet}}$$

This is represented by choice **d.** Notice that you need to have corresponding units in the numerators and corresponding units in the denominators of the proportion. For example, you have inches in the numerator on both sides of the equal sign.

37. Five parts of white plus the 1 part of wheat yields a 6 part mixture. Let x = the number of pounds of white flour present in a 48 lb mixture. Thus, the problem can be restated more usefully as: 5 parts is to 6 parts as x pounds is to 48 pounds, or $\frac{5}{6} = \frac{x}{48}$. Cross multiplying: $(5)(48) = 6x$; $x = \frac{240}{6}$. Thus $x = 40$, choice **d.**

38. Set up an equation and then simplify:

$$p + q = 2(p - q)$$
$$p + q = 2p - 2q$$
$$3q = p$$

p is three times q, so the ratio of p to q is 3:1, choice **e.**

39. **c.** Set up a proportion. It costs \$1.25 per 100 count for paper clips and you want to know how much it will cost for 556 paper clips.

$$\frac{\$1.25}{100 \text{ clips}} = \frac{x}{556 \text{ clips}}$$

Note that only choice **c** is equivalent to this proportion. Choice **a** uses "125," which solves for *cents*, not *dollars*.

40. Make a ratio of white blood cells to red blood cells. The unreduced ratio is 8,000:5,000,000 or 8:5,000. 5,000 divided by 8 equals 625, for a ratio of 1:625, choice **a.**

41. If half the students are female, then you would expect half of the out-of-state students to be female. One half of $\frac{1}{12}$ is $\frac{1}{24}$, choice **b.**

42. To find the distance Ralph can hike in 3 hours, first set up the ratio of the distance he can walk in a certain amount of time. Forty-five minutes is equal to $\frac{3}{4}$ of an hour, or .75 hours. The ratio is thus $\frac{1.3 \text{ miles}}{0.75 \text{ hours}}$. Then set up the second ratio, $\frac{d}{3 \text{ hours}}$. Set these 2 ratios equal to each other. $\frac{1.3}{0.75} = \frac{d}{3}$, choice **b.**

43. Make a ratio for carbon dioxide to oxygen. Using the numbers given in the question, carbon dioxide to oxygen is 35:20,945. Notice that there is a lot more oxygen than carbon dioxide. Choice **a** is wrong because this ratio (20,945:35) specifies a lot more carbon dioxide than oxygen. Because the correct ratio 35:20,945 isn't among the choices, reduce it by dividing it by 5. The new and equivalent ratio is 7:4,189, choice **c**.

44. Choice **d** is correct. The weight in pounds per cubic feet of wet sand is 120. The weight for pumice is 40. The ratio is then 120:40. This reduces to 3:1.

45. If there is a 3:4 ratio of men to women, you can say that you have $3x$ men and $4x$ women. Notice how you preserved the ratio when you introduced the variable. You also know that the total number of people in the study group is $7x$ (because $3x + 4x = 7x$). So, $7x$ represents our total, which you are told is 21. Thus, $x = 3$. The number of men is $3x = 3 \cdot 3 = 9$, choice **c**.

46. Choice **d** is correct. Before the ratio was 5:1 (male:female). The total before was $T_{old} = 5x + 1x = 6x$. Note that $5x$ represents the number of men, $1x$ represents the number of women and $6x$ represents the "old" total. Now, after the 7 women joined, the ratio is 3:2. How do these 7 women affect our formula for the total? Well, no men joined so you still have $5x$, plus the old women and new women, which you can represent as $x + 7$, and the new total is then $6x + 7$. To summarize:

	Before (*old enrollment*)	After (*new enrollment*)	
5:1 ratio {	**Men** = 5x	**Men** = 5x (*no men joined*)	} 3:2 ratio
	Women = 1x	**Women** = 1x + 7 (*7 new women joined*)	
	Total = 6x	**Total** = 5x + 1x + 7	
	Ratio = 5:1	**Ratio** = 3:2	

You can set the new 3:2 ratio equal to the algebraic values that you calculated:

$$\frac{3}{2} = \frac{5x}{x + 7} = \frac{\text{men}}{\text{women}}$$

Cross multiply to get: $3 \cdot (x + 7) = 2 \cdot 5x$, which means $3(x + 7) = 10x$, or $3x + 21 = 10x$. Subtract $3x$ from both sides to yield $21 = 7x$, and $x = 3$. The question asks for the current total, or $5x + 1x + 7$, which equals $5(3) + 1(3) + 7 = 15 + 3 + 7 = 25$.

47. The answer is 4,000, choice **c.** Apply the 3:2:1 ratio to an algebraic formula: $3x + 2x + 1x =$ Total Students. The $3x$ represents the math majors, the $2x$ represents the English majors, and the $1x$ represents the chemistry majors. You know that the total number of students = 12,000, so you have:

$$3x + 2x + 1x = 12,000$$
$$6x = 12,000$$
$$x = 2,000$$

Remember, you are looking for "English majors" = $2x = 2 \times 2,000 = 4,000$

Chapter 13

1. .97 is 97 hundredths, otherwise known as 97 percent, or 97%, choice **a.**

2. 62.5% is $\frac{62.5}{100}$. You should multiply both the numerator and denominator by 10 to move the decimal point, resulting in $\frac{625}{1000}$, and then factor both the numerator and denominator to find out how far you can reduce the fraction. $\frac{625}{1000}$ equals $\frac{(5)(5)(5)(5)}{(5)(5)(5)(8)}$. If you cancel the three 5s that are in both the numerator and denominator, you will get $\frac{5}{8}$, choice **b.**

3. 14% can be written as $\frac{14}{100}$ or .14. Remember that "of" means multiply. Thus 14% of 232 = 0.14 × 232 = 32.48, choice **b.**

4. 44% = $\frac{44}{100}$ or .14. Next, multiply: 0.44 × 5 = 2.2, choice **b.**

5. First, convert 4.5% to a decimal: 0.045. Next, multiply that by $26,000 to find out how much the salary increases: .045 × $26,000 = $1,170. Finally, add the result ($1,170) to the original salary of $26,000 to find out the new salary, $27,170, choice **b.**

6. To change a percent to a decimal, first you have to drop the percent sign, so to change 35% to a decimal, you drop the percent sign and make it 35. Next, you would move the decimal point two digits to the left. 35 is the same as 35.0, so if you move the decimal point two digits to the left you get .35, and .35 (choice **b**) is the same as 35%.

7. First, remove the percent sign to get 42. Next, write the number over 100, to get $\frac{42}{100}$. Lastly, reduce the fraction to get $\frac{21}{50}$, choice **c.**

8. First, move the decimal point two digits to the right: .525 becomes 52.5. Next, add a percent sign: 52.5%, choice **d.**

9. Since the item is marked up by 35%, it is 135% of the original purchasing price. You can multiply the original price by 1.35: $12.20 × 1.35 = $16.47, so choice **c** is correct.

10. This is a two-step problem. First, determine what percent of the trees are *not* oaks by subtracting. 100% – 32% = 68%. Next, change 68% to a decimal and multiply. 0.68 × 400 = 272, choice **b.**

11. 12.5% = .125, and $\frac{3}{8}$ = .375. .125 < .375, thus choice **a** is correct.

12. You need to find 400%, or $\frac{400}{100}$ (which is 4) of 3,400. Remember that *of* means *multiply*. 4 × 30 = 120, choice **c.**

13. Lauren, Jenna, and Rich sold 40%, 15%, and 30%. When combined, these add to 85%, choice **c.**

14. Choice **c** is correct. "20% of $325" is the same as .20 × 325. This is not an answer choice, so you have to look to see which choice expresses the same amount. Choice **c,** 2 × .10(325) = .20 × 325.

15. The correct choice is **b.** If you took 100% of a number, you would have the very same number. Taking 150% of a number will give you a *larger* number. In fact, taking 150% of a number yields a number that is 50% larger than the original.

16. Choice **c** is correct. "Car" represents 12%, "Food" represents 21%, and "Recreation" represents 17%. In adding these three values up, you get 12% + 21% + 17% = 50%, which is $\frac{50}{100}$, or $\frac{1}{2}$ his expenses.

17. "What percentage" can be expressed as $\frac{?}{100}$. "Of 50" means times 50. And "is 12" means = 12. Thus, you have $\frac{?}{100}$ × 50 = 12. Rearranging, $\frac{?}{100} = \frac{12}{500}$. Multiplying both sides by 100 you get ? = $\frac{12}{500}$ × 100, or ? = $\frac{12}{.5}$ = 24%, choice **c.**

18. First, change the percent to a decimal: $7\frac{1}{5}$% = 7.2% = .072. Next, multiply by 465: (.072)(465) = 33.48, which rounded to the nearest tenth is 33.5, so choice **c** is correct.

19. Choice **c** is correct. "33 is 12% of which of the following?" can be represented mathematically as 33 = $\frac{12}{100}$ × ?, or 33 = .12 × ?. Divide 33 by 0.12 (12 percent) to get ? = 275.

20. For this question, you know that 9 out of 75 couldn't attend the wedding, so you would write that out as a fraction: $\frac{9}{75}$. Next, you would divide: 9 ÷ 75 = .12. To change a decimal to a percent, move the decimal point two places to the right, making it 12.0. Add a percent sign to get 12.0%, which is 12%, choice **c.**

21. To express 14% mathematically, you just put the 14 over 100, which gives you $\frac{14}{100}$. You can divide this out to yield .14. If you need 14% of 232, remember that "of" means *times*. This means 14% of 232 = 14% × 232 = $\frac{14}{100}$ × 232 = .14 × 232. Thus, choices **b** and **c** are correct.

22. Convert 3.2% to a decimal by dividing by 100 (or moving the decimal point 2 places to the left): 0.032

Now multiply.

$$\begin{array}{r} 73021 \\ \times\ 0.032 \\ \hline 146042 \\ +\ 219063 \\ \hline 2336.672 \end{array}$$

Since you are working with dollars and cents, round the answer to the hundredths place, $2,336.67. Choice **a** is correct.

23. You can translate the problem to: $16.20 is x percent of $36.00? $\frac{16.20}{36.00} = \frac{x}{100}$; x = 45%. The savings is found by subtracting 100% − 45% = 55%, choice **c**.

24. The graph shows that 28% of the drinks sold (325) are smoothies. 0.28 × 325 = 91, choice **b**.

25. The answer is 378, choice **b**. 7% of the 4,700 men are expected to be colorblind. Thus, you can predict that .07 × 4,700 = 329 men are colorblind. Also, 1% of the 4,900 women, or .01 × 4,900 = 49 women are expected to be colorblind. Therefore, you can predict that 329 + 49 = 378 people are colorblind in Mastic.

26. The correct choice is **b**. "30% of a number" means 30% *times* that number. Mathematically, you write .30 × ? and set this equal to 600. Thus, .30 × ? = 600, and dividing both sides by .30 you get ? = 2,000. You were asked to find 50% of this number, so .50 × 2,000 = 1,000. Choice **d** represents 50% (of *half* of) 600.

27. There are 365 days in a year. 180 days out of 365 days is what percent? Recall that "what percent" can be represented mathematically as $\frac{?}{100}$, or $\frac{x}{100}$. Mathematically, "180 days out of 365 days is what percent?" can be written as $\frac{180}{365} = \frac{x}{100}$. Thus, choice **a** is correct.

28. First, remove the percent sign: $12\frac{1}{2}$. Next, write the number over 100: $\frac{12\frac{1}{2}}{100}$. Then, write the fraction as a division problem: $12\frac{1}{2} \div 100$. Change the mixed number into an improper fraction: $\frac{25}{2} \div 100 = \frac{25}{2} \times \frac{1}{100} = \frac{25}{200}$, which reduces to $\frac{1}{8}$, choice **a**.

29. Choice **d** is correct. Remember 15% = $\frac{15}{100}$ or .15. To find the answer, you should multiply: 0.15 × $300 × 4 televisions = $180.

30. The cost would be 120% of the manufacturer's price. The 120% represents the manufacturer's cost (100%) plus the markup (20%). Because 120% = 1.20, simply multiply 1.20 × $13,000 = $15,600, choice **b**.

31. Start by setting up a proportion. 20 is to 100 as 5 is to what number? This is written as: $\frac{20}{100} = \frac{5}{x}$. 20x = 500: $x = \frac{500}{20}$: x = 25. Choice **c** is correct.

32. Choice **d** is correct. "20% of what number" can be expressed as .20 • ?, "is equal to" simply means =, and "50% of 200" means $\frac{1}{2}$ × 200, or 100. Thus, you have .20 × ? = 100. Dividing both sides by .20 yields ? = 500.

33. The formula for finding simple interest is $I = prt$. (The amount of money deposited is called principal, p. The interest rate per year is represented by r, and t represents the number of years.) Substituting, you have: I = (8000)(.05)(6) = $2400, choice **a**.

34. To calculate the percent increase, use this proportion:

$$\frac{change}{initial} = \frac{?}{100}$$

First, calculate the *change* by looking at the graph. Note that the black bars represent "Charge Card Interest."

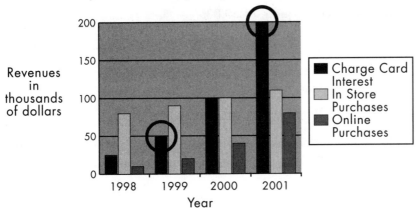

Thus, the *initial* value is 50 (in 1999) and the value in 2001 was 200. The *change* is then 200 − 50 = 150.

$$\frac{change}{initial} = \frac{?}{100} \text{ becomes}$$

$$\frac{150}{50} = \frac{?}{100}$$

Cross multiplying you get 100 × 150 = 50 × ?, or 15,000 = 50 • ?, and dividing both sides by 50 yields ? = 300. Thus, there was a 300% increase, choice **d**.

35. Choice **a** is correct. 72% of 9,125 is (0.72)(9125), or 6,570 males. If 3 out of 5 males were under 25, then 2 out of 5 were 25 or older, so $\frac{2}{5}$(6570) = 2,628 male patients 25 or older.

36. If 60 percent of the people who dined at Jimmy's ordered the pasta special, 40 percent did not order the special. Forty percent of 220 means .40 × 220 = 88, choice **c**.

37. Let x = the unknown number. You have $x + 0.5x = 27$ or $1.5x = 27$. Therefore $x = 18$, choice **d.**

38. First, look at the pie chart to see that "Country" represents 27.5% of sales. You were told that the total sale was 400 discs, so you need to find 27.5% of 400. Another way to express 27.5% is to write $\frac{27.5}{100}$, and "of" means *times*, so you have: $\frac{27.5}{100} \times 400$, choice **d.**

39. a. Use the chart to figure out what the second quotes are:

		Original Quote	Second Quote
K Tech	$12,000	decrease original quote by $\frac{1}{4}$ ⟶	$12,000 - \frac{1}{4}($12,000) = $9,000
L Tech	$13,400	75% of original quote ⟶	.75 × $13,400 = $10,050
M Tech	$11,500	less 15% from original quote ⟶	$11,500 - .15($11,500) = $,9775
N Tech	$15,000	$\frac{7}{8}$ of original offer ⟶	$\frac{7}{8}$ × $15,000 = $13,125

Thus, the best price is K Tech's quote of $9,000.

40. Ask yourself, "92 is 40% of what number?" To write this as an equation, remember that "is" *means* equals, "of" means *times* and "what number" means x. Also, change 40% to .40, so your equation is $92 = (.40)(x)$. Divide both sides by .40 to get $x = 230$. There are 230 kids total because 92 is 40% of 230. You can check your answer: $.4 \times 230 = 92$, choice **c.**

41. Choice **d** is correct. Take V and add 25% of V. 25% = .25 or $\frac{25}{100} = \frac{1}{4}$. Thus, choice **a**, $V + \frac{1}{4}V$ is true. This is the same as $V + .25V$, which is choice **c**. If you actually add choice **c**, you get choice **b**.

42. The new price of the navy blue jacket will be 110% of the old price: 110% of $200 is 1.10 × 200 = $220. Thus, the navy blue jacket will cost $220. The new price of the gray jacket will be 95% of the old price: 95% of 400 is .95 × 400 = $380. Therefore, the sum of their costs will be $220 + $380 = $600, choice **a.**

43. If x is the number of notebooks she buys, she will pay $.80x$ for the books plus $.08(.8x)$ for the tax. This sum must be less than or equal to $12.50. Set up and solve the inequality:

$$(0.80x) + .08(.8x) \leq 12.50$$
$$.80x + .064x \leq 12.50$$
$$.864x \leq 12.50$$
$$x \leq 14.46$$

You must pick 14 (choice **b**), and not 14.46 because she cannot buy .46 of a notebook.

44. Draining half of the 5 gallon tank leaves 2.5 gallons inside. Since you know the solution is a 50–50 mixture, there must be 1.25 gallons of water present at this point. After adding 2 gallons of water, there will be 1.25 + 2, or 3.25 gallons of water (choice **b**) in the final mixture.

45. Two iterations must be done to find the answer:

$$A = P(r)t$$
$$A = \$500 \times 0.08 \times 0.50 = \$20 \text{ (first half-year)}$$
$$A = \$520 \times 0.08 \times 0.50 = \$20.80 \text{ (second half-year)}$$

Therefore, the original amount will grow to: $500 + 20 + 20.80 or 540.80, choice **a.**

46. To solve this problem, use the proportion $\frac{\text{change}}{\text{initial}} = \frac{?}{100}$. Here the change is $340 – $255, or $85. The initial value was $340. Your equation becomes $\frac{85}{340} = \frac{?}{100}$. Multiplying both sides by 100 yields $\frac{85 \times 100}{340} = ?$, and ? = 25. Thus, there was a 25% decrease; choice **d** is correct.

47. Twelve out of 27 times would equal what number out of 100? This is represented by $\frac{12}{27} = \frac{x}{100}$. Multiply both sides by 100 to solve for x. Thus, $x = \frac{(12)(100)}{27}$, choice **d.**

48. To calculate the percent increase, use this proportion:

$$\frac{\text{change}}{\text{initial}} = \frac{?}{100}$$

First, calculate the *change* by looking at the graph. Note that the white bars represent "Oil."

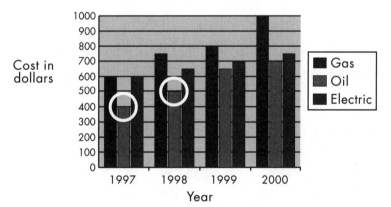

The cost rose from the *initial* $400 in 1997 to $500 in 1998. So, the *change* was $100. Thus, you get:

$$\frac{100}{400} = \frac{?}{100}$$

Cross multiplying, you get: 100 × 100 = 400 × ?, or 10,000 = 400 × ?, and dividing both sides by 400 yields ? = 25. This means the percent increase was 25% (choice **a**).

49. The 10% discount applies to all three items. The school will be paying 90%, which translates into .9. Therefore, the total price is (a + b + c) × 0.9. The average is the total price divided by the number of computers: $0.9 \times \frac{a+b+c}{3}$ (choice **a**).

Chapter 14

1. Choice **b** is correct. First combine like terms: $2a + 1a + 3a = 36$ becomes $6a = 36$. Dividing both sides by 6 and you get $a = 6$.

2. The expression $5n$ means 5 times n. The addition sign before the 7 indicates the phrase *more than*. Choice **a** is correct.

3. Substitute 3 for x in the expression $5 + 4x$ to determine that y equals 17 (choice **d**).

4. Solve this problem with the following equation: $4x - 12 = 20$. Therefore, $4x = 32$, so $x = 8$, choice **d**.

5. Choice **a** is the correct answer. The problem is solved by first determining the $8n = 40$, then dividing 40 by 8.

6. First square 7 to get 49. Then square each of the variables; this means multiplying each exponent by 2. Choice **c**, $49x^6y^4$, is correct.

7. $\frac{1}{3}x + 3 = 8$. In order to solve the equation, all numbers need to be on one side and all x values on the other. Therefore, $\frac{1}{3}x = 5$; $x = 15$, choice **b**.

8. If the number is represented by n, its double is $2n$. Therefore, $n + 2n = 69$; $3n = 69$; $n = 23$, choice **c**.

9. The first step in solving this problem is to add the fractions to get the sum of $\frac{4x}{4}$. This fraction reduces to x, choice **d**.

10. Simply divide 21 by 3 to get the answer: 7 (choice **c**).

11. First, add 3 to both sides:

$$
\begin{array}{rl}
8x - 3 & > 29 \\
+ 3 & + 3 \\
\hline
8x & > 32
\end{array}
$$

Next, divide both sides by 8 to yield $x > 4$, choice **c**.

12. "Alan is 5 years less than twice Helena's age." can be written mathematically as $A = 2H - 5$. Because you are also told that Alan is 27, you know that $27 = 2H - 5$ (choice **d**).

13. *"Three more than three times a number,"* means $3x + 3$. "Is 18" means $= 18$. So you have $3x + 3 = 18$. Subtracting 3 from both sides, you get $3x = 15$. Now, divide both sides by 3, and get $x = 5$.

14. To find the value of j, subtract 4 from both sides leaving $16j = 24$. Then divide 24 by 16 to get a quotient of 1.5, choice **a.**
    b. This answer is incorrect because it adds 4 to 28 instead of subtracting 4.
    c. This answer is incorrect because it incorrectly divides 24 by 16.
    d. This answer is incorrect because it is the difference between the 2 sides of the equation, 20 versus 28.

15. Choice **a** is correct. Since the solution to the problem $x + 25 = 13$ is $x = -12$, choices **b**, **c**, and **d** are all too large to be correct.

16. To find the value of x, simply divide both sides of the equation by 6. $\frac{16}{6} = x$. $\frac{16}{6}$ can be reduced to $\frac{8}{3}$, so the correct answer is choice **c.**

17. Use the formula beginning with the operation in parentheses: 98 minus 32 equals 66. Then multiply 66 by $\frac{5}{9}$, first multiplying 66 by 5 to get 330. 330 divided by 9 is 36.66667, which is rounded up to 36.7, choice **b.**

18. Combine like terms: $x^2 + 2x^2 = 3x^2$; $-3x + 0 = -3x$; $6 - 4 = 2$. Choice **e** is correct.

19. Add like terms: $2x + 6x = 8x$; $-5y + 3y = -2y$; and $5 - 2 = 3$. Putting all terms together, you get: $8x - 2y + 3$, choice **d.**

20. Cross multiplying: $(2x)(48) = (16)(12)$; $96x = 192$. Thus $x = 2$, choice **a.**

21. Seven is added to both sides of the equation, leaving $2x = 11$. Eleven is divided by 2 to give $\frac{11}{2}$, choice **c.**

22. Seven is added to both sides of the equation, giving $1.5x = 19.5$; 19.5 divided by 1.5 gives 13, choice **c.**

23. First, combine like terms: $6x + 9 = 27$. Then subtract 9 from both sides: $6x = 18$. Last, divide each side by 6 to get the answer: $x = 3$, choice **d.**

24. Combine like terms: $3x^2 + x^2 = 4x^2$; $4x + 0 = 4x$; and $-2 + (-5) = -7$. Put them together to get the answer: $4x^2 + 4x - 7$ (choice **b**).

25. Let $x =$ the number sought. Solve this by breaking up the problem into parts: Six less than three times a number $= 3x - 6$, four more than twice the number $= 2x + 4$. Combining terms: $3x - 6 = 2x + 4$. Simplifying: $3x - 2x = 6 + 4$, or $x = 10$, choice **d.**

26. Choice **a** is correct. $x + .30x = 1.95$, so $1.30x = 1.95$, and dividing both sides by 1.30, you get $x = 1.50$.

27. x times $3x^2$ equals $3x^3$; x times y equals xy. Choice **c** is correct.

28. Use 35 for C. $F = (\frac{9}{5} \times 35) + 32$. Therefore $F = 63 + 32$, or $95°$, choice **b**.

29. When you set up a proportion, you need to be careful with units. This question deals with two different units: dollars and pounds. You will set up a proportion with dollars over pounds: $\frac{\text{this many dollars}}{\text{this many pounds}} = \frac{\text{that many dollars}}{\text{that many pounds}}$. Using the numbers in the question, you have $\frac{3.59 \text{ dollars}}{25 \text{ pounds}} = \frac{c \text{ dollars}}{100 \text{ pounds}}$, choice **c**.

30. $(3x^4y^2)(5xy^3)$ first can be changed to $15x^4y^2xy^3$. If you have the same base, when multiplying exponents, you just add the powers. Since x is the same as x^1, when you add the powers of the x terms you get $4 + 1$, or x^5. For the y terms, you add $2 + 3$ to get y^5. Thus, the final answer is $15x^5y^5$, choice **c**.

31. Using the formula *Distance = Rate × Time*, you get $100 = 30 \times Time$, or $Time = \frac{100}{3} = 3\frac{1}{3}$ hours = 3 hours and 20 minutes, choice **b**.

32. To find how much Ian weighs after 3 months, put 3 into the equation for m and put his birth weight, 9.4 pounds, into the equation for b. $(1.2 \times 3) + 9.4 = 13.0$ (choice **d**).
   a. This answer is incorrect because it only adds 1 month's weight to Ian's birth weight.
   b. This answer is incorrect because it only adds 2 months' weight to Ian's birth weight.
   c. This answer is incorrect because it adds the number of months to Ian's birth weight instead of the number of pounds he gained during those months.

33. Choice **b** is correct. Distribute the $3b$. $3b(b + 5) = (3b \times b) + (3b \times 5) = 3b^2 + 15b$.

34. After finding a common denominator, the equation becomes $\frac{4}{12}x + \frac{3}{12}x = 3$. When added, this becomes $\frac{7}{12}x = 3$. By cross multiplying, you get $36x = 7$. Therefore, $x = \frac{36}{7}$, or $5\frac{1}{7}$, choice **d**.

35. $x = \frac{1}{16} \times 54$, which is equivalent to $54 \div 16$, which is 3.375, choice **a**.

36. In order to solve the equation, x needs to be alone on one side of the equation. Subtract 3 from each side of $\frac{1}{3}x + 3 = 8$, thus $\frac{1}{3}x = 5$. Then multiply each side of the equation by 3, thus $x = 15$, choice **b**.

37. If $x = 6$, $y = -2$, and $z = 3$, then $xz - xy = (6)(3) - (6)(-2) = 18 - (-12) = 30$. Divide 30 by z^2, or 9. 30 divided by $9 = \frac{10}{3}$, which equals $3\frac{1}{3}$, choice **c**.

38. $J = 6K$. $J + 2 = 2(K + 2)$, so $6K + 2 = 2K + 4$, which means K equals $\frac{1}{2}$. J equals $6K$, or 3, so choice **a** is correct.

39. The cost (c) is found by multiplying the number of people (n) by the price per ticket ($\$6$) and adding the service charge ($\$7$). $c = 6n + 7$, choice **c**.

40. Find the value of t when $h = 0$, and recognize that time is not measured in negative numbers. When the pebble hits the ground, the height is $h = 0$.

$$0 = -16t^2 + 144$$
$$16t^2 = 144 \qquad \text{Add } 16t^2 \text{ to both sides.}$$
$$t^2 = 9 \qquad \text{Divide both sides by 16.}$$
$$\sqrt{t^2} = \pm\sqrt{9} \qquad \text{Take the square root of both sides.}$$
$$t = \sqrt{3} \qquad \text{Simplify}$$

Since time cannot be negative, $t = 3$, choice **d.**

41. This uses two algebraic equations to solve for the age. Jerry (J) and his grandfather (G) have a sum of ages of 110 years. Therefore, $J + G = 110$. Jerry was $\frac{1}{3}$ as young as his grandfather 15 years ago. Therefore, $J - 15 = \frac{1}{3}(G - 15)$. Either equation can be solved for J or G and substituted into the other. $J = 110 - G$; $110 - G - 15 = \frac{1}{3}G - 5$; $100 = \frac{4}{3}G - 5$; $G = 75$. Choice **b** is correct.

42. Eight is substituted for x. $x^2 = 8 \times 8 = 64$. $\frac{64}{4} = 16$; $16 - 2 = 14$, choice **b.**

43. Insert each pair of x and y values into the equation to determine if each ordered pair is valid. The only pair that is not valid is (5, 21)—choice **c**—since $5(5) - 3 = 22$, not 21.

44. First, substitute the given value for b:

$$12a + \frac{36}{4} = 93 \longrightarrow 12a + 9 = 93$$

Next, isolate a: $12a = 93 - 9 = 84 \longrightarrow a = 84 \div 12 = 7$.

Choice **c** is correct.

45. You need to rearrange the equation $V = \pi r^2 h$, into an equation that has h equal to something. In order to isolate the h, you need to get rid of the πr^2 on the right side of the equation. You can do this by dividing both sides by πr^2. Thus, the equation becomes $\frac{V}{\pi r^2} = h$ (choice **c**).

46. Look at the equation $3x^2 - 2xy^3$ and put a 1 wherever you see an x and a -2 wherever you see a y. The equation becomes $3(1)^2 - 2(1)(-2)^3 = 3(1) - 2(1)(-8) = 3 - (-16) = 3 + 16 = 19$. There are two tricky parts to this question. First, notice that $(-2)^3 = -8$. Also, notice that when subtracting a negative number, you are really just adding a positive number: $3 - (-16) = 3 + +16 = 19$ (choice **d**).

47. To calculate the percent increase, use this proportion:

$$\frac{\text{change}}{\text{initial}} = \frac{I}{100}$$

Here, the change is 366 − 331 = 35, and the initial value was 331. Substituting, you get: $\frac{35}{331} = \frac{I}{100}$ (choice **b**).

48. Let y = the number of ounces you are looking for. Set up a proportion, and then cross multiply and solve for y:

$$\frac{175}{28x} = \frac{75}{y}$$
$$175y = 2100x$$
$$y = 12x \text{ (choice } \mathbf{d})$$

49. Even after scoring only 8 points compared to the Cobras' 13 points, the Tigers were still in the lead. The Tigers' original score plus 8 points is larger than the Cobras' original score plus 13 points. Therefore, $T + 8 > c + 13$ (choice **c**).

  a. This answer is incorrect because it does not describe the situation.
  b. This answer is incorrect because it indicates that the Tigers lost 8 points while the Cobras gained 13 points.
  d. This answer is incorrect because it multiplies the teams' original scores by their additional points and indicates that the Tigers' final score was smaller than the Cobras'.
  e. This answer is incorrect because it adds the Tigers' additional 8 points to the team's original score but multiplies the Cobras' additional points to their original score.

50. Solving this problem requires converting 15 minutes to 0.25 hour, which is the time, then using the formula: 62 mph × 0.25 hour = 15.5 miles (choice **b**).

51. Let D = the unknown distance between farmhouses, in miles. Recall that, given a uniform rate, Distance = Rate × Time or: $D = RT$. You know R = 12 mph and T = 42 minutes. Now convert minutes into hours by establishing the ratio 42 minutes is to 60 minutes as x hours is to 1 hour or: $\frac{42}{60} = \frac{x}{1}$. Cross multiplying: 42 = 60x or x = 0.7 hour. Thus D = (12)(.7) = 8.4 miles (choice **c**).

52. Hilga and Jerome's initial distance apart equals the sum of the distance each travels in 2.5 hours. Using Distance = Rate × Time, or $D = RT$, you know Hilga travels a distance of (2.5)(2.5) = 6.25 miles, and Jerome travels (4)(2.5) = 10 miles. This means that they were 6.25 + 10 = 16.25 miles apart, choice **c**.

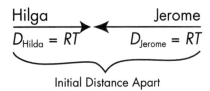

53. In order to factor the original expression, first note what the two terms have in common: You can pull out a 2, a p, and a q^2. You get: $2pq(q - 2pq^2)$ (choice **a**). To check this, you can distribute the $2pq$ to yield the original expression, $2pq^2 - 4p^2q^3$.

54. Choice **c** is correct. The common factor is $4ab$. Divide $16a^3b$ by $4ab$ to get $4a^2$. Then divide -$4ab^2$ by $4ab$ to get $-b$.

55. The correct answer is choice **d**. One way to find which equation was used to create this table is to place the numbers from the table into the given equations. Both the input and output numbers follow the equation Output = 4 × Input - 1. 11 = 4 × 3 - 1, 15 = 4 × 4 - 1, and 19 = 4 × 5 - 1

56. **b.** Use $wd = WD$. Substituting in the given values, you have 6 × 12 = x × 8, or 72 = 8x. Dividing both sides by 8 yields $x = 9$.

Chapter 15

1. The sum of the measures of the angles in a triangle is 180 degrees. 70 degrees + 30 degrees = 100 degrees. 180 degrees – 100 degrees = 80 degrees. Therefore, angle c is 80 degrees, choice **c**.

2. "Adjacent" simply means "next to." Angles 1 and 4 are the only ones NOT adjacent (next to) to each other.

3. All of the angles are acute, and all are different. Therefore, the triangle is acute scalene, choice **a**.

4. Find the slant height using the Pythagorean theorem ($a^2 + b^2 = c^2$): 36 + 64 = 100. The square root of 100 is 10, so that is the measure of the missing side (the slant height). The perimeter is therefore (2 × 18) + (2 × 10) = 56, choice **d**.

5. In order to find the perimeter, the hypotenuse of the triangle must be found. This comes from recognizing that the triangle is a 5-12-13 triangle, or by using the Pythagorean theorem. Therefore, 5 + 12 + 13 = 30, choice **c**.

6. Above the horizontal line you have a 60 degree angle and a 90 degree angle. Therefore, the third angle is 30 degrees. 180 – 60 – 90 = 30. Because angle F is equal to the third angle, angle F = 30 degrees. Choice **c** is correct.

7. If two angles are 60 degrees, the third must also be 60 degrees. This is an equilateral triangle. All sides are therefore equal, and choice **d** is correct.

8. Use the area formula for a circle, $A = \pi r^2$. If $d = 8$, then $r = 4$. $A = \pi r^2$ becomes $A = \pi(4)^2 = \pi(16) = 16\pi$ cm^2, choice **c**.

9. PQ and RS are intersecting lines. The fact that angle POS is a 90-degree angle means that PQ and RS are perpendicular, indicating that all the angles formed by their intersection, including ROQ, measure 90 degrees (choice **b**).

10. An isosceles triangle is defined as a triangle with two equal angles (choice **a**).

11. The angle that is directly above P will equal Q (it is an alternate interior with the given Q). P + Q form a straight line, so they add to 180°. 180 − 40 = 140, so Q = 140° (choice **d**).

12. Choice **e** is the only choice that includes a 90-degree angle and adds to a total of 180.

13. The area of a circle is $A = \pi r^2$. The area of Circle B is $\pi(3)^2$, or 9π. The area of Circle A is $\pi(2)^2$, or 4π. The difference in areas is $9\pi - 4\pi$, or 5π, choice **a.**

14. A polygon is a closed figure made of line segments. A regular polygon has all sides and all angles congruent. Thus, the only regular polygon shown is the triangle, choice **b.**

15. A square is a special case of all of these figures except the trapezoid (choice **d**). A square is a parallelogram, because its opposite sides are parallel. A square is a rectangle because it is a quadrilateral with 90-degree angles. A square is a rhombus because it is a parallelogram with all sides equal in length. However, a square is not a trapezoid because a trapezoid has only two parallel sides.

16. If the pentagons are similar, then the two different pentagons will have similar proportions. Because AB is similar to FG, and AB = 10, and FG = 30, the second pentagon is 3 times as large. Therefore, HI is 3 times as large as CD, which gives 15, choice **c.**

17. Because the trapezoid is isosceles, it can be broken into a rectangle and two right triangles, with the two side lengths of 5 applying to the legs of the trapezoid. Because the difference in the bases is 8, half that will be the length of the leg of each of the triangles. Therefore, the right triangles will have a hypotenuse of 5 and a leg of 4. The Pythagorean Theorem shows that the length of the second leg is 3. The area of the two right triangles is equivalent to a 3 by 4 rectangle, and the other rectangle that makes up the trapezoid is 3 by 10. This gives areas of 12 and 30, which adds up to 42, choice **c.**

18. Point *H* should have the same *x*-coordinate as point *I* and the same *y*-coordinate as point *G*. Therefore, the answer is choice **c**: (−2, −1).

19. The area of a circle is $A = (\pi)(r^2)$; $(\pi)(r^2) = 16\pi$; $r = 4$. The perimeter of a circle is $P = (2)(\pi)(r)$. $P = (2)(\pi)(4) = 8\pi$ inches, choice **c.**

20. DE is 2.5 times greater than AB; therefore, EF is 7.5 and DF is 10. Add the three numbers together to arrive at the perimeter, 22.5 (choice **c**).

21. The Pythagorean theorem states that the square of the length of the hypotenuse of a right triangle is equal to the sum of the squares of the other two sides, so you know that $1^2 + X^2 = (\sqrt{10})^2$, so $1 + X^2 = 10$, so $X^2 = 10 - 1 = 9$, so $X = 3$, choice **b.**

22. Use the Pythagorean theorem to find the missing side: $a^2 + b^2 = c^2$, where c is the hypotenuse. Plug in the numbers: $(12)^2 + (5)^2 = c^2$, or $169 = c^2$. Therefore, $c = 13$, choice **e.**

23. Choice **a** is correct because the x coordinate is always listed first in an ordered pair, as noted by (x, y). Follow the x-axis first and then move up or down the y-axis to the point in question. Here the endpoints are $(-3, 1)$ and $(1, -4)$.

24. When describing the search area, this question tells you that it encompasses a 45-mile radius. When you see the term "radius," you know that you are dealing with a circle. You also know that you need to come up with a formula for T, which is an area in square miles. The area of a circle is πr^2. Thus, $A = \pi r^2$ becomes $T = \pi r^2$. Substituting 45 in for r, your formula becomes $T = \pi(45)^2$. Rearranging, you get choice **b**, $T = 452\pi$.

25. The diagram shows a right triangle with a hypotenuse of 10 ft and one leg equal to 6 ft. If you know how to spot a 6–8–10 right triangle, you are in luck, and you know that the length of the other leg, b, is 8 ft. Otherwise, use the Pythagorean theorem: $a^2 + b^2 = c^2$. This formula becomes $6^2 + b^2 = 10^2$, or $36 + b^2 = 100$, or $b^2 = 64$. Thus $b = 8$, choice **a.**

26. When the sum of two angles is 180 degrees, the angles are supplementary or supplemental to one another. To find the supplement subtract 35 degrees from 180 degrees, or $180 - 35 = 145$, choice **b.**

27. Since line A is parallel to line B, angles in corresponding positions are equal to each other. Therefore, the angle directly above $x°$ is also 125°. Since these two angles form a straight line, their sum must be 180°. Thus, $x = 180 - 125 = 55$, choice **b.**

28. The shaded area is simply the area of the rectangle minus the area of the triangle. The width of the rectangle and the height of the triangle are both 4, because the radius of the circle is 4. You get:

$$A_{rect} - A_{triangle}$$
$$(lw) - (\tfrac{1}{2}bh)$$
$$(8)(4) - \tfrac{1}{2}(8)(4)$$
$$32 - 16$$
$$16 \text{ (choice **e**)}$$

29. Since the triangle is a right isosceles, the non-right angles are 45 degrees, choice **c.**

30. First, calculate the volume of each box. The smaller box measures 16 × 18 × 20 inches, so its volume is 5,760 cubic inches. The dimensions of the larger box are 18 × 20 × 22 inches, so its volume is 7,920 cubic inches. Subtract 5,760 from 7,920 to get a difference of 2,160 cubic inches, answer **c.**

31. The side of the original cube is 2, so its volume is $V = \text{side}^3 = (2)^3 = 8\ \text{units}^3$. When you double its side, the side = 2 × 2 = 4. The new volume is $V = (4)^3 = 64\ \text{units}^3$. When you compare the two volumes, you see that you multiply the old volume (8) by 8 to get the new volume (64, answer choice **d**).

32. A reflection occurs when an image is flipped over a line. Choice **a** is the only answer that has the polygon as a reflection of polygon A across the y-axis.

33. First, you need to determine the length of a side of the square. Notice that each side is the hypotenuse for a right triangle. Using the Pythagorean theorem, you get $(OB)^2 + (OC)^2 = (BC)^2$, or $(3)^2 + (3)^2 = (BC)^2$, and $(BC)^2 = 18$. Thus, $BC = \sqrt{18} = \sqrt{9 \times 2} = 3\sqrt{2}$ feet. Since BC is a side of the square, its area is = 9 × 2 = 18 square feet, choice **d.**

34. If the figure is a regular decagon, it can be divided into ten equal sections by lines passing through the center. Two such lines form the indicated angle, which includes three of the ten sections. $\frac{3}{10}$ of 360 degrees = 108 degrees, choice **d.**

35. The easiest way to calculate the area is to realize that the shaded figure is made up of half a circle of diameter 4 (radius = $\frac{4}{2}$ = 2) on top of a rectangle that is 4 units wide and 6 units tall. The area of a half circle is $(\frac{1}{2})\pi r^2$, and the area of a rectangle is length times width. So the shaded area equals $(\frac{1}{2})\pi(2)^2 + (4)(6) = 24 + 2\pi$, so choice **c** is correct.

36. If angle 1 is 30 degrees, angle 3 must be 60 degrees by right triangle geometry. Because lines A and B are parallel, angles 3 and 4 must be congruent, so angle 4 must also equal 60 degrees. To find angle 5, angle 4 must be subtracted from 180 degrees (supplementary angles add up to 180 degrees). 180 degrees minus 60 degrees equals 120 degrees, choice **c.**

37. Because the radius of the hemisphere is 3, and it is the same as half the base of the triangle, the base must be 6. Therefore, the area of the triangle is $\frac{1}{2}bh$ = 12. The area of the circle is πr^2 which is equal to 9π. Therefore, the half-circle's area is $\frac{9\pi}{2}$. Adding gives $\frac{9\pi}{2}$ + 12, choice **d.**

38. If the triangle is reflected about the y-axis, the resulting triangle will be a mirror image of the given triangle, located the same distance from the axes. The x coordinate of point R will now be a negative number, but the y coordinate will still be positive. The coordinates of the new point R will be (–5, 6), choice **a.**

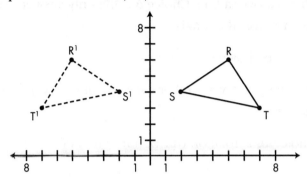

39. Use the Pythagorean theorem ($a^2 + b^2 = c^2$). The distance from Jason to the rock wall is 125 m, so $a = 125$. The hypotenuse of the triangle in the diagram is 341 m, so $c = 341$. Using these values yields the equation $125^2 + b^2 = 341^2$. Solve the equation for b.

$$b^2 = 341^2 - 125^2; \; b^2 = 116,281 - 15,625; \; b^2 = 100,656$$
$$b = \sqrt{100,656} = 317.3, \text{ choice } \textbf{a.}$$

40. Triangle ABC and triangle DAE are similar. This means that their sides will be in proportion. Side AB will be in proportion with side AD. On the figure you can see that $AB = 3$. You are given that $DB = 6$, so you know that $AD = 9$. Thus the triangles are in a 3:9 ratio, which reduces to a 1:3 ratio. This helps us because if $AC = 2$, then AE will be three times as long, or 6 (choice **b**).

41. Choice **d** is correct. The perimeter formula for a rectangle is $P = 2l + 2w$. Here the length is $2 - a$, and the width is a. Putting these values into your formula you get $L = 2(2 - a) + 2(a) = 4 - 4a + 4a = 4$.

42. The line that crosses both parallel lines will create the same angles about both lines. There is an angle marked "$x - 6$" under line segment $\overline{AB}$, so you can mark an angle "$x - 6$" under line segment $\overline{CD}$. Now, notice that $2x$ and $x - 6$ combine to make a straight line. Since a straight line is 180 degrees, write: $2x + (x - 6) = 180$, or $3x - 6 = 180$, or $3x = 186$, or $x = 62°$, answer choice **b.**

43. The diameter of the outer circle (the pool plus the walk) = 30 + 4 + 4 = 38 feet. Therefore, the radius of the outer circle is 19 feet, and its area = $\pi r^2 = \pi \times (19)^2 = 361\pi$ square feet. The diameter of the inner circle (just the pool) = 30 feet, and its radius is 15 feet. Thus, the area of the inner circle = $\pi r^2 = \pi \times (15)^2 = 225\pi$ square feet. Therefore, the area of the walk = $361\pi - 225\pi = 136\pi$ square feet, choice **b.**

44. The shaded area is the difference between the area of the square and the circle. Because the radius is 1, a side of the square is 2. The area of the square is 2(2), and the area of the circle is $\pi r^2 = \pi 1^2 = \pi$. Therefore, the answer is $4 - \pi$ (choice **e**).

45. A reflection occurs when an image is flipped over a line. Choice **a** is the only answer that has triangle ABC as a reflection of triangle XYZ over the x-axis.

46. Point M is at (4, 0). It is on the line $x = 4$, so choice **c** is correct.

47. Choice **d** is correct. Line q runs through the point $x = -3$. For every point on the y-axis, line q is at $x = -3$. The equation of line q is $x = -3$.

48. The correct order, as represented in choice **d**, is rotation (turn), translation (slide), reflection (flip).

49. To find the volume of water in the bathtub, multiply the length by the width by the height of water. 70 in × 25 in × 2 in = 3500 in^3, choice **b**.

50. The dimensions of Pedro's doghouse must equal a volume of 31.32 cubic feet. 2.7 ft × 2.9 ft × 4 ft = 31.32 cubic feet, choice **a**.

51. The diamond (choice **a**) will tessellate:

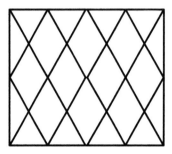

The other choices listed do NOT tessellate because there are gaps between the shapes as you tile them atop a surface:

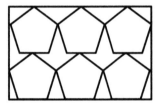 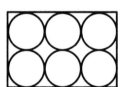 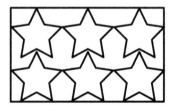

52. The distance between Plattville and Quincy is the hypotenuse of a right triangle with sides of length 80 and 60. The length of the hypotenuse equals the square root of 80^2 plus 60^2, which equals the square root of 6,400 plus 3,600, which equals the square root of 10,000, which equals 100 miles (choice **a**).

Chapter 16

1. To find the mean, add the numbers then divide the sum by the number of addends: 49 + 54 + 67 + 75 + 75 = 320. Then, 320 ÷ 5 = 64, choice **c.**

2. The mode is the number that appears *most frequently*, in this case, $\sqrt{3}$ (choice **c**).

3. This is a two-step problem. First, add the three numbers: 22 + 25 + 19 = 66. Now divide the sum by 3 to find the average: 66 ÷ 3 = 22, choice **c.**

4. Choice **c** is correct. The median is the number in the *middle* of the series—in this case, 20.

5. The mean is the average. To calculate the average you add all the numbers up, and then divide by the number of tests: 92 + 89 + 96 + 93 + 93 + 83 = 546. Next, divide: 546 ÷ 6 = 91, choice **b.**

6. Since there are two *middle numbers* in this set—30 and 40—the median is the average of the two, or 35, choice **b.**

7. The mode is the number that appears most frequently in a series—in this case, it is 9, choice **c.**

8. The median value is the middle value when the numbers are listed in order. This is 10 inches, answer choice **b.**

9. To calculate the average, use this formula:

$$\text{Average} = \frac{\text{sum of all values}}{\text{\# of values}}$$

   The sum of all the values is: 54 + 61 + 70 + 75 = 260. Divide 260 by 4 to get 65, choice **b.**

10. There are a total of 5 + 12 + 7 socks, or 24 socks in his drawer. Since 5 are blue, the odds of Derrick pulling out a blue sock are 5:24, choice **c.**

11. There are a total of 12 tokens. Therefore, the probability that the first token drawn is red = $\frac{4}{12} = \frac{1}{3}$, choice **b.**

12. **b.** To find the median score, you first must list all of the scores in order: 3 7 8 10 12 13 14. The middle number will be your median: 3 7 8 **10** 12 13 14. Hence, 10 is the median. Note that if there are ever two middle numbers (i.e. when taking the median of an even number of numbers), you simply take the average of the 2 middle numbers.

13. **a.** The mode of a set of numbers is the number that appears the most. Looking at the numbers: 35 52 17 23 51 52 18 32, you see that 52 appears twice.

$$35 \boxed{52} \ 17 \ 23 \ 51 \ \boxed{52} \ 18 \ 32$$

Thus, the mode is 52. Note that choice **c** represents the median, and choice **b** represents the average of the given numbers.

14. **a.** The formula for calculating the mean (average) is:

$$\text{Mean} = \frac{\text{sum of all values}}{\text{\# of values}}$$

The sum of all the values given is: 75 + 81 + 93 + 77 + 84 = 410. The number of values (scores) is 5. Thus, the mean = $\frac{410}{5}$ = 82, choice **a**.

15. Because the term *mean* is another term for the term *average,* you know that choice **d** must be wrong. You will need to calculate the mean and the median. The formula for calculating the mean (average) is:

$$\text{Mean} = \frac{\text{sum of all values}}{\text{\# of values}}$$

Here the sum of all the values is 12 + 14 + 15 + 19 + 20 + 22 = 102, and the number of values is 6. Thus the average is $\frac{102}{6}$ = 17, choice **c**.

16. Choice **b** is correct. To figure out the probability for the given outcome, you need to calculate the total possible outcomes. You know that the record company brought 300 rap CDs, 500 rock CDs, 200 easy listening CDs, and 400 country CDs. The total possible outcomes equal 300 + 500 + 200 + 400 = 1,400. The outcomes that fit the criteria in the question = 200. This is because 200 easy listening CDs will be given out. This means that the chance of getting an easy listening CD will be $\frac{200}{1,400}$. This reduces to $\frac{1}{7}$.

17. To find the number of different combinations, multiply the 3 numbers together. The product of 6 × 9 × 11 is 594, choice **c**.

18. To find the reasonable average of these 3 years, first round each year to the closest 50, giving memberships of 500, 550, and 600. The average of these 3 numbers is 550, choice **d**.

19. The mode of a group of numbers is the number that occurs most frequently. Since Rita has 4 grandparents and 4 nieces, 4 (choice **b**) is the most frequent number and is the mode.

20. To find the mean of the numbers given, add the 4 numbers and divide by 4. 28 + 44 + 64 + 56 = 192. $\frac{192}{4}$ = 48, choice **c**.

21. To find the probability use the following formula:

$$\frac{\text{number of white marbles}}{\text{total number of marbles}}$$

$\frac{16}{80} = \frac{1}{5}$, choice **c.**

22. The mean is the *average*. To find the average, add 522.75 + 498.25 + 530 to get 1,551. Then divide by the number of paychecks (3): 1,551 ÷ 3 = 517 (choice **a**). It is not answer **b** because that is the middle number, which is the median.

23. Yellow beans + orange beans = 12. There are 30 total beans. $\frac{12}{30}$ is reduced to $\frac{2}{5}$, choice **b.**

24. The two drawings are independent of each other; therefore, the probability that Mrs. Fikstad will draw Benjamin's name again is the same as if he had not been picked the first time. He has a 1 in 26 chance of being drawn again, so choice **b** is correct.

25. Using the fundamental counting principle, multiply 3 choices by 2 choices by 3 choices to get 18 total outfits (choice **d**).

26. Choice **c** is correct. First, add the number of patients to find the total: 63. Then divide the number of patients by the number of nursing assistants: 63 divided by 7 is 9.

27. There are 2 choices of burgers, 2 choices of side dishes, and 3 choices of desserts. Thus, the total number of choices is: 2 × 2 × 3 = 12, choice **c.**

28. Jack has 6 types of wrapping paper to choose from, 5 cards to choose from, and 3 bows to choose from. The total possible choices would then be: 6 × 5 × 3 = 90, choice **d.**

29. Choice **a** is correct. All 6 possible outcomes: 1, 2, 3, 4, 5, 6. Only 2 possibilities (5 and 6) are greater than 4. $\frac{2}{6} = \frac{1}{3}$.

30. Here, the order matters, and you have 8 available places:

$$_8P_8 = 8 \times 7 \times 6 \times 5 \times 4 \times 3 \times 2 \times 1 = 40,320. \text{ Choice } \textbf{d} \text{ is correct.}$$

31. Choice **c** is correct. The total number or tickets sold was 5 + 3 + 7 + 9 = 24. Of these 24, J.T. purchased 3. This means J.T. has a $\frac{3}{24} = \frac{1}{8}$ chance of winning.

32. The recruit's three best times are 54, 54, and 57. To find the average, add the three numbers and divide the sum by three. The average is 55 seconds, choice **b.**

33. c. Here, the order matters, and you have 4 available places:

$$_4P_4 = 4 \times 3 \times 2 \times 1 = 24.$$

Alternatively, if you listed the possibilities, you would get:

A B Sammy C D	A D Sammy B C
A B Sammy D C	A D Sammy C B
B A Sammy C D	D A Sammy B C
B A Sammy D C	D A Sammy C B
A C Sammy B D	B D Sammy A C
A C Sammy D B	B D Sammy C A
C A Sammy B D	D B Sammy A C
C A Sammy D B	D B Sammy C A
C B Sammy A D	C D Sammy A B
C B Sammy D A	C D Sammy B A
B C Sammy A D	D C Sammy A B
B C Sammy D A	D C Sammy B A

34. Here you have 6 in all and 3 choices to make. Also, the order matters because the question asks about "arrangements." You use: $_6P_3 = 6 \times 5 \times 4 = 120$, choice **a.**

35. 4 shirts with an average price of $9 yields: $4 \times 9 = \$36$ total. You can subtract out the $15 and $17 shirts, so you know $36 - 15 - 17$, or $14 was spent on the other 2 shirts. Just look for the answer choice that adds to $14. Choice **d** is the only option that fits these criteria.

36. A score of 130 would give a mean of 166.6 and a median of 163.
A score of 145 would give a mean of 169.6 and a median of 163.
A score of 168 would give a mean of 174.2 and a median of 168.
A score of 177 would give a mean of 176 and a median of 177.
A score of 270 would give a mean of 194.6 and a median of 192.
177 (choice **d**) is the only one that has a median greater than the mean.

37. There is a total of 20 socks, and 16 socks are navy or black, and, therefore, not white. The probability that the first sock drawn will not be white is $\frac{16}{20} = \frac{4}{5}$, choice **d.**

38. Here you need to know the formula for calculating the average, which is also known as the mean:

$$\text{Average} = \frac{\text{sum of all values}}{\text{\# of values}}$$

Here you know that the average is 13 and that 5 CDs were purchased. You have $14 = \frac{(\text{sum of all values})}{5}$. Multiplying both sides by 5, you get 65 = sum of all CDs. You know that she bought 3 CDs at $12 each, a fourth for $15 and you need to figure out what the fifth CD cost. Put a "?" in for the fifth CD.

$$65 = \text{sum of all CDs}$$
$$65 = 12 + 12 + 12 + 15 + ?$$
$$65 = 36 + 15 + ?$$
$$65 = 51 + ?$$
$$14 = ?$$

This means that the fifth CD cost $14, choice **c**.

39. Choice **a** is correct. First calculate the number of possible outcomes. The possibilities are: 1, 2, 3, 4, 5, or 6. Thus, there are 6 possible outcomes. Next, underline the outcomes that satisfy the condition given in the question. Which of these numbers are multiples of 3? 1, 2, **3**, 4, 5, **6**. Notice that only 2 outcomes out of a total of 6 outcomes are multiples of 3. Thus the answer would be $\frac{2}{6}$, which reduces to $\frac{1}{3}$.

40. To find the average, you use the following formula:

$$\text{Average (mean)} = \frac{\text{sum of all values}}{\text{\# of values}}$$

Here you know the average is $18.95, and that the number of values = 4 (there are 4 books). Substituting, you get:

$$\$18.95 = \frac{\text{sum of all values}}{4}$$

Cross multiplying, you get $18.95 × 4 = *sum of all values*, which means $75.80 = *sum of all values*. So, the 4 books totaled $75.80, and you know the price of 3 of these books. Therefore, you can subtract off the price of the 3 books to find out the cost of the fourth: $75.80 − $25.25 − $14.95 − $19.95 = $15.65; choice **c** is correct.

41. Here, the order does not matter: If the five names are A, B, C, D, and E, picking ABC is the same as BCA. That is why you use the formula for combinations. All = 5 because there are 5 names, and $c = 3$ because you will choose 3. Thus, our formula

$$\text{ALL}_c\text{CHOSEN} = \frac{_a P_c}{c!}$$

becomes:

$$\text{ALL}_c\text{CHOSEN} = \frac{_5 P_3}{3!}$$

On top, you start taking the factorial of 5, but you stop after 3 spots. On the bottom you take 3 factorial:

$$\frac{5}{3} \times \frac{4}{2} \times \frac{3}{1}$$

The two threes cancel, so you have $\frac{5 \times 4}{2 \times 1}$, which is $\frac{20}{2}$, or 10 choice **d**.

42. Here, the order does not matter. Two of 10 will get the part. Use the formula for combinations. You use:

$$\text{ALL}_c\text{CHOSEN} = \frac{_a P_c}{c!}$$

All = 10 because there are 10 dancers auditioning, and $c = 2$ because only 2 will make it. Our formula becomes:

$$\text{ALL}_c\text{CHOSEN} = \frac{_{10} P_2}{2!}$$

On top, you start taking the factorial of 10, but you stop after 2 spots. On the bottom you take 2 factorial:

$$\frac{10 \times 9}{2 \times 1}$$

This is $\frac{90}{2}$, or 45, so choice **c** is correct.

D

Glossary of Mathematics Terms

Base   A number used as a repeated factor in an exponential expression. In 8^5, 8 is the base number.

Base 10   see *Decimal numbers.*

Binary System   One of the simplest numbering systems. The base of the binary system is 2, which means that only the digits 0 and 1 can appear in a binary representation of any number.

Circumference   The distance around the outside of a circle.

Composite number   Any integer that can be divided evenly by a number other than itself and 1. All numbers are either prime or composite.

Counting numbers   Include all whole numbers, with the exception of zero.

Decimal   A number in the base 10 number system. Each place value in a decimal number is worth ten times the place value of the digit to its right.

Denominator   The bottom number in a fraction. The denominator of $\frac{1}{2}$ is 2.

Diameter   A chord which passes through the center of the circle and has endpoints on the circle.

Difference   The result of subtracting one number from another.

Divisible by   Capable of being evenly divided by a given number, without a remainder.

Dividend   The number in a division problem that is being divided. In $32 \div 4 = 8$, 32 is the dividend.

Even number   A counting number that is divisible by two.

Expanded notation   A method of writing numbers as the sum of their units (hundreds, tens, ones, etc.). The expanded notation for 378 is $300 + 70 + 8$.

Exponent   A number that indicates an operation of repeated multiplication. For instance, 3^4 indicates that the number 3 should be multiplied by itself 4 times.

Factor   One of two or more numbers or variables that are being multiplied together.

Factorial   The product of all integers from 1 up to the integer in question, symbolized by !. 4! means "4 factorial," or $4 \times 3 \times 2 \times 1$.

Fractal   A geometric figure that is self-similar; that is, any smaller piece of the figure will have roughly the same shape as the whole.

Improper fraction   A fraction whose numerator is the same size as or larger than its denominator. Improper fractions are equal to or greater than one.

Integer   All of the *whole numbers* and negatives too. Examples are $-3, -2, -1, 0, 1, 2,$ and 3. Note that integers *do not* include fractions or decimals.

Multiple of   A multiple of a number has that number as one of its factors. Thirty is a multiple of six; it is also a multiple of five.

Negative number   A real number whose value is less than zero.

Numerator   The top number in a fraction. The numerator of $\frac{1}{4}$ is 1.

Odd number   A counting number that is not divisible by two.

Percent   A ratio or fraction whose denominator is assumed to be 100, expressed using the % sign; 98% is equal to $\frac{98}{100}$.

Perimeter   The distance around the outside of a polygon.

Polygon   A closed two-dimensional shape made up of several line segments that are joined together.

Positive number   A real number whose value is greater than zero.

Prime number   A real number that is divisible by only two positive factors: one and itself.

Product   The result when two numbers are multiplied together.

Proper fraction   A fraction whose denominator is larger than its numerator. Proper fractions are equal to less than one.

Proportion   A relationship between two equivalent sets of fractions in the form $\frac{a}{b} = \frac{c}{d}$.

Quotient   The result when one number is divided into another.

Radical   The symbol used to signify a root operation.

Radius   Any line segment from the center of the circle to a point on the circle. The radius of a circle is equal to half its diameter.

Ratio   The relationship between two things, expressed as a proportion.

Real numbers   Include fractions and decimals in addition to *integers*.

Reciprocal   One of two numbers which, when multiplied together, give a product of one. For instance, since $\frac{3}{2} \times \frac{2}{3}$ is equal to 1, $\frac{3}{2}$ is the reciprocal of $\frac{2}{3}$.

Remainder   The amount left over after a division problem using whole numbers. Divisible numbers always have a remainder of zero.

Root (square root)   One of two (or more) equal factors of a number. The square root of 36 is 6, because 6 • 6 = 36. The cube root of 27 is 3 because 3 • 3 • 3 = 27.

Simplify terms   To combine like terms and reduce an equation to its most basic form.

Variable   A letter, often x, used to represent an unknown number value in a problem.

Whole numbers   0, 1, 2, 3, and so on. They do not include negatives, fractions, or decimals.

E

Resources for Students

► BOOKS

The following is a list of recommended books for learners in the middle school years, but you may find that your child reads above or below the level of some books. These titles are a mixture of old classics and new favorites. They can be found at your local library or bookstore, or ordered online from sites like Powells.com or Amazon.com. Remember that these recommendations are just the tip of the iceberg; there are many great books for middle-school-aged readers. For more suggestions, visit the American Library Association's book lists at www.ala.org/yalsa/booklists/index.html.

Fiction and Literature

Alcott, Louisa May. *Little Women*

Babbitt, Natalie. *Tuck Everlasting*

Bauer, Joan. *Hope Was Here*

Block, Francesca Lia. *Girl Goddess #9*

Burnett, Frances Hodgson. *The Secret Garden*

Cisneros, Sandra. *The House on Mango Street*

Cormier, Robert. *The Chocolate War*

Dorris, Michael. *Morning Girl*

George, Jean Craighead. *My Side of the Mountain*

Hinton, S.E. *The Outsiders*

Juster, Norman. *The Phantom Tollbooth*

Knowles, John. *A Separate Peace*

L'Engle, Madeleine. *A Wrinkle in Time*

Lowry, Lois. *Number the Stars*

Lowry, Lois. *The Giver*

Potok, Chaim. *The Chosen*

Paterson, Katherine. *Lyddie*

Rowling, J.K. *Harry Potter and the Sorcerer's Stone*

Smith, Betty. *A Tree Grows in Brooklyn*

Smith, Dodie. *I Capture the Castle*

Taylor, Mildred. *Roll of Thunder, Hear My Cry*

Townsend, Sue. *The Secret Diary of Adrian Mole, Aged $13\frac{3}{4}$*

Biography/Autobiography

Angelou, Maya. *I Know Why the Caged Bird Sings*

Frank, Anne. *Anne Frank: The Diary of a Young Girl*

Fulghum, Robert. *All I Really Need to Know I Learned in Kindergarten*

Rosen, Michael. *Shakespeare: His Work and His World*

Wright, Richard. *Black Boy*

Writing

Hanson, Anne. *Visual Writing: Diagramming Your Ideas to Communicate Effectively*

Goldberg, Natalie. *Writing Down the Bones*

Rae, Colleen. *Movies in the Mind: How to Build a Short Story*

Science

Ballard, Robert. *Exploring the Titanic*

Cobb, Vicki. *Science Experiments You Can Eat*

Goodall, Jane. *My Life with the Chimpanzees*

Jones, Charlotte. *Fingerprints and Talking Bones: How Real Life Crimes Are Solved*

Lauber, Patricia. *Seeing Earth from Space*

Macaulay, David. *The Way Things Work*

Mowat, Farley. *Never Cry Wolf*

National Geographic Society. *Why on Earth?*

Ronan, Colin. *Science Explained*

Social Studies/History

Bachrach, Susan. *Tell Them We Remember: The Story of The Holocaust*

Beals, Melba. *Warriors Don't Cry: A Searing Memoir of the Battle to Integrate Little Rock's Central High*

Brandenburg, J. *Sand and Fog: Adventures in Southern Africa*

Coleman, Penny. *Rosie the Riveter*

D'Aulaire, Ingri and Edgar. *D'Aulaire's Book of Greek Myths*

Dash, Joan. *We Shall Not Be Moved*

Hoose, Phillip M. *We Were There, Too!: Young People in U.S. History*

Houston, Jeanne Wakatsuki. *Farewell to Manzanar: A True Story of Japanese American Experience During and After the World War II Internment*

Jiang, Ji-Li. *Red Scarf Girl*

Metzer, Milton. *Brother, Can You Spare a Dime?: The Great Depression 1929–1933*

Morin, Isobel. *Our Changing Constitution*

Racine, Ned. *Visual Communication: Understanding Maps, Charts, Diagrams, and Schematics*

Mathematics

Burns, Marilyn. *The I Hate Mathematics Book*

Great Source Education Group. *Math on Call*

Pappas, Theoni. *Fractals, Googols and Other Mathematical Tales*

Sobanski, Jessika. *Visual Math: See How Math Makes Sense*

Tang, Greg. *The Grapes of Math: Mind Stretching Math Riddles*

Thompson, Virginia. *Family Math: The Middle School Years, Algebraic Reasoning and Number Sense*

Wright, Joseph. *Math Games for Middle School: Challenges and Skill-Builders for Students at Every Level*

▶ MAGAZINES

Boys' Life
This is a great general interest magazine for boys. Read about a wide variety of topics.

Creative Kids
Appropriately named, this magazine is meant to encourage your teen's creativity.

Cricket
This is a general interest magazine with stories, recipes, science articles, and games.

Dig
Does your teen want to be an archaeologist? *Dig* is a perfect magazine for her. Mummies, dinosaurs, and ancient civilizations fill its pages.

Explore!
This magazine sets out to answer the question "How does the world work?" There are plenty of adventure, science, and technology stories from all over the world.

Girls' Life
This magazine has plenty of advice, stories, celebrity interviews, and other topics of interest for girls.

Kid's Wall Street News
Show me the money! This magazine is a great introduction to saving, investing, and learning about the economy.

National Geographic World
With great articles about wildlife and world cultures, this award-winning magazine is perfect for pleasure reading.

Sports Illustrated for Kids
Have your teen sports fanatic check out *Sports Illustrated for Kids* and read all about his favorite teams, players, and sports events!

Teen Voices
A great magazine written by and for teen girls that focuses on real-life topics.

Time for Kids
From the editors of *Time* comes this current events magazine filled with great articles, photos, and maps.

▶ CD-ROMs and Software

General

Excel @ Middle School. Twelve complete subjects are covered, with pretests, posttests, and study pages.

Middle School Advantage 2002. Offers students ages 11 and older opportunities to enrich their knowledge of U.S. history, vocabulary, grammar, life science, earth science, Spanish, typing, prealgebra, algebra, and geometry.

New Millennium Encyclopedia & Home Reference Library Deluxe 2002. A multimedia compilation of eight complete reference works, including *Roget's Thesaurus, Webster's Dictionary,* atlas, almanac and more. Over 170,000 total entries in the form of articles, video and audio clips, and photographs.

Math

StudyWorks Middle School Deluxe Math 5.0. Comprehensive math activities and lessons to prepare students for state examination standards. Includes unlimited access to StudyWorks online, and a bonus title, *Middle School Deluxe Science,* which provides material on a variety of science topics.

Science

The New Way Things Work. This CD-ROM is a great way to learn about machine and inventions that changed the world.

Night Sky Interactive. Learn all about planets, stars, and comets with this interactive software. There is animation and narration.

Language

Rosetta Stone Spanish Explorer. Help your learner learn or improve her Spanish with this quality program complete with native speakers as teachers. Cost: $19.99

Rosetta Stone French Explorer. Parlez-vous français? If your family is studying French this year, try this fun interactive program.

Social Studies

Masks: Faces of the Pacific. This CD-ROM is a unique alternative to most programs. Learn about the history and culture surrounding the masks from the Pacific Rim.

History of the World 2.0. Complete with biographies, histories, and articles, this program is a must for history buffs.

Music

Magix Music Maker 2000. If your child has an interest in music, give him the tools to compose it right on the computer.

▶ INTERNET

Note: At the time of publication, the websites listed here were current. Due to the ever-changing nature of the Web, we cannot guarantee their continued existence or content. Parents should always supervise their children while they are on the Internet.

Homeschool-Related Web Resource

Apricot Pie: www.apricotpie.com. Message boards, chat and articles written by and for teen homeschoolers.

Homeschool Teens and College—Homeschooled Teenagers' Web Sites: www. homeschoolteenscollege.net/teenwebs.htm.

General Web Resources

Exploratorium: www.exploratorium.edu. The famous San Francisco museum by the same name hosts this site. The museum is dedicated to science, art, and human perception. Here you will find exhibitions from the museum, activities, and resources for projects.

Hot Popcorn: www.hotpopcorn.com. If your child loves movies, music, and television, this is a great site for him or her to sound-off. Visitors can write their own reviews of movies, as well as get all the latest entertainment news.

Internet Public Library Teen Division: www.ipl.org/teen. Links to teen-friendly websites of all kinds, selected by a librarian and teen advisory panel.

The Jason Project: www.jasonproject.org. Homeschoolers can register to follow Dr. Robert Ballard—who discovered the RMS *Titanic*—and his crew on their deep sea expeditions. The project includes print curricula, live satellite broadcasts and video supplements.

Los Angeles County Museum of Art: www.lacma.org. The Los Angeles County Museum of Art features works of art online. There is also a feature that allows your teen to offer his opinion about a work of art.

Metropolitan Museum of Art: www.metmuseum.org. New York's Metropolitan Museum of Art features 5,000 years of artwork. This is an amazing site that will allow your child to learn about art and artists throughout history.

Roots & Shoots: vax.wcsu.edu/cyberchimp/roots/rsindex.html. Learn how the Roots & Shoots program teaches young people about environmental awareness and community service—and then join up yourself!

Searchopolis: www.searchopolis.com. Filtered Internet searches for middle and high school students.

Surf Monkey: www.surfmonkey.com. The content on this site is sure to please your child. Their wonderful links are organized by categories such as *playful, artsy, brainy, spacey, newsworthy, techie, worldly,* and *starstruck.*

Teen Hoopla: www.ala.org/teenhoopla. Maintained by the American Library Association, this site offers book reviews, message boards, and links to websites created by and for teenagers.

TeenLit Writer's Workshop: www.teenlit.com/workshop. Advice and links to other resources for young writers on topics including punctuation, overcoming writer's block, editing marks, and avoiding clichés.

▶ EDUCATIONAL VIDEOS/DVDs

Your child's favorite movies are probably not documentaries or nature films—but educational videos don't have to be boring! For a selection of smart, teen-friendly films that you and your child can watch together and discuss, visit the documentary section of your video store, or check out these resources:

The American Library Association's Young Adult Library Services Association (YALSA) selects a list of outstanding videos for young adults each year. The committee that selects the videos is a mixture of teenagers and youth librarians. Past selections have ranged from "Triumph of the Nerds," a biography of Bill Gates, to "Rights from the Heart," a series of vignettes examining the issue of human rights around the world. View current and past recommendations online at www.ala.org/yalsa/booklists/video.

www.Classroomvisuals.com is a mail-order video site. For an annual fee, you can order five videos at a time, for two weeks' viewing, postage paid both ways, delivered to and picked up from your front step. This site lists thousands of videos—from PBS and the Discovery and History channels to biographies to movie classics—both educational and entertainment videos.

▶ AUDIO RESOURCES

August House Audio (www.augusthouse.com) publishes a wonderful variety of storytellers on CD and cassette for all ages.

See the American Library Association's selection of the best audio books for young adults at www.ala.org/yalsa/booklists/audio.

Boomerang! is a monthly 70-minute audio magazine for, by, and about kids. (800-333-7858)

Audio Memory (www.audiomemory.com) uses music to help kids learn math, geography, history, and much more.

If you have a fast Internet connection, it's even possible to download full-length audio books in Real Audio or MP3 format, sometimes at no charge. To see what's available, visit www.mp3lit.com or broadcast.yahoo.com.

And for great music and interesting commentary, try tuning in to your local public radio station. A listing of stations by city or zip code is available at www.npr.org.

Resources for Parents

► BOOKS

General Homeschooling Information

Beechick, Ruth. *You Can Teach Your Child Successfully: Grades 4–8* (Pollock Pines, CA: Arrow Press, 1992).

Cohen, Cafi. *Homeschooling: The Teen Years: Your Complete Guide to Successfully Homeschooling the 13- To 18-Year Old* (Roseville, CA: Prima, 2000).

Colfax, David and Micki Colfax. *Homeschooling for Excellence* (New York: Warner Books, 1988).

Dobson, Linda, ed. *The Homeschooling Book of Answers* (Roseville, CA: Prima, 1998).

Griffith, Mary. *Homeschooling Handbook.* 2nd ed. (Roseville, CA: Prima, 1999).

Guterson, David. *Family Matters: Why Homeschooling Makes Sense* (New York: Harvest Books, 1993).

Hendrickson, Borg. *Home School: Taking the First Step* (Sheridan, WY: Mountain Meadow Press, 1994).

Llewellyn, Grace, ed. *Real Lives: Eleven Teenagers Who Don't Go to School* (Eugene, OR: Lowry House, 1993).

Llewellyn, Grace. *The Teenage Liberation Handbook: How to Quit School and Get a Real Life and Education* (Eugene, OR: Lowry House, 1998).

Ransom, Martha. *Complete Idiot's Guide to Homeschooling* (New York: Alpha Books, 2001).

Curriculum

Hendrickson, Borg. *How to Write a Low-Cost/No-Cost Curriculum for Your Home-School Child* (Sheridan, WY: Mountain Meadow Press, 1998).

Hirch, E.D., ed. *What Your 6th Grader Needs to Know: Fundamentals of a Good 6th Grade Education* (New York: Delta Books, 1995).

Henry, Shari. *Homeschooling: The Middle Years: Your Complete Guide to Successfully Homeschooling the 8- To 12-Year Old Child* (Roseville, CA: Prima, 1999).

Leppert, Mary, et al. *Homeschooling Almanac 2002–2003* (Roseville, CA: Prima, 2001).

Rupp, Rebecca. *The Complete Home Learning Source Book* (New York: Three Rivers Press, Random House, 1998).

Rupp, Rebecca. *Home Learning Year by Year: How to Design a Homeschool Curriculum from Preschool Through High School* (New York: Three Rivers Press, Random House, 2000).

► MAGAZINES, PERIODICALS, AND NEWSPAPERS

Home Education Magazine (6 issues/year)
P.O. Box 1083
Tonasket WA, 98855-1083
800-236-3278
www.home-ed-magazine.com

Home Educator's Family Times (6 issues/year)

www.homeeducator.com/FamilyTimes/index.htm—subscriptions to the print version are also
available.

John Holt's Growing Without Schooling Magazine (6 issues/year)

John Holt's Bookstore

2380 Massachusetts Avenue, Suite 104

Cambridge, MA 02140-1226

888-925-9298

www.holtgws.com

The Link, A Homeschool Newspaper (bi-monthly, no cost)

587 North Ventu Park Road, Suite F-911

Newbury Park, CA, 91320

888-470-4513

www.homeschoolnewslink.com

At Home in America (newsletter produced by Homeschool Associates)

25 Adams Avenue

Lewiston, ME 04240

207-777-1700

www.athomeinamerica.com

▶ INTERNET

Web Resources for Homeschooling Parents

The Busy Person's Guide to Homeschooling Grades 7–12:
www.wz.com/education/HomeSchoolingGrades7to12.html. A collection of links to Web
resources, rated and reviewed by homeschoolers.

California Homeschool Network Curriculum and Resource List:
www.cahomeschoolnet.org/Resources.htm. A variety of books, websites, and other resources
for curriculum development and other homeschooling needs.

Design-a-Study Guides: www.designastudy.com. Everything you need to know to design your
own unit study or create a custom curriculum.

Eclectic Homeschool Online: www.eho.org. An online magazine for creative homeschoolers.

Family Unschoolers Network: www.unschooling.org. Resources and support for support for
unschooling, homeschooling, and self-directed learning.

Finding Homeschool Support on the Internet—Freeware and Shareware:
www.geocities.com/Athens/8259/sware.html. Annotated listing of places to find free or low-
cost educational computer programs online.

Homefires: The Journal of Homeschooling Online: www.homefires.com. This site by a home-schooling parent provides many new approaches to homeschooling—among them Carschooling®, a collection of resources and teaching methods that can be used while traveling.

Homeschool.com: Your Virtual Home School: www.homeschool.com. Online courses, resource guide, support groups, and message boards.

Homeschool Teens and College: www.homeschoolteenscollege.net. Articles, reviews, and product advice for parents who are homeschooling children from 11 to 18.

Learn in Freedom!: www.learninfreedom.org. Extensive bibliographies, articles, and subject-specific resource guides from homeschoolers and unschoolers.

Multiple Intelligences—Inventory and Informational Site: www.surfaquarium.com/im.htm. Information on the many types of intelligence and learning styles children possess, many of which are frequently undervalued in traditional schools.

The On-Line Books Page: http://digital.library.upenn.edu/books. An index of over 14,000 books which are freely available on the Internet.

PEP: Parents, Educators and Publishers: www.microweb.com/pepsite. Lots of information on children's software programs.

Online Reading Lists for Middle Schoolers

Carol Hurst's Children's Literature Site: www.carolhurst.com. A huge number of book listings with capsules and ratings. Searchable by author, age group, and curriculum area.

The Children's Literature Web Guide: Internet Resources Related to Books for Children and Young Adults: www.acs.ucalgary.ca/~dkbrown. Links, discussion boards, commentary, and recommendations for all ages.

John Holt's Reading List (Growing Without Schooling): www.holtgws.com/jhrl.htm. Extensive list of parenting, homeschooling, and children's books.

Lion's House Middle and High School Reading List: www.lionshouse.org/education/bl.htm. Focuses mostly on well-known "classic" books, with helpful links to online versions of the books where available.

Little Red School House and Elizabeth Irwin High School's Middle School Reading List: www.lrei.org/html/reading.htm. This is a very good, comprehensive list with age group recommendations and links to additional sites.

Teen Reads: www.teenreads.com. Aimed at a teenage audience, this site features reviews by teenagers, book lists, message boards, author interviews, and a weekly newsletter.

Homeschooling Parents' Organizations

One of the best resources for a homeschooling parent is the support, knowledge, and advice of other homeschooling families. This list of national, state, and local homeschooling parents' groups will help you get an idea of the kinds of organizations that are available to you. This list is not comprehensive, but is designed to give you a start in networking with other families in your area.

▶ NATIONAL HOMESCHOOLING PARENTS' ORGANIZATIONS

Alternative Education Resource Organization
    (AERO)
417 Roslyn Road
Roslyn Heights, NY 11577
www.edrev.org

American Homeschool Association
P.O. Box 3142
Palmer, AK 99645
800-236-3278
www.americanhomeschoolassociation.org

National Challenged Homeschoolers Associated
    Network
P.O. Box 39
Porthill, ID 83853
208-267-6246
www.nathhan.com

National Home Education Network
P.O. Box 41067
Long Beach, CA 90853
www.nhen.org

National Home Education Research Institute
P.O. Box 13939
Salem, OR 97309
503-364-1490
www.nheri.org

▶ STATE/LOCAL HOMESCHOOLING PARENTS' ORGANIZATIONS

If your state is not listed here, no information about state groups was available at press time. To find a group in your area, contact one of the national organizations above, or ask your local school board.

Alabama
Baldwin Regional Association of Independent
    Non-Traditional Schools
P.O. Box 1765
Bay Minette, AL 36507-1765
www.homestead.com/wearebrains

North Alabama Home Educators
P.O. Box 3054
Huntsville, AL 35810
http://northalabamahomeeducators.freeservers.
    com

Alaska

Alaska Homeschool Network
www.akhomeschool.net

Arizona

Active Arizona Homeschoolers
4101 West Mulberry Drive
Phoenix, AZ 85019
http://members.tripod.com/home4school

Arizona Families for Home Education
P.O. Box 2035
Chandler, AZ 85244-2035
www.afhe.org

Arkansas

Home Educators of Arkansas
P.O. Box 192455
Little Rock, AR 72219
www.geocities.com/Heartland/Garden/4555

California

California Coalition for People for Alternative
    Learning Situations (CC-Pals)
P.O. Box 92
Escondido, CA 92025

California Homeschool Network
P.O. Box 55485
Hayward, CA 94545
800-327-5339
www.cahomeschoolnet.org

HomeSchool Association of California
P.O. Box 868
Davis, CA 95617
888-HSC-4440
www.hsc.org

Colorado

Boulder County Home Educators' Association
www.bchea.com

Colorado Springs Homeschool Support Group
P.O. Box 26117
Colorado Springs, CO 80936-6117
719-598-2636
www.hschool.com

West River Unschoolers
2420 North 1st Street
Grand Junction, CO 81501
970-241-4137

Connecticut

Connecticut Home Educators' Association
203-781-8569
www.cthomeschoolers.com

Delaware

Delaware Home Education Association
70 Tiverton Circle
Newark, DE 19702
www.dheaonline.org

Florida

Florida Parent Educators Association
P.O. Box 50685
Jackson Beach, FL 32240-0685
800-ASK-FPEA
www.fpea.com

West Florida Home Education Support League
P.O. Box 11720
Pensacola, FL 32524-1720
850-981-1222
www.whfesl.org

Georgia

Home Education Information Resource
P.O. Box 2111
Roswell, GA 30077-2111
404-681-4347
www.heir.org

Hawaii

Hawaii Homeschoolers Association
P.O. Box 893476
Mililani HI 96789
808-944-3339

Idaho

Snake River Home Educators' Association
204 5th Street
Idaho Falls, ID 83401
http://home.rmci.net/portela/SRHEA.html

Illinois

Grassroots Homeschoolers
918 Princeton Avenue
Matteson, IL 60443
grassrootshs.tripod.com

Illinois Home Oriented Unique Schooling
    Experience (HOUSE)
www.geocities.com/illinoishouse/index.html

Indiana

Life Education and Resource Network (LEARN)
812-336-1110
www.bloomington.in.us/~learn

Iowa

Iowans Dedicated to Educational Alternatives
    (IDEA)
P.O. Box 17
Teeds Grove, IA 52771
http://home.plutonium.net/~pdiltz/idea

Kansas

Central Kansas Home Educators
Route 1, Box 130
Lyons, KS 67554
316-897-6631

Johnson County Parent Educators
P.O. Box 14391
Lenexa, KS 66285-4391
www.jcpe.org

Kentucky

Kentucky Home Education Association
P.O. Box 81
Winchester, KY 40392-0081
ww4.choice.net/~buglet/KHEApage/
    KHEAhome.html

Louisiana

Louisiana Home Education Network
PMB 700
602 W. Prien Lake Road
Lake Charles, LA 70601
www.la-home-education.com

Maine

Homeschool Support Network
P.O. Box 708
Gray, ME 04039
888-300-8434
www.homeeducator.com/HSN

Maine Home Education Association
c/o Ann Bagala
56 Long Hill Road
Gray, ME 04039
www.geocities.com/mainehomeed

Maryland

Family Unschoolers Network/North County
    Home Educators
1688 Belhaven Woods Court
Pasadena, MD 21122-3727
410-360-7330
www.unschooling.org

Maryland Home Education Association
9085 Flamepool Way
Columbia, MD 21045
410-730-0073
www.mhea.com

Massachusetts

Cape Cod Homeschoolers
P.O. Box 1735
Onset, MA 02558
www.capecodhomeschoolers.com

The Family Resource Center
19 Cedarview Street
Salem, MA 01970
www.familyrc.com

Homeschooling Together
c/o Sophia Sayigh
24 Avon Place
Arlington, MA 02474
http://people.ne.mediaone.net/jrsladkey/hst

Massachusetts Home Learning Association
P.O. Box 1558
Marston's Mills, MA 02648
www.mhla.org

Pathfinder Center
256 North Pleasant Street
Amherst, MA 01002
413-253-9412
www.pathfindercenter.org

Minnesota

Minnesota Homeschoolers' Alliance
P.O. Box 23072
Richfield, MN 55423
612-288-9662 / 888-346-7622
www.homeschoolers.org

Mississippi

Home Educators of Central Mississippi
c/o Alan Bowen
1500 Beverly Drive
Clinton, MS 39056-3507
www2.netdoor.com/~nfgcgrb

Mississippi Home Educators Association
P.O. Box 945
Brookhaven, MS 39601
601-833-9110
www.mhea.org

Missouri

Families for Home Education
P.O. Box 800
Platte City, MO 64079-0800
www.microlink.net/~fhe

St. Louis Homeschool Network
c/o Karen Karabell
4147 West Pine
St. Louis, MO 63108
314-534-1171

St. Louis Secular Homeschoolers Co-Op
www.stlsecularhomeschool.org

Montana

Bozeman Homeschool Network
8799 Huffman Lane
Bozeman, MT 59715
406-586-1025

Montana Coalition of Home Educators
P.O. Box 43
Gallatin Gateway, MT 59730
www.mtche.org

Nevada

Homeschool MeltingPot
1000 North Green Valley Parkway #440-231
Henderson, NV 89014
702-320-4840
www.angelfire.com/nv/homeschoolmeltingpot

Northern Nevada Home Schools, Inc.
P.O. Box 21323
Reno, NV 89515
775-852-NNHS
www.angelfire.com/nv/NNHS

New Hampshire

Homeschooling Friends
204 Brackett Road
New Durham, NH 03855-2330
www.homeschoolingfriends.org

New Hampshire Homeschooling Coalition
P.O. Box 2224
Concord, NH 03302
www.nhhomeschooling.org

New Jersey

Homeschoolers Support Network
P.O. Box 56198
Trenton, NJ 08638-7198
www.homeschoolsupport.org

New Jersey Homeschool Association
P.O. Box 1386
Medford, NJ 08055
www.geocities.com/Athens/Agora/3009

Unschoolers Network
2 Smith Street
Farmingdale, NJ 07727
732-938-2473

New Mexico

New Mexico Family Educators
P.O. Box 92776
Albuquerque, NM 87199-2276
505-275-7053

New York

Alliance for Parental Involvement in Education
P.O. Box 59
East Chatham, NY 12060

Home Education Exchange of the Southern
    Tier
P.O. Box 85
Southview Station
Binghamton, NY 13903-0085

New York City Home Educators Alliance
8 East 2nd Street
New York, NY 10003
www.nychea.com

Tri-County Homeschoolers
P.O. Box 190
Ossining NY 10562
www.croton.com/home-ed

North Carolina

Families Learning Together
1670 NC 33 West
Chocowinity, NC 27817
http://fltnc.cjb.net

Greensboro Home Educators
P.O. Box 78018
Greensboro, NC 27427-8018
http://members.nbci.com/ghe_sw

Ohio

Ohio Home Educators Network
P.O. Box 38132
Olmsted Falls, OH 44138-8132
www.grafixbynix.com/ohen

Oklahoma

Home Educators' Resource Network (HERO)
    of Oklahoma
302 North Coolidge
Enid, OK 73703-381
www.oklahomahomeschooling.org

Oregon

Homeschool Information & Services Network
    (HIS Net
1044 Bismark
Klamath Falls, OR 97601
www.efn.org/~hisnet

Oregon City Public Schools Linkup
(A Parent Designed and Monitored Program
    for Homeschooling Families)
1404 Seventh Street
Oregon City, OR 97045
503-657-2434
http://linkup.orecity.k12.or.us

Oregon Home Education Network
P.O. Box 218
Beaverton, OR 97075-0218
503-321-5166
www.teleport.com/~ohen

Pennsylvania

Pennsylvania Home Education Network
285 Allegheny Street
Meadville, PA 16335
www.phen.org

Pennsylvania Home School Connection
c/o Wendy Bush
650 Company Farm Road
Aspers, PA 17304
717-528-8850
www.homeschoolheadlines.com/hspa.htm

Rhode Island

S.O.S. for Home Schoolers
55 West Log Bridge Road
Coventry, RI 02816
401-392-3386

South Carolina

South Carolina Association of Independent
    Home Schools
P.O. Box 2104
Irmo, SC 29063-2104
803-551-1003
http://members.aol.com/scaihs/scaihs.htm

South Dakota

South Dakota Home School Association
8801 E. 38th Street
Sioux Falls SD 57110-6704
www.southdakotahomeschool.com

Tennessee

Eclectic Homeschoolers of Tennessee
3135 Lakeland Drive
Nashville, TN 37214
615-889-4938
E-mail: learninghappens@home.com

Texas

Houston Alternative Education Alliance
    (HAEA)
P.O. Box 11280
Houston, TX 77293
281-590-3688

Houston Unschoolers Group
9625 Exeter Road
Houston, TX 77093
713-695-4888
www.geocities.com/Athens/Delphi/1794/hug

Utah

Utah Home Education Association
P.O. Box 1492
Riverton, UT 84065-1492
www.utah-uhea.org

Vermont

Vermont Association of Home Educators
RR 1, Box 847
Bethel, VT 05032
802-234-6804

Virginia

Virginia Home Education Association
P.O. Box 5131
Charlottesville, VA 22905
540-832-3578
www.vhea.org

Washington

Teaching Parents Association
P.O. Box 1934
Woodinville, WA 98072-1934
206-505-1561 x1274
www.washtpa.org

Washington Homeschool Organization
6632 S. 191st Place, Suite E-100
Kent, WA 98032-2117
425-251-0439
www.washhomeschool.org

West Virginia

West Virginia Home Educators Association
P.O. Box 3707
Charleston, W.V. 25337
800-736-WVHE
http://wvheahome.homestead.com

Wisconsin

Wisconsin Parents Association
P.O. Box 2502
Madison, WI 53701-2502
608-283-3131
www.homeschooling-wpa.org

Washington, D.C.

Bolling Area Home Educators
c/o Tammy Jensen
P.O. Box 8401
Washington, D.C. 20336
202-574-1217

Puerto Rico

T'CHERs
P.O. Box 867
Boqueron, PR 00622
www.geocities.com/tchers2001

▶ WEB RESOURCES FOR FINDING A SUPPORT GROUP

About.com listings: http://homeschooling.about.com/education/homeschooling/mbody.htm
Growing Without Schooling: www.holtgws.com
Jon's Homeschool Resource: www.midnightbeach.com/hs